THE
FINANCIAL ADMINISTRATION
OF IRELAND

J. B. O'CONNELL, Ph. D., M.A. (Cantab.)

Late Finance Officer, Department of Defence, Dublin

MOUNT SALUS PRESS LIMITED

DUBLIN

First printing — October, 1960.

.

Printed and published for the author by
MOUNT SALUS PRESS LTD., DUBLIN

PREFACE

In 1934 I published *The Financial Administration of Saorstát Éireann*, the object of which was to do for the financial system of the Saorstát what a number of books had done for the system in Great Britain. The work was published on my personal responsibility, and though it had no official status or support, it was, I gratefully acknowledge, favourably received by Irish newspapers, and by journals dealing with the civil service, accountancy, banking and law.

That work has been out of print for a long time, and though I was frequently urged to republish it before my retirement from the civil service, I had neither the time nor the opportunity to do so. After my retirement I gave, I must confess, very little thought to the subject until February, 1958, when the Institute of Public Administration, deeming the work to be of value to the public service, offered to reprint and republish it, if I would undertake a new edition taking into consideration any developments since it was first issued. I, therefore, undertook the task, but, when it was completed, I again decided, for various reasons, to republish on my own responsibility, so that although most probably the work would not have been written but for the Institute's invitation, the responsibility both for its form and its content is entirely mine. Hence this book is neither official nor semi-official.

In this edition the earlier work has been completely re-shaped. Some parts of it have been omitted as being no longer of importance, while others, for the opposite reason, have been treated at greater length. Thus, for example, the organs of financial administration, formerly dealt with rather cursorily, have now been given their proper setting in the light of the new Constitution.

There have been many developments since 1934. In 1937, for instance, came the new Constitution which, being incapable of amendment except by referendum, may be taken as finally defining the administrative, executive and other organs of the State. In 1950 there was formally introduced the "Voted Capital Services", the existence of which, it is said, had always been recognised in the annual Budget, when a deduction for Capital items had usually been made before arriving at the amount of expenditure chargeable against current revenue. Following on this and closely associated with it came the Capital Budget financed entirely by borrowing and the consequent huge increase in the Public Debt. In External Affairs, Ireland in 1934 had only four ministers abroad, a High Commissioner in Great Britain, and Consuls in four American cities. She was associated with the British Commonwealth and the only international organisation of which she was a member was the League of Nations. Finally, there is the considerable growth — far more considerable than is commonly realised — in the number of financial, industrial and commercial enterprises sponsored by the State requiring now for capital purposes almost as much money as the Central Fund Services. Of those dealth with elsewhere only four in their present form existed in 1934.

These developments, national and international, have made the subject of State finance more complicated than ever before, and the ordinary citizen is at a loss at times to understand its meaning or purpose. This is not the work of a specialist, but by collecting material from many sources and by avoiding technicalities I have tried to act as a guide through the different paths of our financial administration. For that purpose, while retaining the main features of

3

the former book, which perhaps stressed more the system than its content, I have now endeavoured to describe the more important of our public services, the activities and finances of some of the State-sponsored Bodies, and the functions of the International Institutions of which the State is a member. With this general view of the subject, the reader may be able to understand better the services on which the money of the public is expended. I can only hope that those who found the first edition useful will find this equally so.

Finally, it is my duty to record my sincere thanks to those friends who have helped me by their advice and support to compile this work and to correct its proofs. My debt to them is more than I can say.

MONKSTOWN,   J. B. O'CONNELL.
CO. DUBLIN.
OCTOBER, 1960.

CONTENTS

Chapter

APPENDIX

To The Late
REV. EDMUND M. FITZGERALD, C.C.

Chapter I

The Organs of Financial Administration

THE CONSTITUTION

1. The title of this work is " The Financial Administration of Ireland " and by " Ireland " is meant the sovereign, independent, democratic state called " Éire " or in the English language " Ireland." The national territory of that state consists of the whole island of Ireland, its islands and the territorial seas, but its laws, pending the re-integration of the national territory, has the like area and extent of application as the laws of Saorstát Éireann and the like extra territorial effect.[1]

2. The Irish Constitution, which has been in operation since 29th December, 1937, has an important article dealing with the administration or management of the State. Article 6 runs as follows:

" All powers of government, legislative, executive and judicial, derive, under God, from the people, whose right it is to designate the rulers of the State, and, in final appeal, to decide all questions of national policy, according to the requirements of the common good. These powers of government are exercisable only by or on the authority of the organs of State established by this Constitution."

3. In dealing, therefore, with the financial administration of Ireland, it is necessary at the outset to determine the constitutional organs of the State which are in one way or another concerned with that administration. The principal organs established by the Constitution are: The President, The National Parliament, The Government, The Attorney General, The Council of State, The Comptroller and Auditor General and The Courts. The President is concerned with financial administration only in so far as he is a constitutent factor of the National Parliament, or Oireachtas. The Council of State, which acts in an advisory capacity in certain matters to the President, is only consulted on financial matters, if and when the Senate requests the President to refer a bill, purporting to be a money bill, to a Committee of Privileges. The functions of the Courts are purely judicial and not executive, administrative or legislative: and the Attorney General is involved only in his capacity as Parliamentary Draftsman in preparing bills (including money bills) approved by the Government, for submission to the Oireachtas. The remaining organs, the Government, the National Parliament, and the Comptroller and Auditor General are the special constitutional organs which, in their appropriate spheres, exercise the financial powers of the State, and we have, therefore, in the course

---

1. Cons. Arts. 2, 3, 4 and 5.

of this work to show how these organs are constituted and how they operate.

THE GOVERNMENT

4. All the executive, including, therefore, the administrative powers of the State are vested by the Constitution in the Government, which is, in effect, an executive council, or cabinet, consisting of not less than seven and not more than fifteen members or ministers. The head of the Government, the Taoiseach, or Prime Minister, is appointed by the President on the nomination of Dáil Éireann, and the other ministers are also appointed by him on the nomination of the Taoiseach, who also nominates one member, called the Tánaiste, to act for him in the event of death, incapacity or absence. The Taoiseach, the Tánaiste and the Minister for Finance must be members of Dáil Éireann, and not more than two other executive ministers may be Senators.[2]

The Government acts collectively and is thus responsible for the departments of State administered by its members. The organisation and distribution of business among the departments, and the designation of the ministers in charge thereof are regulated by law.[3] We are thus led to consider briefly the Departments of State, the functions of the Ministers controlling them, and the Staff serving in them.

THE DEPARTMENTS OF STATE

5. The Acts which establish the Departments of State and distribute the public services between them are the Ministers and Secretaries Acts, 1924-1959. These statutes describe in the most general terms the powers, duties, and functions of each department, but the actual services administered by them are shown in the annual book of " Estimates for the Public Services." In a subsequent chapter we shall deal with the main services of each department, but meanwhile we shall deal briefly with the effect of the statutes.

6. The Principal Act of 1924 established eleven departments — The President of the Executive Council (now the Taoiseach); Finance; Justice; Local Government and Public Health; Education; Lands and Agriculture; Industry and Commerce; Fisheries; Posts and Telegraphs; Defence; and External Affairs. In addition to prescribing their general functions, the Act in its schedules specifically transferred to each department services previously administered by the former British Government. Thus, to the

2. Cons. Art. 28.
3. Cons. Art. 28, 12.

Department of Finance was assigned the general administration of the Public Finance including the collection and expenditure of the revenues from whatever source arising (save as may be otherwise provided by law); and to it were also assigned, in particular, the functions formally administered by the British Treasury in Ireland, the Revenue Commissioners, the Paymaster General, the Commissioners of Public Works, the Civil Service Commission, the Commissioners of Valuation and Boundary Survey, the Ordnance Survey, the Stationery Office, the Post Office Savings Bank, and the Registrar of Friendly Societies.

7. By an Act of 1928 the Irish Land Commission was transferred from the Department of Agriculture to that of Fisheries, and the Minister's general functions regarding agriculture were re-defined, but there were still only eleven departments.

An Act of 1939 established the Department of Supplies for regulating supplies and services essential to the life of the community, but the department ceased in 1946, and under the Minister for Supplies (Transfer of Functions) Act of that year any of its remaining functions were transferred to Industry and Commerce. The Act of 1939 vested in the Government the power to transfer the administration of any public department, and to allocate to any department the business of any public service not expressly allocated to any department. Cases of doubt are resolved by the Taoiseach, who may from time to time assign a particular department to a member of the Government, and may assign more than one department to the same person.

An Act of 1946 created two new departments, Public Health and Social Welfare. No fresh functions were defined, which means that the former took over the Health, and the latter the Insurance and Social Services previously administered by the Department of Local Government and Public Health. The new title of Department of Local Government was given by S. R. O. 16/1947.

An Act of 1956 set up the Department of the Gaeltacht to promote the cultural, social and economic welfare of the Gaeltacht. In effect, it took over certain services formerly administered by the Department of Lands and Fisheries.

An Act of 1959 established the Department of Transport and Power and to it were transferred certain functions formerly performed by the Department of Industry and Commerce.

MINISTERS

8. At the head of each Department of State is the Minister to whom it has been assigned by the Taoiseach. Each is directly

11

responsible to the Government, and indirectly to the Dail, for ensuring that the policy relating to his Department is duly carried out, but that in no way derogates from the collective responsibility of his colleagues in the Government. Beyond seeing that his orders are dealt with speedily and efficiently, he does not as a rule interfere with the day-to-day working of the Department. The Government may be likened to a Board of Directors in the industrial sphere, and each Minister to a Managing Director in his particular department. The one decides the policy and the other carries it out.

Each Minister is a " Corporation Sole," has perpetual succession, an official seal, and may sue, and (subject to the " Fiat " of the Attorney General) be sued under his own style or name. He may acquire, hold and dispose of land for the purpose of his Department.

Under the Act of 1939, it is not necessary for every member of the Government to be in charge of a Department. Any member not so charged is known as a " Minister without portfolio," and the Government may assign him a style or title to be judicially and officially noticed.

PARLIAMENTARY SECRETARIES

9. Parliamentary Secretaries are not mentioned in the Constitution, but the Ministers and Secretaries Act of 1924 empowered the Government to appoint, on the nomination of the Taoiseach, members of the Oireachtas not exceeding seven to act as such either to the Government or to Ministers. Not more than one may be appointed to any one department. A Parliamentary Secretary holds office as long as he is a member of the Oireachtas and as long as the nominating Taoiseach holds office, but the Government may remove him at any time from office.

The Act of 1924 prescribed that the duties and powers of such Secretaries would be those delegated or assigned to them from time to time by the Government, but the Act of 1939 prescribed that the Government might, at the request of the Minister, delegate all the powers and duties of the Minister under any Act, or any of his statutory powers or duties to a Parliament Secretary. Any such delegation vests in the Secretary and the powers or duties are exercisable in his own name, but (a) they must be performed under the control of the Minister; (b) they vest concurrently in the Minister so that they may be exercised either by the latter or by the Secretary; (c) the Minister is still responsible to the Government. The delegation may be revoked at any time by the Government, or it may cease by the Minister ceasing to hold office.

SECRETARIES

10. The life of Dáil Éireann is by law limited to five years, but a government remains in office until its successor is appointed. It is, however, dependent on the support of the Dáil, which in turn depends on the changing views of the electorate, so that there is always an element of relative uncertainty and instability about any Government. But the life of the body politic is continuous, so that if the public services on which it depends are not to be subject to interruption, there must be an organ of executive administration which is permanent and stable, and entirely removed from the fluctuations of politics. That organ is present in the Secretaries of the different departments and the staff of Civil Servants working under them.

In the Ministers and Secretaries Act of 1924, the permanent head of each department is called the Principal Officer, but he is officially known as its Secretary. The word in the context of state administration has not the ordinary meaning, but connotes the chief administrative officer of the department. To continue the simile already employed, he may be described as the works manager of the department. He is appointed by the Government on the recommendation of the Minister, and is directly responsible to the latter. A Secretary's functions are not defined by law, and, except in such minor matters as staffing, etc., they will vary with the services assigned by law to the different departments. This implies that in general he should have an intimate acquaintance with the work of each of the department's branches, and in particular a thorough knowledge of the Acts governing the department, and of the Orders, Rules and Regulations made thereunder.

ACCOUNTING OFFICERS

11. In addition to his function as Secretary, the principal officer generally, though not necessarily, has the important financial function of what is called " Accounting Officer," and, as such, he is one of the principal organs of financial administration. The appointment is made directly by the Minister for Finance, and is governed by section 22 of the Exchequer and Audit Act, 1866. Having prescribed that " Appropriation Accounts "—that is, accounts for the appropriation of the several supply grants comprised in the Appropriation Act of each year—should be prepared by departments and rendered to the Comptroller and Auditor General, the Treasury, and the House of Commons, it provided that the term " Department " should be construed as including any public officer or officers to whom that duty should be assigned by the Treasury. The section, it will be noted, does not employ the term " Accounting Officer."

A Treasury Minute of the 14th August, 1872, addressed to the Committee of Public Accounts, however, said: " Some term should be employed which shall clearly denote the relation in which officers appointed to render Appropriation Accounts stand towards Parliament as responsible for the financial administration of the grant for the services under the control of their departments, while it should at the same time avoid ascribing to them a character which properly belongs only to persons possessing a technical knowledge of book-keeping and accounts. It appears that the designation of ' Accounting Officer ' will sufficiently meet both of these requirements." The Committee agreed with the suggestion and the term was adopted. The term really means " accountable," that is, the officer accountable to Parliament for the expenditure of the grant.

12. Any officer of a Department may be appointed its Accounting Officer, but in practice Secretaries answer for the expenditure of the branches or offices directly under their control; but other officers, always the heads or principals, are appointed to account for the expenditure of branches which they directly operate, and which are not under the immediate administration of the Secretaries. Thus, in the case of the Revenue Commissioners, the Office of Public Works, the Valuation Office, and the Stationery Office, which are offices or branches of the Department of Finance, the accounting officer is not the Secretary of that Department, but other officers in those branches are appointed to answer for the expenditure.

13. Although the appointment of the Secretary as Accounting Officer is made by the Minister for Finance, he is directly responsible to the Dáil, as represented by the Committee of Public Accounts, for the expenditure recorded in his accounts. The Minister is responsible for seeking and obtaining from the Dáil the supply or money required for the services of his Department, but once that supply has been granted, the Secretary, as Accounting Officer, is directly accountable for its proper and regular expenditure.

14. The functions of Principal Officers as Secretaries vary with departments according to the specifically distinct services allotted to each, but their functions as Accouning Officers are always the same in every respect. As an Accounting Officer is one of the chief pivots in the financial administration of the State, it is necessary to outline his duties. These are not defined, but from the general consideration that he is responsible to Parliament for the financial administration of the departmental grant, and also from the particular comments made from time to time by the Committee of

Public Accounts, his duties may be summarised as follows:—

(1) In general it may be said that in all financial matters, the responsibility is personal and cannot be delegated or diverted. It is not merely theoretical but practical, and cases are on record in which Accounting Officers have been surcharged for improper or irregular expenditure.

(2) He is responsible for seeing that all expenditure is duly authorised. For that purpose he should ensure that the general system of paying, accounting, and auditing rests on a sound basis, so that he may be able to rely on the certified statements of his subordinates. If the latter be faced with expenditure of an unusual or exceptional nature, they should consult the Accounting Officer before making payment, and failure to do so may incur the risk of a personal disallowance.

(3) He is responsible for seeing that there is no deviation from regulations, or from established order and procedure without the explicit concurrence of Finance.

(4) He is responsible for securing that his department is run in an economical manner. If a new service is to be introduced, or an existing service extended, he is bound to represent to his Minister the financial implications of the proposals.

(5) If the Minister orders expenditure which, in the opinion of the **Accounting Officer**, is irregular or improper, the latter must state in writing his objections, and should not proceed with the expenditure until the Minister in reply repeats his order in writing.

(6) If an Accounting Officer be appointed during a period of account, and has no personal knowledge of expenditure incurred before his appointment, he should take steps to satisfy himself that the accounts for the period previous to his appointment are correct before using them as the basis of the appropriation account, which he will be rendering. If not satisfied he should not sign the account unconditionally but subject to qualification as to the specific items for which he feels unable to accept responsibility. His predecessor will then have to answer for the items.

(7) An Accounting Officer who has relinquished his appointment after signing an account is liable for all matters in that account, and must, if required, attend for examination before the Committee of Public Accounts.

THE CIVIL SERVICE COMMISSION

15. Under each Principal Officer, in his dual capacity, there is a staff of Civil Servants working under him. The Ministers and Secretaries Act of 1924 prescribed that each Minister may appoint

such officers and servants to serve in his Department as he may, with the sanction of the Minister for Finance, determine, but every appointment so made must be subject to the provisions of the Civil Service Regulation Act, 1923, or any Act amending or replacing it. The terms and conditions of appointment of all such officers were to be prescribed by the Minister for Finance who was also to determine from time to time their salaries and remuneration.

16.   The Civil Service Regulation Act, 1923 was replaced by a similar Act in 1924 and this was amended in 1926. Both Acts dealt both with the Commission and with the Civil Service, but in 1956 there appeared two new Acts — the Civil Service Commissioners Act, and the Civil Service Regulation Act. The former repealed the whole Act of 1924 " so far as unrepealed," but the latter repealed only Section 9 of the Act of 1924 and certain sections of the Ministers and Secretaries Act of 1924 dealing with the terms and conditions of appointment of Civil Servants.

17.   The Civil Service Commissioners Act, 1956, establishes a Commission of three persons appointed by, and holding office at the will and pleasure of the Government, and it prescribes that no person may be appointed to an established post in the Service, unless he is appointed by the Commission as a result of a competitive examination, but this does not apply to a person appointed " in the public interest " by the Government. A similar Commission was appointed for dealing with appointments by Local Authorities under the Local Authorities (Officers and Employers) Act, 1926.

18.   The competition may be a written examination, or an oral examination, or an interview, or a practical test, or any other test considered to be appropriate, but not more than one of the tests need be competitive. The selection of successful candidates must be according to merit, and the filling of posts for which they are required must be approved by the Minister for Finance.

The Act does not apply to certain scheduled positions such as porters, door keepers, adult messengers, night watchmen, charwomen, cleaners, artisans, or to a person hired to perform only subordinate duties or ordinary labour as and when required.

19.   In practice the Commissions consist of the Chairman of Dáil Éireann and four — two for each Commission — high ranking Civil Servants. The examinations are of the same standard and subjects as the ordinary examinations held in the schools — primary and secondary — and in the Universities throughout the State. No subjects bearing on administration or kindred subjects are included. After the examinations, the Commission sends to the Department of Finance a list of successful candidates, and at the same time

assigns them to the departments in which there are vacancies. Hence, though in law the Minister appoints the Civil Servant, he has not, in fact, anything to do with the appointment, but simply accepts those assigned to his Department.

THE CIVIL SERVICE [4]

20. The Civil Service Regulations Act, 1956, declares that the Civil Servant holds office at the will and pleasure of the Government, and empowers the Minister for Finance to make and unmake regulations concerning the control of the Service, the classification and unclassification, the numbers and remuneration of Civil Servants, and the fixing of the terms and conditions of their service.

21. The Act is not helpful as to what constitutes the Civil Service or the Civil Servant, but for our present purpose we may describe a Civil Servant as a person employed either permanently or temporarily — that is, as established or unestablished — in a department of State with the consent of the Minister for Finance. Now in 1955, excluding members of the Defence Forces, the Garda Síochána, Teachers, etc., there were 43,000 names on the State's civil pay-roll. Of that number some were casual workers, and others were paid on a piece-work, fee, or capitation basis. They numbered about 9,617 persons, but they were not civil servants, because they were not engaged in the departments, and also because they were excluded by the schedule already mentioned to the Commissioners' Act. Excluding that category of miscellaneous employees, there were in 1955 some 33,383 persons costing about £14m. a year who occupied established or unestablished posts in the Service.

22. In the official census of 1955, these officers were arranged in eight groups [5]:

(1) *The Administrative and Executive Group,* ranging, in what is called the General Service Grade, from Secretaries to Executive Officers and also including analogous departmental classes. The cost was £2.6m. a year and there were 23 unestablished officers out of a total of 2,619.

(2) *The Clerical Group,* ranging in the General Service Grades from Staff Officers to Writing Assistants. Here there were 6,485 costing £2.9m. a year, of which 727 were unestablished.

(3) *The Typing Group,* another General Service Grade, of 941 persons — 89 unestablished — costing £323,000 a year.

(4) *The Professional and Technical Group,* such as Architects,

---

4. See Appendix, para. 352.
5. *Administration,* Vol. 3, Nos. 2-3.

Engineers, Doctors, Lawyers, etc., numbering 2,343 (679 unestablished), costing £1.7m. a year.

(5) *The Inspectorate Group,* of 765 persons — 187 established — costing £448,000 a year.

(6) *The Minor Supervising and Manipulative Group,* mainly Post Office employees totalling 15,341 persons — 9,268 unestablished — costing £4.8m. a year.

(7) *The Ancillary Group* of messengers, cleaners, etc., numbering 2,375 persons, 482 being unestablished, and costing £577,000 annually.

(8) *The Industrial Group* of gardeners, labourers, etc., comprising 2,514 unestablished employees and costing £.9m. yearly.

To interpret these figures correctly, it is to be noted that not less than 16,609 civil servants were employed in the Post Office at a cost of £5m. annually. That Department is regarded as being run on a commercial basis and in 1957 it made a profit of £30,000. Hence, excluding the Post Office, the fact remains that in the other departments there were 17,314 Civil Servants costing £9m. a year.

23. The Irish Civil Service was based and organised on the British model, and was, therefore, geared to administer an empire rather than a small state. The Minister for Finance has frankly admitted that " it is too elaborate for our needs," and requires " simplification." Steps have been taken during the last few years to reorganise the system and in his Budget Statement in 1959 he announced " that the views of Heads of Departments had been sought on proposals for reorganising the Civil Service structure." [6]

24. The Civil Servant, in his official capacity, is responsible to the Government, to his Minister, and to the public. Although in law he is appointed by his Minister, the latter acts as a member of the Government and he is, therefore, responsible to the Government. His relation to it is not the ordinary contractual relationship subsisting between employee and employer. It is rather a kind of informal contact implying security of tenure, and, after the lapse, of a certain period, the right — but not the absolute right — to a pension, provided, however, that the person must serve subject to any regulations promulgated from time to time by the Minister for Finance, and provided also that his office is held at the will and pleasure of the Government.

25. To the Minister he is bound at all times to carry out loyally his policy and orders, no matter what may be their merits or consequences. In doing so, he is entitled to the Minister's protection, and if any question be raised either in Parliament or elsewhere, he

---

6. See Appendix, para. 353.

has a right to be defended by the Minister. If, however, he errs by excess or defect in matters of major importance, he forfeits the right of ministerial defence or protection.

26. To the public the Civil Servant has the duty of dealing justly and expeditiously with each citizen's claim howsoever arising. If a claimant feels that he has been unjustly treated, he may make representations to the Minister personally, or by means of a Dáil Question, but if that fails and the matter is one of importance, his only remedy would be to sue the Minister in the ordinary courts of law. There both plaintiff and defendant are subject to the same Rule of Law, and the action will be tried not in accordance with any special statute or rule of administrative law, but in accordance with the principles of Common Law, and what will be tried is not the justice, but the legality of the alleged grievance. This method of inquiry is in sharp contrast with that used in France, where the case would be investigated by a special tribunal, the Council of State (Conseil d'État), which has its own personnel, laws, functions and procedure, and is quite distinct and separate from the ordinary courts of the State. Its members are not lawyers or civil servants, but persons versed in political, social, and administrative sciences.[7] Its judicial functions are exercised in accordance with a special code of Administrative Law (Droit Administratif) which is "the sum of the principles which govern the relation between French citizens as individuals, and the administration, as representatives of the State"[8] and which should not be confused with Laws of Administration found in our Statute Books.

27. Civil Servants are frequently accused of "bureaucracy," that is, of exercising quasi-judicial and quasi-legislative functions in the making of statutory instruments, orders, rules, regulations, schemes, etc., in virtue of powers conferred on Ministers by statutes, and the instruments are pictured as the product of the unfettered discretion of irresponsible civil servants. In reply it is sufficient to point out:

(1) In 1929 a Select Committee of the House of Commons reported that Delegated Legislation is both legitimate and constitutionally desirable for certain purposes, within certain limits, and under certain safeguards, because of the great pressure on Parliamentary time, the technical nature of modern legislation, the difficulty of foreseeing the administrative machinery required to meet all contingencies and local conditions for which provision must eventually be made, the flexibility it provides for constant

7. *Administration*, Vol. 3, Nos. 2, 3.
8. Diecy. Law of the Constitution, page 382.

adaptation to unknown future conditions without the necessity of amending Legislation, the opportunity it affords of utilising the lessons of experience, and the frequent need under modern conditions of immediate legislative action.

(2) A similar Committee in 1944 reported that such Legislation is unavoidable under modern conditions.

(3) The discretion exercised is not unfettered, because (a) before their making, the instruments have to be approved by the Government and by the Parliamentary Draftsman, and (b) after they are made they are examined by a Select Committee of the Seanad set up in 1954 to ensure not only that they are in strict conformity with the parent statutes, but also that they do not contain any unusual use of the powers conferred by them.

Under modern conditions there is no alternative to delegated legislation. Its critics may say that it has been abused, but they do not say it should be abolished. If it did not exist, it would have been necessary to invent it.

THE NATIONAL PARLIAMENT

28. Another organ of financial administration established by the Constitution is the National Parliament, called the Oireachtas, which consists of the President and of two Houses of Parliament — a House of Representatives called Dáil Éireann, and a Senate called Seanad Éireann. The sole and exclusive power of making laws for the State is vested in the Oireachtas, but it may not make any laws repugnant to the Constitution, and may not declare acts to be infringements of the law which were not so at the date of their commission.[9]

THE PRESIDENT

29. The President is elected by the direct vote of the people, that is, by citizens having the right to vote at an election for members of the Dáil. He holds office for seven years but may be re-elected once and only once for another term of Office. The Dáil is summoned or dissolved by the President on the advice of the Taoiseach, but there is vested in him an absolute discretion to refuse to dissolve the Dáil on the advice of a Taoiseach who has ceased to retain the support of a majority in that House.[10]

30. A Bill passed or deemed to have been passed by both Houses is presented to the President by the Taoiseach for his signature and its proclamation as a law, and ordinarily it must be

9. Cons. Art. 15.
10. Cons. Art. 12.

signed between the fifth and seventh day of its presentation. It becomes law on the date of signature, unless a contrary intention is apparent, and promulgation is effected by proclamation in the official gazette, Iris Oifigiúil.

31.   In the event of the President's incapacity, absence, or death, his powers and functions are exercised by a Commission consisting of the Chief Justice and the Chairmen of both Houses of the Oireachtas. For nomination as President candidates require twenty members of the Oireachtas or four administrative County Councils.

DÁIL ÉIREANN

32.   The constitution [11] declares every citizen without distinction of sex, who has attained the age of 21, and who is not placed under disability or incapacity by the Constitution or by law to be eligible for membership of Dáil Éireann.   The Constitution renders the President, the Judiciary and the Comptroller and Auditor General incapable, and the Law incapacitates bankrupts, persons guilty of corrupt election practices, members of the Gárdaí and Defence Forces, Civil Servants, and persons undergoing a sentence of imprisonment with hard labour for a period exceeding six months or of penal servitude.

33.   Every person, regardless of sex, who has attained the age of 21 is entitled to be registered as a Dáil elector in any one constituency in which he is ordinarily resident, or in which he occupies a business premises on the qualifying date. If qualified to vote in more than one constituency, the person may elect the one in which he wishes to be registered.

34.   For the purpose of electing members to the Dáil, the State is divided into constituencies determined by law, but the total number of members may not be less than one member for each 30,000 or more than one member for each 20,000 of the population. The Constituencies must be revised every 12 years, but each must have at least three members.   The Electoral Act of 1923 fixed the number of Deputies at 153 including six University representatives, but in 1937 that representation was abolished, and the number of Deputies reduced to 138.   Ten years later, the number was increased to 147 and under the Electoral (Amendment) Act, 1959, the number of constituencies has now been reduced from 40 to 39, and the Deputies from 147 to 144.   Alterations in constituencies do not take effect during the life of the Dáil sitting when revision takes place. The life of a Dáil is fixed at seven years by the Constitution, but a shorter period may be determined by law.   The Electoral (Amend-

11. Arts. 16 and 17.

ment) Act, 1927, fixes the maximum duration without a dissolution at five years.

35. Members of the Dáil are elected on the system of proportional representation by means of the single transferable vote, and the Electoral Act, 1923, defines the term " transferable vote " as " a vote (a) capable of being given so as to indicate the voter's preference for the candidates in order; and (b) capable of being transferred to the next choice, when the vote is not required to give a prior choice the necessary quota of votes, or when, owing to the deficiency in the number of votes given for a prior choice, that choice is eliminated from the list of candidates." By " quota " is meant the number of votes sufficient to elect a candidate. It is obtained by dividing the total number of first preference votes cast in the Constituency for all candidates by the number of vacancies to be filled plus one, and by increasing the result by one. Candidates must be nominated by ten registered electors of the Constituency including one as proposer and another as assentor.

SEANAD ÉIREANN

36. The Constitution [12] sets the number of Senators at 60, made up of: (a) 11 nominated by the Taoiseach; (b) 3 elected by the National University and 3 by Dublin University; and (c) 43 elected from panels containing the names of persons having knowledge and practical experience of (1) the National Language and Culture, Literature, Art, Education, and such professional interests as may be defined by Law; (2) Agriculture and Fisheries; (3) Labour; (4) Industry and Commerce, including banking, finance, accountancy, engineering and architecture; (5) Public Administration and Social Services including voluntary social activities. Not more than 11 and not less than 5 members may be elected from any one panel and election is on the system of proportional representation by means of the single transferable vote and by secret postal ballot. Provision may, however, be made by law for the direct election by any functional, or vocational group, or association, or council of as many members in substitution for an equal number of members to be elected from the corresponding panels.

37. Under the Seanad Éireann (Panel Members) Acts, for the purpose of nominations to the panels, a Register of Nominating Bodies is kept, and the number which may be nominated to each panel is fixed — 6 for the First Panel, 14 for the Second, 14 for the Third, 12 for the Fourth, and 8 for the Fifth. Under the same Acts, each panel is divided into two sub-

---

12. Arts. 18 and 19.

panels, one for the Nominating Bodies, and the other for the Oireachtas. Any four members of the Oireachtas may nominate any one person but not more, and may not join in the nomination of more than one person in any particular panel.

38. Under the Acts the number to be elected from each panel is: (a) 5 from the First, with at least 2 from each sub-panel; (b) 11 from each of the Second and Third panels with at least 4 from each sub-panel; (c) 9 from the Fourth with at least 3 from each of the sub-panels; and (d) 7 from the Fifth with at least 3 from each sub-panel.

39. The electors consist of (1) Members of the Dáil elected after a dissolution; (2) Members of the old Seanad; (3) Members of every County Council or County Borough. In all, the electors number about 800.

Senators under the Constitution hold office until the next general election for their House which must take place not later than 90 days after a dissolution of the Dáil.

40. The Seanad Éireann (University Members) Act, 1937, prescribes the method of electing the three members from each of the two Universities to the Seanad. The election is on the system of proportional representation by means of the single transferable vote, and the franchise embraces any person who is a citizen of Ireland, who has attained the age af 21, and who has a degree (other than an honorary degree) in the University concerned. A Register of Electors is kept in each University, and the voting is entirely by post. Candidates require two registered electors as proposer and seconder, and eight assentors who may subscribe as many papers as there are vacancies.

LEGISLATION

41. As regards Legislation the Constitution [13] prescribes: (1) Every Bill initiated and passed in the Dáil, must be sent to the Seanad, and conversely every Bill initiated and passed in the Seanad must be introduced in the Dáil; (2) A Bill passed by either House and accepted by the other is deemed to have been passed by both Houses; (3) If a Bill initiated and passed in the Dáil, is amended by the Seanad, the Dáil must consider every such amendment, but if a Bill initiated and passed in the Seanad is amended in the Dáil, it is considered a Bill initiated in the Dáil; (4) If within 90 days (or a longer period agreed by both Houses) of a Bill being sent by the Dáil to the Seanad, it is either rejected, or passed with amendments to which the Dáil does not agree, or if it is neither passed

13. Arts. 20-27.

(with or without amendments), nor rejected by the Seanad, the Bill is deemed to have been passed by both Houses, if and when a resolution to that effect is passed by the Dáil within 180 days after the expiration of the 90 days. This also applies to a Bill initiated and passed in the Seanad and amended in the Dáil and, therefore, deemed to be initiated in the latter, but here the 90 days counts from the day on which the Bill as amended is sent to the Seanad; (5) A Money Bill can be initiated only in the Dáil, but it is sent in the usual way to the Seanad for its recommendations but not for amendment. It must be returned to the Dáil within 21 days and the Dáil may accept or reject any recommendations made. If it is not returned within the 21 days, or if it is returned with recommendations not accepted by the Dáil, it is deemed to have passed both Houses at the expiration of the 21 days.

42.   A Money Bill means " a Bill which contains only provisions dealing with all or any of the following subjects, namely, the imposition, repeal, remission, alteration or regulation of taxation; the imposition for the payment of debt, or other financial purposes of charges on public moneys, or the variation or repeal of any such charges; supply; the appropriation, receipt, custody, issue or audit of accounts of public money; the raising or guarantee of any loan or the repayment thereof; matters subordinate and incidental to these matters or any of them. In this definition the expressions ' taxation,' ' public money ' and ' loan ' respectively do not include any taxation, money or loan raised by local authorities or bodies for local purposes. The Chairman of Dáil Éireann shall certify any Bill which, in his opinion, is a Money Bill to be a Money Bill, and his certificate shall be final and conclusive, unless the question whether the Bill is or is not a Money Bill is referred to a Committee of Privileges." If the Senate with 30 members present request the President to refer a Bill purporting to be a Money Bill to such a Committee, he may, after consulting the Council of State, comply with the request, and the Committee will then consist of an equal number of members of both Houses presided over by a judge of the Supreme Court.

43.   The Constitution [14] also prescribes that " Dáil Éireann may not pass any vote or resolution, and no law shall be enacted for the appropriation of revenue or other public moneys, unless the purpose of the appropriation shall have been recommended to Dáil Éireann by a message from the Government signed by the Taoiseach." This is known as the " Right of Initiative," and means that the right of

---

14. Art. 17, 2.

initiating public expenditure is the exclusive right of the Government.

44. A Public Bill originates at ministerial level, when the Minister indicates to the Secretary of his department the proposals the Government has in mind. They may involve a completely new Bill, that is, Direct Legislation; or they may mean amending or extending existing legislation, that is, Legislation by Reference. The procedure to be followed by departments is carefully regulated, and may be summarised thus: (1) All other departments concerned with the proposals, but especially the Department of Finance, must be consulted; (2) A memorandum must then be submitted to the Government setting out the proposals, their cost, and the views of other departments; (3) If the Government agrees, the department prepares a Draft, other departments concerned being again consulted; (4) If Finance agrees, the Draft is sent to the Government with a covering explanatory memorandum, and authority is sought to have a Bill drafted; (5) The Draft is then sent to the Attorney General to have a Bill drafted by the Parliamentary Draftsman; (6) Copies of the Bill so drafted in typescript are then sent to Finance by the promoting department; (7) Finance then arranges for what is called the " White Paper Print " of the Bill; (8) The promoting department sends this Print to the Government asking leave to introduce the Bill in the Dáil; (9) When the Government approves certified copies of the Bill are sent to the Clerk of the Dáil.

45. Every Bill contains a Long and a Short Title, e.g., The Expiring Laws Act, 1947, has as long title, " An Act to continue for a limited period certain Expiring Enactments," In case of urgency it suffices to send for the time being certified copies of the titles. The Clerk has the title printed on the Dail's Order Paper, its daily Agenda, and the Bill thus reaches the first of the five stages it has to go through before being sent to the Seanad. These stages are not prescribed by the Constitution or by Law but by the Standing Orders of the House.

46. The Stages [15] of the Legislative Process are briefly as follows:

First Stage. If, as is usual in the case of Public Bills, the ministerial motion for leave to introduce is agreed, an order is made for its second reading and for its printing. This is known as the " Green Paper Print."

Second Stage. On the motion that " The Bill be now read a second time," a debate confined to the general principle of the Bill

---

15. S.O.s 85-100.

takes place, and only amendments of a general nature, e.g., to omit the word " now " are permitted, no direct negatives being allowed. If on a division there is an equality of votes, the Chairman has a casting vote.

Third State. This is known as the Committee Stage because all the Bill's provisions must be examined in Committee in detail. For the better understanding of this stage it is necessary to outline the chief committees connected with the work of the Dáil. They are (a) Committee of Selection [16]. Eleven members are appointed at the beginning of each session to nominate deputies to serve on Special and Select Committees; (b) Special Committees [17] appointed to deal with Private Members' Bills which have passed a second reading or with Public Bills which, after that reading, are referred either in whole or in part for the Committee's recommendations; (c) Select Committees [18] appointed on the motion of the Dáil to take evidence on any matter or Bill. It may be empowered to send for papers, persons and records, and if so empowered its report must be recommitted to a Committee of the Whole Dáil; (d) Committee of Whole Dáil [19] — The Dáil is so called when it considers a Bill in detail, and it goes into Committee whenever it reaches business to be considered in Committee. The Ceann Comhairle nominates a panel of Deputies, one of whom is to act as chairman. Its setting is notionally continuous, so that instead of a motion to adjourn, a motion " to report progress " must be moved; (e) Committee on Finance [20] — The Committee of the Whole Dáil is so called when it considers a motion for any aid, grant or charge on the public revenue, or for any charge upon the people and it must report back before any resolution or vote of the Dáil be taken. Any motion or amendment proposing to increase the amount named may be moved only by a member of the Government.

47. There are two phases in bills dealing directly with public money. There is a resolution to grant the supply named, and a resolution to make good the supply so granted. As regards the annual estimates, for instance, a resolution to grant the supply is moved first for each estimate separately in the Committee, and when all the Estimates have been completed, the Minister for Finance moves that the Dáil " agree with the Committee on Finance in the Resolutions of Supply reported in respect of the several Estimates."

16. S.O. 72.
17. S.O. 87.
18. S.O. 67.
19. S.O. 62.
20. S.O. 115.

If the Dail agrees, he moves in Committee, "that towards making good the supply granted for the service of the year ending on the 31st March, 19—, the sum of £x be granted out of the Central Fund." On the Committee and the Dáil assenting, leave is given to introduce the Bill necessary to implement the resolution. According to the Standing Orders of the House when the Dáil has completed its consideration of the resolutions or votes, a Bill must be introduced by the Minister for Finance or by some other Minister acting on his behalf.

48. A Money Resolution — e.g. "that it is expedient to authorise such payments out of moneys provided by the Oireachtas as are necessary to give effect" to the Act — is not a Resolution of Supply, because no specific sum is stated. When a Bill deals only indirectly or incidentally with public money, it is accompanied by such a resolution which can be moved at any time prior to the Committee Stage of the Bill itself. Its effect is not to grant or to make good supply. In a sense it is largely procedural, but being incidental to money matters which will follow in due course, it would appear to have the effect of making the Bill a Money Bill.

49. In the Committee Stage a Bill is considered section by section. Any section may be amended or a new section inserted provided that it is relevant to the subject matter, within the Title, and not in conflict with the Bill as read a second time.

Fourth Stage. This is called the Report Stage, because the Dail in Committee is deemed to have reported on it by passing or amending it. Amendments may be moved but they may not be amendments rejected in Committee.

Fifth Stage. Here the Bill receives final consideration. Only verbal amendments are allowed, but during the progress of the Bill corrections of a verbal or formal nature may be made by the Clerk under the direction of the Chair. Versional and other corrections must be formally moved and dealt with as amendments.

50. Immediately after a Bill, which in his opinion is a Money Bill, has passed its fifth stage, the Ceann Comhairle issues his certificate to the effect. Exact copies of the Bill certified by the Clerk of the Dáil are then sent to the Senate. The procedure of five stages is also followed in the Senate, but a Bill received from one House by the other is deemed to have passed its first stage. When a Bill has passed or is deemed to have passed both Houses, it is sent by the Taoiseach to the President for signature and promulgation.

CHAPTER II

Estimates of Expenditure : Central Fund and Capital Services

THE CONSTITUTION

51.   As far as financial matters are concerned, the Constitution deals with them in three different Articles.   In Article 28, when dealing with the Government, it says in Section 4, Subsection 5 :

"The Government shall prepare Estimates of the Receipts and Estimates of the Expenditure of the State for each financial year, and shall present them to Dáil Éireann for consideration."

52.   Article 17 is devoted entirely to the subject of Finance :

"As soon as possible after the presentation to Dáil Éireann under Article 28 of this Constitution of the Estimates of Receipts and the Estimates of Expenditure of the State for any financial year, Dáil Éireann shall consider such Estimates " ; " Save in so far as may be provided by specific enactment in each case, the legislation required to give effect to the Financial Resolutions of each year shall be enacted within that year " ; " Dáil Éireann shall not pass any vote or resolution, and no law shall be enacted for the appropriation of revenue or other public moneys unless the purpose of the appropriation shall be recommended to Dáil Éireann by a message from the Government signed by the Taoiseach."

53.   The third Article of the Constitution dealing with Finance is Article 11 which says :

"All revenues of the State from whatever source arising shall, subject to such exception as may be provided by law, form one fund, and shall be appropriated for the purposes and in the manner and subject to the charges and liabilities determined and imposed by law."

The Fund referred to is the Central Fund, with which we shall deal at a later stage.

THE FINANCIAL YEAR

54.   First, then, we have to deal with the Financial Year, that is, with the annual period for which the State's accounts are made up.   The choice of the period is entirely a matter of convenience, and there is no really compelling reason why one period should be

---

Standing Order 117 of Dáil Éireann states :

"The yearly Estimates for the Public Services shall be presented to the Dáil and circulated to members not less than fourteen days prior to the consideration thereof and not later than the first day of April; provided that supplementary or additional estimates, not included therein, may be brought forward on leave given by the Dáil after motion made on notice."

chosen rather than another. Generally speaking, however, it would seem that the period chosen is either the Calendar Year, or that beginning on July 1st, or that commencing on April 1st each year. The first period is followed by such countries as Austria, Belgium, France, Spain and Switzerland; the second, by Australia, Italy, Norway, Portugal, Sweden and the United States of America; and the third, by Great Britain, Denmark, New Zealand, South Africa and Ireland. From the diversity of practice in neighbouring states, it is clear that climatic conditions do not determine the period, and indeed within the past few years there was some question in Ireland of substituting the calendar for the present financial year.

ESTIMATES OF EXPENDITURE — ALL SERVICES [1]

55. Confining attention for the present to Estimates of Expenditure, it is to be noted at the outset that all the expenditure of the State may be divided under three main headings according as it relates to Supply Services, to Central Fund Services or to what may be called Capital Services.

56. Supply Services are temporary annual charges on the Central Fund authorised for specific purposes as set out in the annual Appropriation Act. They are, therefore, recurring charges in that they come each year under the review and criticism of Parliament. They are, in effect, estimates for the cost of the public services administered by each department, so that the terms " Supply Services " and " Public Services " are interchangeable.

57. Central Fund Services are permanent charges on the Central Fund authorised for specific purposes by continuing Acts of Parliament. The Acts are continuing in the sense that they remain in force until repealed, so that they do not come annually under the review of Parliament. In effect they may be considered as continuing grants to the Minister for Finance for certain well defined purposes set out in the governing statutes.

58. Capital Services may be considered to consist of advances of money made under continuing statutes either to State-sponsored Bodies or to certain Capital Funds established by the statutes.

59. In a White Paper — " Estimates of Receipts and Expenditure " — presented to the Dáil by the Government at the beginning of each financial year in accordance with Article 28 of the Constitution, summaries and details of the estimated expenditure on each of the three services are given. Thus for 1959/60 the totals on each of the services and the Road Fund were:

---

1. See Appendix, para. 354.

		£000
1.	Supply Services	115,547
2.	Central Fund Services (excluding Road Fund)	22,427
3.	Capital Services	16,560
4.	Payments to Road Fund	5,550

TOTAL   £160,084

From these figures it is clear that the main bulk of the State's expenditure falls on the Supply Services, and it is with the financial administration of that outlay that this book is chiefly concerned.

ESTIMATES OF EXPENDITURE — CENTRAL FUND SERVICES [2]

60. The same White Paper details the estimated expenditure on the Central Fund Services for 1959/60 as follows:

		£000
1.	Service of Public Debt	
	Interest	14,127
	Sinking Fund, etc.	6,868
2.	Local Taxation Grants	
	Agricultural Grant	599
	Exchequer Contribution	2
	Customs and Excise Duties Grant ...	87
	Licence Duties Grant	260
	Estate Duty Grant	165
3.	Judicial Salaries, etc.	
	Judicial Salaries	140
	Judicial Pensions, etc.	20
	Other Salaries and Allowances ...	17
	Other Pensions, etc.	17
	Expenses of Returning Officers ...	125
4.	Payments to Road Fund	5,550

TOTAL   £27,977

As regards the term "Central Fund Services," it should be noted that it is not connected in any way with the annual Central Fund Act which deals exclusively with the Supply Services. The services here referred to are governed by permanent or continuing statutes passed either by the Oireachtas or formerly by the British Parliament and continued in force by the Irish Government.

SERVICE OF PUBLIC DEBT

61. This Debt is sometimes called the "National Debt," and it means the debt created by the Central Government as distinct

---

2. See Appendix, para. 357.

from that created by Local Authorities under specific Statutes enabling them to do so. We shall be dealing later more fully with the subject. At the end of March, 1959, the Public Debt amounted to £360m. and the annual interest payable thereon was estimated at £14m. In accordance with the issue terms of the various State loans, a sinking fund for each of them is formed by periodically setting aside revenue and allowing it to accumulate at interest for the specific purpose of reducing the principal of the loan. The amount so set aside in 1959/60 was £6.8m. The sum stated does not include the remuneration (£66,300) paid to the Bank of Ireland for the management of Government Stocks.

AGRICULTURAL GRANT

62.   This Grant is paid to County Councils to enable them without loss to themselves to make allowances, by way of rate abatements, to the rated occupiers of agricultural land in their areas. The figure given here, £599,000, is governed by Section 47 of the Local Government (Ireland) Act, 1898. It is borne on the Central Fund and is distinct from the Supplementary Agricultural Grant which is voted annually as one of the Supply Services. Under the Act of 1898 it was a fixed amount of £727,655 for the whole of Ireland, and gave relief to the extent of half the rates paid on agricultural land in the standard year 1896/97.

In 1922, the amount apportioned to Saorstát Éireann was £599,000. Between 1922 and 1946, the amount of the Grant was increased by means of the Supplementary Grant and the basis of its distribution altered.

In 1946, under the Rates on Agricultural Land (Relief) Act, the Grant was again increased, but, instead of being payable in advance, it was related to the actual rates struck by the County Councils in any particular year, and was to be the amount needed to give relief on the following basis: (a) A Primary Allowance of three-fifths of the general rate in the £ on the land valuation up to £20; (b) A Supplementary Allowance of one-fifth of the general rate in the £ on the land valuation over £20; (c) An Employment Allowance at the rate of 10/- in the £ on the land valuation over £20, provided that the allowance should not exceed £6-10-0 for each adult workman at work on the holding during the whole of the preceding calendar year.

In 1953 another Relief Act abolished the Supplementary Allowance, increased the Employment Allowance, and left the Primary Allowance unchanged. The Employment Allowance was increased to £17 in respect of each qualified workman, provided that the total of the allowances should not exceed the rates on the land valuation over £20. This Act was to operate for three years, but it was renewed for a similar period in 1956 and 1959.

The Supplementary Agricultural Grant for 1959/60 is £4.8m. in addition to the £599,000 granted under the Act of 1898, so that the total relief is £5.4m. In 1958/59 the grants relieved farmers to the extent of 44 per cent of the rates levied on agricultural land, but its value as an agent of productivity has recently been the subject of adverse criticism. The Capital Investment Advisory Committee recommended its abolition, and Mr. Whitaker says of it: " Much attention has been focussed recently on this subvention and on the question of its aid to agricultural production. The employment allowance (some £1.3m. out of a total of £5.62m.) is a wage subsidy, introduced in the early thirties as an inducement to farmers to increase the amount of their hired labour. It was never an effective inducement and in the conditions of to-day is a complete anachronism." [3]

OTHER LOCAL TAXATION GRANTS

63. These include: (i) the Exchequer Contribution. Originally this was payable under the Purchase of Land (Ireland) Act, 1891, but under the Labourers (Ireland) Act, 1906 — the basis of Acts providing houses for rural workers — it became a direct subsidy for the purpose of rural housing, and was allocated in proportion to the number of cottages built in each county up to 1906. It is payable annually in reduction of loan charges incurred on cottages built up to 1906; (ii) the Grant under the Local Government (Ireland) Act, 1898, the object of which was to relieve the local rates of the cost of maintaining the insane poor, and the Act provided that certain local licence duties should be assigned for this purpose; (iii) under old British Statutes a portion of the local Customs and Excise and Estate Duties were also payable into the Local Taxation and other Accounts, the object again being to relieve the burden on the rates. Thus, duties on Liquor Licences were meant to pay one-half of the salaries of doctors, nurses and teachers in poor law institutions including one-half of the cost of maintenance, and the product of the Estate Duties was intended for the pay and pensions of those officers. The grants and payments continue but the basis of their distribution ceased in 1947/48.

JUDICIAL AND OTHER SALARIES AND PENSIONS

64. The pensions of Civil Servants are governed by the

3. Economic Development, p. 130.

Superannuation Acts, 1934 to 1956, and their salaries by regulations made from time to time by the Minister for Finance. Both are part of the Supply Services and are, therefore, annually reviewed by the Dáil — the salaries being provided under each departmental vote, and the pensions under the Vote for Superannuation and Retired Allowances. The salaries and pensions, however, of the members of the Judiciary are Central Fund Services and are prescribed by the Courts of Justice Act, 1924 to 1959, and continue in force until repealed or amended. The Salaries referred to here are those of five Judges of the Supreme Court, seven of the High Court, and ten of the Circuit Courts, together with those of 41 Justices of the District Courts. The salaries of the staffs attached to these Courts are Supply Services and are borne on Votes 29 to 33.

65. *Other Salaries and Allowances* include the salaries of the President, the Comptroller and Auditor General, Allowances to two Leaders of Opposition Parties, Compensation to King's Inns Library and Sundry Allowances to the Lord Mayor and Citizens of Dublin and the Librarian of Marsh's Library. The salary of the President is provided by the Presidential Establishment Acts, but the salaries, allowances and expenses of the Establishment itself are borne on Vote 1 of the Supply Services. The Allowances paid to two Leaders of Opposition Parties are provided by the Ministers and Parliamentary Secretaries Acts, and the salary of the Comptroller and Auditor General by the Acts of that title. The compensation paid to King's Inns Library is for loss of right to free copies of books, and the Sundry Allowances are paid under an old Act of George III.

66. *Other Pensions.* The reference here is to the pensions paid to former Comptrollers and Auditors General, and to former holders of Ministerial or Secretarial Offices including the widows of the latter.

67. *Expenses of Returning Officers* are paid under Electoral Acts to officers presiding at, and superintending, elections to the Dáil and Seanad.

THE ROAD FUND

68. The revenue derived from the Motor Vehicles etc. Duties is earmarked for the Road Fund. Licence Duties on mechanically-driven vehicles were first introduced in 1909 when a Road Board was set up to build new and to improve old roads. In 1919 its functions were transferred to the Ministry of Transport, and in 1922 to the Department of Local Government. Under the Roads Act of 1920 County Councils and County Borough Corporations, known as the " Licensing Authorities," were made responsible for the registration of vehicles, and the collection of licence duties and of fees for driving

licences. The rates of motor taxation are fixed by the Finance Acts. The Road Fund is fed by the licence and driving duties, by fees on petrol pumps, and by fines and penalties enforced under the Road Acts. All such receipts are paid into a Central Motor Tax Account, and thence transferred through the Exchequer to the Road Fund. Under the Road (Advances) Acts, 1926 to 1948, the Minister for Finance may from time to time make advances, repayable with interest to the Fund, within a limit of £5m. On 31st March, 1959, the repayable advances outstanding were £1.7m. Under the Road Fund (Grants and Advances) (Temporary Provisions) Act, 1959, the Minister for Finance may, in each of the five financial years beginning in 1959/60, make to the Fund an advance of £200,000, all such advances with interest payable thereon being a charge on the Fund.

ACCOUNT OF THE CENTRAL FUND SERVICES

69. The account for the Central Fund Services is kept by the Department of Finance, and under Section 12 of the Exchequer and Audit Acts, 1866-1921, Finance has to send to the Auditor General at the end of each quarter an account of the transactions on the Fund for that period, and the Act empowers the Comptroller to grant further credits in respect of any outstanding charges. If, on the other hand, there is not sufficient money in the account to meet these charges he may, at the request of the Department, issue a Deficiency Certificate to the Bank which may then make advances up to the amount certified. An Exchequer Record of all transactions is kept by the Comptroller's Office. At the end of the year the account for the period is rendered, and is published as an Appendix to the Report of the Committee of Public Accounts. Thus, the account for 1957/58 was as follows:—

	Estimated Expenditure £	Actual Expenditure £	Less than Estimated £	More than Estimated £
Central Fund:—				
Service of Public Debt	15,973,000	15,903,382	69,618	
Payments to Local Taxation a/c ...	1,175,486	1,190,912		15,426
Payments to Capital Fund	3,000,000	4,275,000		1,275,000
Other Central Fund Services	201,514	507,309		305,795
Road Fund ...	5,750,000	4,762,000	988,000	28,000
Total of Central Fund Services ...	£26,100,000	26,638,603	1,057,618	1,596.221

It will be noted that while in the case of the Supply Services the comparison in the Appropriation Account is between " Grant " and " Expenditure ", the comparison here is between Estimate and Expenditure, because the Acts governing the Central Fund Services are regarded as giving continuing grants to the Minister for Finance.

ESTIMATES OF EXPENDITURE — CAPITAL SERVICES [4]

70. The Estimates for " Capital and Other Issues " for 1959/60 were as follows:—

		£000
1.	Electricity (Supply) Acts, 1927-58	1,000
2.	Turf Development Acts, 1946-59	1,410
3.	Irish Shipping Ltd. Acts, 1947-59	2,030
4.	Sea Fisheries Acts, 1952 and 1956	240
5.	Industrial Credit Acts, 1933 and 1958 ...	2,400
6.	Air Navigation & Transport Acts, 1936-1950	490
7.	Telephone Capital Acts, 1924-1956	1,610
8.	Local Loans Fund Acts, 1935-1956	6,500
9.	Road Fund (Advances) Acts, 1926 and 1948	200
10.	Finance Acts, 1953 (Sec. 16) and 1954 (Sec. 22)	200
11.	Bretton Woods Agreements Acts, 1957 ...	—
12.	International Finance Corporation Act, 1958	—
13.	Trade Loans (Guarantee) Acts, 1939-1954 ...	30
14.	Insurance Act, 1953 (Section 2 (4)) ...	—
15.	Gaeltacht Industries Act, 1957	90
16.	Payment to Shannon Free Airport Development Coy. Ltd.	360

TOTAL £16,560

71. The advances contemplated above are issues from the Central Fund in accordance with the statutes referred to. The Road Fund has already been dealt with, and Items 1 to 6 inclusive will be considered in the chapter on State-Sponsored Bodies. Meanwhile the explanation of the other items is briefly as follows:—

72. *Telephone Capital Acts.* These authorise the Minister for Finance to advance from time to time any money needed for the development of the telephonic system of the State. Advances are made through the Exchequer from the Post Office Savings Bank, and they are repaid by means of annuities extending over a period of not less than 25 years. These annuities are provided by means

---

4. See Appendix, para. 358.

of moneys voted annually by Parliament in the Vote for the Department of Posts and Telegraphs. The Telephone Capital Repayments for 1959/60 is estimated at £1.3m. The Act of 1956 permits further advances up to £6m. On 31st March, 1959, the State had contracted a liability of £15.2m. in respect of debt created under the Acts.

73. *Local Loans Fund Acts.* The Local Loans Fund is a fund outside the Exchequer from which loans are made on certain conditions to Local Authorities for certain capital purposes. The Authorities have power to borrow with the sanction of the Minister for Local Government or, where health projects of a capital nature are involved, the Minister for Health. They borrow temporarily from the Banks or other financial agencies to meet short-term deficiencies pending the receipt of rates or other revenue, or pending the raising of capital by long-term loans. The latter are chiefly obtained from the Fund which is controlled by the Minister for Finance, but County Councils, County Boroughs and Borough Corporations and Urban District Councils have also the power, with the consent of the Minister, to borrow by the creation and issue of Stock — a power exercised by the Corporations of Cork and Dublin in recent years.

Up to 1922 the service of the loans was administered through the Local Loans Fund of the United Kingdom established by the National Debt and Local Loans Act, 1887, and was managed by the National Debt Commissioners. Between 1922 and 1935, pending the making of suitable arrangements for the continuation of the service in Ireland, an informal plan was adopted by which the money collected in the Irish State in respect of loans made before 1st April, 1922, was paid into the Exchequer, but for local loans made after that date, a non-statutory Local Loans Fund was set up and operated as a self-contained fund outside of the Exchequer, being financed by voted grants-in-aid. On 1st May, 1935, the Capital thus provided amounted to £5.6m.

The present statutory Local Loans Fund began in 1935. It took over the entire assets of the informal Fund and the amounts outstanding in respect of loans issued before 1st April, 1922. As against these assets the Fund was deemed to be liable for about £12m. as an Exchequer advance. Since 1935 the capital of the Fund has been increased under succeeding Statutes by means of Exchequer advances. These Acts do not expressly limit the extent to which the Fund may borrow, but they do limit the aggregate amount of moneys issued from the Fund in respect of local loans. Thus the Act of 1956 sets the limit at £110m. On 31st March, 1960, the Fund owed the State £93.3m.

The main capital purposes for which the loans are used by the Local Authorities are Housing, Drainage, Land Improvements, Mental Hospitals, County Homes and Vocational Education.

74. *Finance Acts, 1953 and 1954.* The Acts empower the Minister for Finance to accept in payment of Death Duties the surrender of 5 per cent National Loan 1962/72, or 4½ per cent 1973/78. Hence, the estimate is the sum which may be required from the Central Fund during 1959/60, to enable the Minister to take up any stock so surrendered.

75. *Bretton Woods Agreements Act, 1957.* By this Act the Irish Government became a member of the two organisations known as "The International Monetary Fund" and "The International Bank for Reconstruction" established in July, 1944, at Bretton Woods in the United States of America. One of the many objects of these Institutions is to assist by means of loans, repayable over a period of from three to five years, the national development of member states, when their own financial resources are insufficient to do so, and to that end to give expert advice by official surveys. To become a member it is necessary to join both the Fund and the Bank. For that purpose quotas are allotted, that is, the part or share which each member must contribute to the total amount of the Institutions' capital. Ireland's quota or subscription to each Institution was £30m. The deposit with the Fund is made by payment in gold of either 25 per cent of its quota, or 10 per cent of its net holdings of gold and United States dollars, whichever is the less. The 10 per cent of Ireland's holdings in gold and dollars on the relevant date (May, 1957) was £1.6m. and that represented 15 per cent of its quota. The remaining 85 per cent was payable in Irish Currency and was met by non-negotiable, non-interest bearing notes. The subscription to the Bank as distinct from the Fund was payable in the following manner: (a) 20 per cent in gold or U.S. dollars on joining but subject to these provisos: (1) 2 per cent of the price of each share in gold or dollars on joining; (2) 18 per cent in Irish Currency when required by the Bank to meet its obligations, but 8 per cent would be called within 12 months of joining; (b) 80 per cent when called by the Bank to meet its obligations payable either in gold or dollars or Irish currency. The value both of the deposit and of the shares is repayable, if a State withdraws from the Institutions.

76. *International Finance Corporation Act, 1958.* By this Act Ireland became a member of this Corporation, the purpose of which "is to further economic development by encouraging the growth of private enterprise in member countries, particularly in the less developed countries." The Corporation thus supplements the

activities of the International Bank. It may invest in productive private enterprises in the territories of its members, notwithstanding the fact of the existence of a government or other public interest in such enterprises. Its authorised capital is $100,000,000 divided into 100,000 shares having a par value of one thousand U.S. dollars each. To become a member Ireland had to buy 350 share units of $1,000 each. This would give her about 600 votes out of a total of about 106,048 — each member having 250 votes together with one extra vote for each share held. Up to 1960 the State paid to the three Institutions the sum of £4.2m. in subscriptions and payments.

77. *International Development Association.* This is a new Institution and will be an affiliate of the World Bank. Its main object will be to make easy payment loans to underdeveloped countries on favourable interest rates and long repayment terms— the repayment being partly at least in the currency of the borrowers. It will have a capital of £357m. of which the United States of America will subscribe about £114m. and Great Britain £85.6m. Some sixty nations may become members, and their subscriptions will be in proportion to their ability to pay.

78. *Shannon Free Airport Development Coy. Ltd.* This Company was, without any special statute, incorporated as a limited liability company under the Companies Acts in January, 1959. Its purpose is to develop at Shannon Airport transatlantic traffic, tourist facilities and freight traffic. To that end it can do all things which are calculated, either directly or indirecly, to facilitate the establishment of commercial, industrial and trading enterprises, including the purchase of land, the construction of buildings, and the making of grants to other persons or companies for those purposes. The Company's aim is to make the Airport an industrial centre by attracting to the area enterprises which will engage in the import and export of materials and finished products by air.

The main object of the Shannon Free Airport Development Act, 1959, is to provide capital and grants for the Company. The Act provides (1) that the Minister for Finance may with money out of the Central Fund take up shares in the Company within an aggregate of £1½m. (2) that out of moneys voted by the Oireachtas he may make grants up to £½m. to enable the Company to carry out its purposes and to meet its running expenses; (3) that if the grants be used to provide machinery and equipment for industrial undertakings they may not exceed one-half of their cost. A grant-in-aid of £50,000 was provided for the Company in 1959/60, but this was subsequently raised to £190,000 by a Supplementary Estimate.

79. *Insurance Act,* 1953. This amends the law relating to the

insurance business and empowers the Minister for Industry and Commerce to give guarantees with respect to the insurance of risks in connection with external trade.

80. *Gaeltacht Industries Act,* 1957. The purpose of this Act was to make better provision for the organisation, conduct and development of the Rural Industries formerly administered by the Department of the Gaeltacht; to provide for the initiation of new industries and productive schemes of employment in the Gaeltacht; to establish a board to be called Gaeltarra Éireann; to define its powers and duties, and to transfer to it the rural industries. Section 26 provides for capital repayment advances to the Board within a limit of £500,000, and Section 25 for its administrative expenses out of voted moneys. The estimate for 1959/60 was for a Grant-in-aid of £110,000.

81. *Trade Loans (Guarantee) Acts,* 1939 *to* 1954. These Acts empower the Minister for Industry and Commerce, after consulting an Advisory Committee and under conditions and terms agreed by the Minister for Finance, (1) to guarantee or to grant loans for capital or manufacturing undertakings, that is, any undertakings involving capital expenditure, the object of which is the production or manufacture in Ireland of goods or articles for sale, or for the erection or equipment in Ireland of dwelling houses (including the acquisition and development of land for that purpose), provided that the application of the proceeds is calculated to promote employment in Ireland; (2) to grant or to guarantee loans in order to reduce the retail prices of essential commodities, that is, commodities taken into account by the Minister in compiling the cost of living index number, or commodities deemed by the Minister to be essential. No loan was to be granted for less than £500, and the aggregate capital amount of the loans granted was not to exceed £1m., subsequently raised in 1953 to £1½m. Advances were to be made out of the Central Fund, and any not repaid after two years from the date of the advance were to be repaid out of moneys voted by the Oireachtas. Quarterly statements of loans granted or guaranteed giving their amounts, purposes and conditions were to be laid before the Oireachtas together with an annual statement of the sums outstanding and of those repaid. In the Estimates for 1959/60, in the Vote for Repayment of Trade Loans Advances, there is a sum of £113,000. Four companies were involved. The amount of the Guaranteed Loans was £129,000, the amount advanced £125,996, and the amount to be repaid to the Central Fund £113,000.

CHAPTER III

Estimates of Expenditure: Supply Services

PREPARATION OF THE ESTIMATES

82. The Estimates of Expenditure on the Supply Services, commonly called simply "The Estimates," are statements of the probable cost of carrying out the public services of the State. They are the main foundation of the whole financial fabric of government, because they determine to a very large extent the amount of revenue to be raised and the consequent taxation to be imposed on the citizens. The word "Budget" is sometimes used in the same sense as we have used "Estimate," but ordinarily the former denotes a statement not only of the probable expenditure, but also of the anticipated revenue, together with the financial proposals founded thereon.

83. The collection and expenditure of the State's revenues are a particular function of the Minister for Finance, and it is his Department, therefore, which initiates the call to each department of State for an estimate of its financial needs for the coming year. The Department of Finance itself has four main divisions: (1) Finance, which deals with revenue, loans, the public debt, estimates, money bills, the Central Fund, banking, currency and financial procedure; (2) Supply, which deals with the expenditure of grants voted by the Dáil; (3) Establishment, which is concerned with the personnel, remuneration and organisation of the Civil Service; and (4) Planning, dealing with economic matters.

84. Much preliminary work is performed before the Estimates emerge into the light of day. The initial step is taken by the Department of Finance in the October of the current year, when it issues its annual "Estimates Circular" directing each Accounting Officer to submit by December 1st the estimate for his department for the coming year. The Circular usually stresses the need for economy, the necessity of accurate estimation, the care which should be taken regarding any new proposals for increased expenditure, and the necessity of complying strictly with the "Standing Instructions to Accounting Officers" issued by the Department.

The Standing Instructions deal exclusively with the method of preparing the Estimates. The main instructions may be, briefly, summarised as follows:—

(a) The printed Estimate Forms forwarded with the Circular must be filled up in quadruplicate.

(b) There must accompany the Forms statements in triplicate " explaining and justifying seriatim the amounts provided in the Estimate under each Sub-head of expenditure."

(c) No provision should be inserted for any matter or service not already sanctioned by the Department of Finance. If in an exceptional case this may be necessary, then the proposal should be submitted for sanction immediately so as to allow of due consideration before the Estimates assume their final form.

(d) Authority for a new or increased expenditure must not be inferred from the fact of its having been from any cause printed in the Estimate before the proper official sanction has been given.

85. With the receipt of the Circular each department must give active consideration to its estimate. During the past months problems will have arisen, and new proposals will have come forward, and no doubt they will have received due attention, but the time has now come to see how they can be fitted into the financial programme for the coming year. In framing its estimate each department must follow the method of " Gross Estimation " — that is, expenditure and receipts must be shown separately in the estimate and accounts without any deduction. This is opposed to " Net Estimation," where the estimate and accounts show only the balance of expenditure over receipts or conversely.

86. When the various problems arising out of the proposals have been settled during the early months of the new calendar year, the " Book of Estimates for Public Services " makes its appearance in March. Each estimate now receives the title of Vote and is given a number. By " Vote " is meant the amount of grant or supply for each department to be submitted for the vote of the Dáil and the estimates appear as numbered on the Order Paper.

86A. The Estimates for 1959/60 contain 66 Votes totalling a gross sum of £123,215,366, or, after deducting receipts of £7,668,296 (called Appropriations-in-Aid) a net sum of £115,547,070. Of that total the pay item alone of the Civil Service, the Defence Forces, the Gárda Síochán and the Teachers, excluding the cost of Industrial Staff, amounts to about £34m. — Civil Service £17m., Defence Forces £3m., Gárda Síochána £4m. and Teachers £10m. The cost of the £34m. is spread over the most of the Votes, and it would, therefore, serve no useful purpose, even if it were not beyond the limits of this work, to treat each Vote separately. Instead, it

41

is proposed to take the 14 Departments listed in Chapter I, to summarise their costs, and then to deal briefly with the more important services administered by them.[1]

The nett cost of each Department is as follows:—

		£		
1.	The Dept. of the Taoiseach	28,130	Vote	3
2.	The Dept. of Finance ...	15,516,540	Votes	1, 2, 4, 6-25
3.	The Dept. of Justice	5,878,020	,,	26-34
4.	The Dept. of Education ...	15,578,870	,,	36-44
5.	The Dept. of Posts & Telegraphs	10,012,500	,,	55-56
6.	The Dept. of Defence ...	8,401,450	,,	57-58
7.	The Dept. of External Affairs	522,710	,,	59-60
8.	The Dept. of Industry & Commerce	5,259,220	,,	50-54 & 66
9.	The Dept. of Agriculture ...	11,344,960	,,	49
10.	The Dept. of Local Govt. ...	4,475,120	,,	35
11.	The Dept. of Lands & Fisheries	4,417,450	,,	45-47
12.	The Dept. of Health ...	8,259,350	,,	64-65
13.	The Dept. of Social Welfare	25,334,600	,,	61-63
14.	The Dept. of the Gaeltacht ...	481,700	,,	48
	Audit Office	36,450	,,	5

Total: £115,547,070

VOTED CAPITAL SERVICES [2]

87. Included in the figure of £115,547,070, there is an amount of £14,419,495 in respect of Capital Services, and, therefore, that must be added to the total in para. 70 for such services. The items are spread over 11 Votes and may be summarised thus:

Vote 9, Public Works and Buildings, includes £2.6m. for New Works, Arterial Drainage and for the purchase of Sites, Buildings and Equipment.

Vote 35, Local Government, bears a sum of £1.7m. for Grants, under the Housing Acts.

Vote 43, Universities and Colleges, has £55,000 for the clearance of a site in Cork, for additional accommodation in Galway; and for the redemption of Capital Expenditure in Trinity College.

1. See Appendix, para. 355.
2. See Appendix, para. 356.

Vote 46, Forestry, contains £1.3m. for the acquisition of land, and for forest development and management.

Vote 47, Fisheries, provides £154,800 for a grant-in-aid to the Fisheries Board, for the purchase of an Exploratory Fishing Vessel for Pond Fish Culture, and for a grant to the Salmon Conservancy Fund.

Vote 48, Roinn na Gaeltachta, contains a grant of £90,000 for houses.

Vote 49, Agriculture, has £6.5m. for Bovine Tuberculosis, the Land Project, Lime and Fertilisers Subsidies, Farm Buildings Scheme and for the improvement of Poultry and Egg production.

Vote 50, Industry and Commerce, provides two Grants-in-Aid, one for Industrial Development (£200,000) and the other (£500,000) for An Foras Tionscal.

Vote 51, Transport and Marine Services, has a grant of £214,990 for the permanent improvement of Harbours.

Vote 52, Aviation and Meterological Services, contains £961,875 for constructional Works at Shannon, Dublin and Cork Airports, and for the purchase of lands, buildings and equipment.

Vote 54, Tourism, provides two Grants-in-Aid for Resort Development (£100,000) and for additional Bedroom Accommodation (£50,000).

Provision is made in the Central Fund Services for the redemption over a thirty-year period of borrowings incurred for these voted capital services.

DEPARTMENT OF FINANCE

88. This Department is responsible either directly or indirectly for the financial administration of the Votes for the President's Establishment; Houses of the Oireachtas; Department of the Taoiseach; Central Statistics Office; The Minister's Office; Office of the Revenue Commissioners; Office of Public Works; Public Works and Buildings; Employment and Emergency Schemes; Management of Government Stocks; State Laboratory; Civil Service Commission; An Chomhairle Ealaíon; Commissions and Special Inquiries; Superannuation and Retired Allowances; Secret Service; Expenses under the Electoral and Juries Acts; Supplementary Agricultural Grant; Law Charges; Miscellaneous Expenses; Stationery Office; Valuation and Boundary Survey; Ordnance Survey; and Rates on Government Property. Apart from the Supplementary Agricultural Grant, which has already been dealt with, the following services included above would seem to call for comment:

88A. *New Works, etc.* (Vote 9). In the voted capital services there is included £1.6m. for the building and alteration of National Schools. This represents a long-term programme extending over some twenty years. In 1922 there were about 4,800 National Schools in the Irish State, and since then about 25 per cent. has been replaced by new schools. Of the remaining 3,600, about 750 are listed for replacement, and some 300 require major improvements or extensions.

88B. *Arterial Drainage.* In Vote 9 there is included as a Capital Service £546,000 for Arterial as distinct from River Drainage. Under Sec. 9 of the Arterial Drainage Act, 1945, the Commissioners of Public Works are authorised to carry out such drainage schemes as are confirmed by order made by the Minister for Finance. The cost of maintenance is, under the Acts 1945-55, recoverable from the Councils of the Counties in which the benefited lands are situated. The estimated cost of six Catchment Drainage Schemes is £4.6m. and the estimated expenditure to 31st March, 1959, was £4.4m. Of the scheme generally Mr. Whitaker says: " The position is that the policy of having three major and one or two minor schemes always in progress entails an annual outlay of close on £1m. to cover administrative and engineering charges, wages and materials and the maintenance, repair and replacement of machinery and plant. The cost must be regarded as high when it is borne in mind that it represents in recent schemes from £40 to £60 per acre of land improved, and that the improvement in the annual value of the drained land is reduced to a very small net amount when allowance is made for the cost of maintenance. There does not seem to be very good ground for increasing this form of State aid to agriculture until more immediate needs are fully met." [1]

88C. *Employment and Emergency Schemes.* This Vote (No. 10) provides grants to Local Authorities towards their expenditure on road and amenity schemes in order to provide employment, the distribution of the grants being related to the number of unemployed in each area. Urban and Rural Employment schemes cover the provision of road amenity and development schemes in town and country: Minor Employment schemes, the construction and repair of accommodation and bog roads; Development Works, the provision of roads and drainage to help the production of turf by landowners, voluntary organisations, business firms and others. The local contribution in recent years for special employment schemes has been 20 per cent. in Dublin and Dún Laoghaire; 17 per cent. in Cork and Limerick; 14 per cent. in Waterford, and it averages 12 per cent. in 55 other urban areas.

---

1. Economic Development, p. 128.

88D. *Miscellaneous Expenses* (Vote 21) is mainly made up of Grants-in-Aid to the Incorporated Council of Law Reporting for Ireland, the Abbey Theatre, and to such cultural institutions as the Royal Zoological Society, the Royal Irish Academy and the Royal Irish Academy of Music.

DEPARTMENT OF JUSTICE

89. This Department administers the Votes for the Minister's Office; the Gárda Síochána including Pensions, Allowances and Gratuities in respect of its members; Prisons, the District Court, the Circuit Court, the Supreme and High Courts, the Land Registry and Registry of Deeds, the Public Record Office and Charitable Donations and Bequests.

DEPARTMENT OF LOCAL GOVERNMENT

90. This Department (Vote 35) has a single vote for £4.5m., about 80 per cent. of which provides for housing grants and subsidies. The main items are:

90A. *Contribution towards Housing Loan Charges of Local Authorities* £1.8m. Borrowing for urban and local housing schemes is primarily the business of Local Authorities, but the State comes to their aid by contributing a proportion of the loan charges incurred by them. For urban housing the Housing (Financial and Miscellaneous Provisions) Acts, 1932-58, permit the State to contribute up to $66\frac{2}{3}$ per cent. of the annual loan charges where the Minister of Local Government is satisfied that the houses are needed for the accommodation of (i) persons displaced by the collapse or destruction of their former dwellings or by any of the operations of the Authority under the Housing of the Working Classes Acts, or (ii) persons in need of re-housing on medical, compassionate or other similar grounds whose circumstances would not permit them to be re-housed otherwise. The limit is $33\frac{1}{3}$ per cent. of the charge for any other housing schemes. The maximum period over which the subsidy may be spread is 50 years, and in measuring the subsidy the capital cost is limited to £1,500 for each house, and £2,000 for flats.

For rural housing a contribution up to 60 per cent. of the loan charges is allowed, the capital cost for each house ranking for the subsidy being £1,000 for unserviced, and £1,500 for serviced cottages. The contribution is conditioned by the houses being let at such rents as the Authorities may, with the approval of the Minister, determine.

In addition to providing houses, County Councils are empowered to make loans under the Small Dwellings Acquisition Acts to persons building houses for their own accommodation. The limit of the market value of such houses, the maximum advance payable thereon, and the maximum period of repayment have varied from time to time.

90B. *Interest Subsidy towards Loan Charges of Local Authorities* on certain loans advanced from the Local Loans Fund in respect of Housing Schemes (£231,000). The loans refer to the money borrowed by Local Authorities for the purposes of the Housing of the Working Classes Acts or the Labourers' Acts and the subsidy is the difference between the loan charges incurred and the loan charges on the same amount calculated at such lesser rate or rates of interest as may be determined by the Minister.

90C. *Grants under the Housing (Financial and Miscellaneous Provisions) Acts,* 1932-58, £1.7m. The Acts allow the Minister, with the consent of the Minister for Finance to make to any private person a grant not exceeding certain specified limits prescribed in the Acts for the purpose of purchasing, erecting, reconstructing and improving dwelling houses.

90D *Contributions towards Loan Charges of Local Authorities in respect of Sanitary Service Works* (£345,000). This refers to the capital cost of Sanitary Service Schemes including Swimming Pools. To encourage the expansion of water and sewerage schemes, it is now proposed to raise the contribution payable to the Authorities. The Exchequer will in future bear about 52 per cent. of their cost, and the repayment of the loans will be based on an annuity instead of the present instalment system, the repayment of the loans being extended from 30 to 50 years. The total cost is estimated at £35m.

90E. *Grant to supplement the Road Fund* (£200,000). In addition to the repayable advances mentioned in para. 68, the Act of 1959 also provides that an annual grant of £200,000 may be made to supplement the Fund for a period of five years out of moneys provided by the Oireachtas. Its purpose is to deal with the special problems created by the closure of railway lines and by particular major industrial undertakings.

DEPARTMENT OF EDUCATION

91. This Department is financially responsible for the administration of the Votes for the Minister's Office; Primary Education; Secondary Education; Technical Instruction; Science and Art; Reformatory and Industrial Schools; Dublin Institute for Advanced Studies; Universities and Colleges, and the National Gallery. The more important items are:

91A. *Training of Teachers* (£209,230). This includes grants in respect of students in four Training Colleges at Drumcondra,

Blackrock, Limerick and Dublin, repayable advances to students in respect of fees, and the cost of six Preparatory Colleges* which are situated in Co. Cork, Co. Dublin, Co. Mayo, Co. Kerry, Co. Donegal and Galway.

91B. *Primary Education.* The total of £10m. includes £1m. for the superannuation of National Teachers which is offset by £66,500, being the income from the securities which were formerly part of the National School Teachers' Pension Fund and by £26,598 from the Church Temporalities Fund. The Primary Schools, numbering about 4,870, are divided into 4,440 Classifications Schools and 430 Capitation Schools. The teachers in the former, numbering about 10,000, are in receipt of salaries paid direct by the Department (£6.5m.) and those in the latter, about 3,300, by annual capitation grants (£2m.) based on the rate of from £14-12-0 to £16-7-0 on the first 100 pupils, and from £10 to £11 on the remainder. The Capitation are Monastery or Convent schools, and if a lay Assistant is appointed the salary is paid by the Department and deducted from the Grant payable to the school.

91C. *Secondary Education.* There are about 485 Secondary Schools in the State employing some 4,570 teachers. The schools are not State-owned, but the State assists them financially, and especially by contributing capitation grants to the Managers of the schools, and incremental salary grants to teachers. The capitation grants range from £4 to £8 for pupils under 12 years of age, from £6 to £11 for junior, and £8 to £16 for senior pupils according to the number of attendances during the school year. The amount of capitation grant is £800,000 for 1959/60, including £30,750 payable in respect of teachers' salaries under the Intermediate Education (Ireland) Act, 1914. As regards the Incremental Salary Grant, the teachers are paid on a scale rising from a minimum basic pay by increments to a prescribed maximum. The basic salary is paid by the managers, but the yearly increments by the State. The pensions of secondary teachers are not paid by the State, but out of a fund to which the teachers themselves contribute.

91D. *Technical Instruction.* Technical Instruction or Vocational Education is in the hands of the Local Authorities of 4 County Boroughs, 7 Urban Districts and 27 (there are two in Co. Tipperary) County Councils. There are about 190 permanent Vocational Schools in the State. The instruction is imparted by about 1,430 whole-time and 2,000 part-time teachers. There are six

---

* The system of Preparatory Colleges for Teachers is being abolished and is to be replaced by a greater number of Secondary and University scholarships for Gaeltacht students. Five of the six colleges are to become secondary schools.

training centres for the teachers — two for Domestic Science in Co. Dublin and Co. Sligo, two for Metal Work in Cork and Dublin, one for Woodwork in Cork and another for Rural Science. During the day courses are held for Whole-Time Continuation Education, for Technical Education of apprentices, and for Miscellaneous Subjects. At night instruction is also given in Miscellaneous Subjects. In three of the County Boroughs, Compulsory Continuation Courses are also held.

The Vocational Committees are financed by contributions from the Rating Authorities and by Grants from this Vote. The main items in the Vote for 1959/60 are: (i) Grants to Committees, £1.1m.; (ii) Training of Teachers, £38,267; (iii) Payments in respect of Pensions, £45,500; (iv) Payments in respect of loans for Capital purposes, £49,940; (v) Grants to schools not established and maintained by Vocational Committees, £21,759.

91E. *Science and Art.* About 50 per cent. of this Vote for £205,020 is devoted to the development of the Irish language, including publications in Irish, dramatic productions in Irish, University Scholarships, Colleges providing courses in Irish, periodicals and newspapers in Irish and short films in Irish. In addition there are grants to such societies as Comdháil Náisiúnta na Gaeilge, An tOireachtas, the Irish Folklore Commission, the Irish Committee of Historical Studies and the National Film Institute of Ireland.

91F. *Reformatory and Industrial Schools.* The State maintains 3 Reformatory Schools, 50 Industrial Schools and one Place of Detention. Youthful offenders against the law are sent to the Reformatories, and to the Industrial Schools are committed neglected children such as those without a home, or a fixed place of abode, or without proper parental control, or children found guilty of offences punishable by imprisonment in the case of an adult. Local Authorities make grants to both schools in respect of persons committed from their areas, but for the most part they depend on capitation grants made by the State in respect of each person maintained. In 1959/60 the State grant for reformatories was estimated at £14,665 and that for the industrial schools at £249,375.

91G. *Dublin Institute for Advanced Studies.* This Vote (No. 42) provides grants totalling £78,450 for the administrative expenses of the Institute, for the School of Celtic Studies, for the School of Theoretical Physics, for the School of Cosmic Physics, and for buildings.

91H. *Universities and Colleges.* This Vote (No. 43) is also taken up with grants totalling £1m. for the National University, for University Colleges at Dublin, Cork and Galway, for Maynooth College, for Trinity College and for the College of Surgeons.

DEPARTMENT OF AGRICULTURE

The main services administered by this Department are:

92. *Agricultural Schools and Farms.* The Department maintains its own Schools and Farms at Athenry, Ballyhaise, Clonakilty, Johnstown Castle, Cork and Dunsany. In addition it provides grants for Private Schools, Colleges and the Universities.

92A. *Production Grants* are provided for the improvement of Milk, Live-stock, Poultry and Eggs.

92B. *County Committees of Agriculture.* There is a County Committee of Agriculture, a body corporate, in each of the 26 Counties of the State. They employ 178 instructors, and instruction is given in agriculture, horticulture, bee-keeping and improvement of live-stock. The Committees are financed (i) by proceeds of the local county rates of not less than twice and not more than 15 times the produce of a rate of one penny in the pound, and (ii) by a State grant divided in 1959/60 into a Normal Grant of £285,000 and £5,500 to provide sea sand for agricultural purposes. In 1956/57 the Committees received £287,620 from Central Funds and £272,511 from the proceeds of the rates. They have power to borrow.

In addition to the schemes operated by the Committees special schemes are undertaken by the Government at an estimated cost of £216,087. Included in them is the *Parish Plan* under which some 25 parish agents are employed in 14 counties to supplement the advisory services of the Committee. The agents assist by lectures, planned demonstrations, advice as to the keeping of records and accounts and by notes of agricultural interest in the local newspapers.

92C. *The Agricultural Institute (An Foras Talúntais).* This Institute has been made possible through the generosity of the U.S.A. Government. By an agreement with the Irish Government a sum of £1.8m. was diverted from the American Counterpart Special Account for the establishment of the Institute. Of that sum £1m. is to form an Endowment Fund to provide a permanent income, and the remainder to form a Capital Fund for financing the cost of suitable premises and equipment and to develop and extend its main function, that of agricultural research. The Agriculture (An Foras Talúntais) Act, 1958, establishing the Institute also provides for an annual State contribution, and for 1959/60 a sum of £50,000 is taken in the Estimates. Its functions are to promote and undertake agricultural research, and for that purpose to make capital grants for research facilities, to advise on research programmes and to publish the results of its research work. The administration of the Institute will be in the hands of a Council consisting of a Chairman appointed by the President, and twelve members by the Government, of which five are to be nominated by agricultural and rural organisations and four by Universities. A director will control its activities subject to the Council's direction. Under the Johnstown Castle Agricultural College (Amdt.) Act, 1959, the College was vested in the Institute.

92D. *Farm Buildings and Water Supplies Schemes.* The estimated cost of these schemes for 1959/60 is £758,671. Under the first scheme grants are made to rated occupiers of agricultural land towards the cost of construction of new farm buildings, the extension and repair of existing buildings, the laying and repairing of roadways, paths and farmyards, and the construction of tanks, silos and cattle enclosures. Grants for newly-constructed buildings vary according to the nature of the work undertaken, but for the improvement of existing buildings they are paid on the basis of 50 per cent. of the approved estimated cost of labour subject to a maximum grant for each building equal to three-fifths of the grant for a new building of the same class. For other approved works the basis is 50 per cent. of the estimated labour cost. Under the second scheme grants are given towards the cost of installing piped water supplies in the kitchens of farm dwellings and in the case of participants in the Bovine Tuberculosis Eradication Scheme for the extension of such supplies to the farmyards and farms. The basis in this case is 50 per cent. of the approved estimated cost subject to a maximum of £100 for each installation. No grant is payable for any work estimated to cost less than £10.

92E. *Land Project.* Under the Land Reclamation Act, 1949, State assistance is provided for field drainage, land reclamation, the construction and improvement of watercourses, the removal of unnecessary fences or any ancillary operation. An applicant may elect to have his land treated under either Section A or Section B of the Project. Under A the farmer himself does the work aided by a grant of two-thirds of the estimated cost of the work subject to a maximum of £30 an acre. Under Section B, abandoned in 1959, the Department undertook the work either by direct labour or by contractors and the farmer paid two-fifths of the estimated cost, subject to a maximum of £12 an acre and to the condition that work estimated to cost the State more than £30 an acre would not be undertaken. In 1955, however, it was agreed that work estimated to involve a higher expenditure might be undertaken if the farmer agreed to contribute 50 per cent. of the excess. The contributions under B were paid by additions to the Land Purchase Annuities.

In connection with the Project, there is also since 1950/51 a *Fertilisers Scheme* under which farmers who pay Land Annuities may have their lands tested for lime and manurial deficiencies at a fee of 1/- per acre. They are supplied on special terms with the quantities of lime and phosphates shown by the tests to be required. A farmer who elects for this scheme must deposit at least 10 per cent. of the cost, and must repay the balance by means of an addition to his Land Purchase Annuity.

For grants under the Project Schemes the estimates for 1959/60 provide £1.4m. and for fertilisers £155,000. From 1949 to the end of 1957, the Project cost some £17m. including £10m. for grants to farmers and payments to contractors, with about £1.1m. for lime and fertilisers. The yearly cost of the Project (Section B) was about £900,000 and there is a doubt about its economic value. Mr. Whitaker says: " If, as seems clear in the case of Section B, the cost is uneconomic, the Land Project is merely a case of misdirected State aid; indeed to the extent that, even under Section A farmers carry out small reclamation works merely to qualify for the State Grant, it is fast becoming a social service." [2]

92F. *Lime and Fertilisers Subsidies.* A Lime Subsidy of £485,000 relates to Ground Limestone for which there are about 50 grinding plants operating throughout the State. As from March, 1951, the cost of delivering ground limestone from the producing centres to the farmers' holdings was paid by the State to the carriers, provided that the producers undertook to make the limestone available at a price not exceeding 16/- a ton. Since June, 1957, the transport subsidy is payable only in respect of deliveries not exceeding 35 miles in Counties Wicklow and Wexford and 30 miles in other counties, or if there is no grinding plant within these distances, the distance from the nearest approved plant to the purchaser.

During 1956/57 it was decided that Superphosphate should be made available on the home market at world prices, and accordingly the customs duty on imported superphosphate was removed and provision made for an appropriate subsidy to home manufacturers. On the native product a subsidy of £180,000 and on the imported £1.75m. is provided for 1959/60.

92G. *Bovine Tuberculosis Eradication Scheme.* A vital problem at present facing Irish agriculture is the eradication of

2. Economic Development, page 129.

Bovine Tuberculosis for on its solution depends our future trade with Britain, our chief market for cattle. The Bovine Tuberculosis Eradication Scheme was begun in September, 1954, and its urgency has recently been stressed by the fact that a similar scheme in Britain will have been completed about March, 1960, and after that time no untested cattle may be imported into that country.

Up to October, 1957, participation in the scheme was voluntary, but after that date compulsion was applied in what are called " Clearance Areas." All herd-owners in these areas are allowed free testing, free professional advice, and the purchase of reactors — that is, cattle which give a positive reaction to the tuberculin test — at full current market value. Each herd is tested once a year, reactors must be moved out of the area if not purchased by the Department, and must be isolated pending removal and disinfection of the premises.

In what are termed " Intensive Areas " the same facilities as regards annual testing, professional advice and purchase of reactors are afforded herd-owners until the areas are declared Clearance Areas.

In the remaining parts of the country, an " Accredited Herds Scheme " operates. Here the herd-owners are given an initial and final test of their cattle free of charge. Before a herd may be registered it must have two complete clear tests within a year and both premises and management must be of a satisfactory standard.

At present store cattle which have passed a single test within 14 days of shipment are allowed into Britain but must be isolated for two months and then pass another test before being allowed into an attested herd. But accredited herds have the same status as British attested herds and may be exported without further testing or isolation.

During 1957/58 an allocation of £423,000 from the National Development Fund was spent on the Scheme in two clearance areas in the West and £700,000 of the American Grant Counterpart Fund was used in other areas. For 1959/60 a sum of £3.5m. is provided for the Scheme.

92H. *Grants for Pasteurisation of Separated Milk, etc.* Intimately associated with the problem of the Bovine Tuberculosis Eradication Scheme is that of the pasteurisation of milk, and one of the measures taken for that purpose is that all registered creameries and cream-separating stations must, not later than 1st January, 1959, be equipped with plant for the pasteurisation of separated milk by a specified method, and must so pasteurise all separated milk returned to suppliers or disposed of for animal feeding. Grants of 50 per cent. of the cost of approved plants are made to the creameries, and £200,000 is provided for that purpose in 1959/60. An agreement of 31st March, 1955, between the Irish and American Governments provided for the use of funds of the American Counterpart Special Account up to £500,000 to recoup the grants paid in respect of expenditure incurred by creameries after the date of the agreement.

92I. *Payments to Pigs and Bacon Commission.* On the expiration in April, 1956, of the agreement between the Irish and British Governments relating to the exports of Irish pigs and pig meat, it was decided to introduce a scheme — the Export Price Guarantee Scheme — to subsidise, when necessary, the price of Grade A bacon exported to the British market. The scheme is administered through a corporate body, the Pigs and Bacon Commission, and is financed from the proceeds of a levy on bacon pigs purchased by curers, and a State contribution not exceeding one-half the amount of the subsidy. Under the scheme a minimum price is guaranteed to producers and an export price to the bacon curers. A compulsory export quota system operates. The Exchequer contribution for 1959/60 is estimated at £550,000.

92J. *Subsidies on Dairy Produce.* Since 9th May, 1957, there has been no home market subsidy or maximum price control on creamery butter, but in order to continue the then existing price level for milk supplies to creameries the Butter Marketing Committee decided to maintain the price to creameries for butter at a level equivalent to the net return obtainable by the creameries on their sales prior to the 9th May, 1957. That in turn was based on the maximum wholesale price increased by the amount of the subsidies which were withdrawn and which were 48/8 per cwt. sales allowance, 3/- production allowance and 9/4 special levy for cold storage. In effect, therefore, the price both of milk and of butter was guaranteed.

The Butter Marketing Committee distributes butter in County Dublin, and supplies merchants and creameries elsewhere when they cannot obtain their requirements in the ordinary way. It keeps certain supplies in cold storage for winter use and it handles the export of surplus creamery butter.

When home demand for creamery butter has been fully satisfied there is often a surplus which has to be exported. The amount of the surplus varies from year to year. In 1957/58, for instance, it was 366,101 cwt. For the purpose of exporting any surplus, licences are issued by the Marketing Committee and the most of it is sold in Great Britain. The price obtained is usually less than that paid to the creameries by the Committee, and the difference is made good by a subsidy from the Exchequer. Up to 1958/59 there was a 100 per cent. subsidisation of these exports, but thereafter the Exchequer will bear only two-thirds, the remainder to be contributed by the dairy industry by means of a levy on butter production.

The proceeds of any levy will be paid into the Dairy Produce (Price Stabilisation) Fund. Ordinarily, the income of the Fund is derived from levies on the home sales of creamery butter and cheese, and is used to defray the administrative expenses of the Butter Marketing Committee, any deficit in its trading account, and the cost of cold storage of creamery butter for winter consumption. If, for any reason, butter has to be imported for home consumption, any loss sustained on its sale is met out of the Fund.

During 1956/57 the Exchequer paid in respect of losses on butter exports £25,342, in 1957/58 £2.8m., and in 1958/59 £2m. The provision for 1959/60 is £1m.

92K. *Losses on disposal of Wheat and Payments to Wheat Growers, etc.* The purpose of the provision under this sub-head is (i) to recoup An Bord Gráin in respect of losses arising from the purchase and resale of wheat and (ii) to enable authorised wheat purchasers to make ex-gratia payments in respect of the 1958 crop, and for miscellaneous expenses.

Usually in the past it was possible to fix the guaranteed price of Irish millable wheat without fear that there would be any unreasonable quantity surplus to home requirements. But in the cereal year 1957/58, when the price, marketing and disposal of such wheat was controlled, and when requirements of about 300,000 tons to be used in the flour millers' grist had been satisfied, there remained a surplus of 95,000 tons for which there was no market at an economic price. Some of it, therefore, had to be sold as animal feed, some was exported, and some was sold to flour millers at the animal feed price of the extra amount of wheat required to enable them to reduce the flour extraction rate from 80 per cent. to 72 per cent.

The cost to the Exchequer in the disposal of the surplus was £1.45m. and as a result it was decided that the guaranteed price will in future be sold as animal feed or exported — the loss being spread over all wheat growers.

CHAPTER IV

Estimates of Expenditure Supply Service (Continued)

DEPARTMENT OF SOCIAL WELFARE

93. The Department of Social Welfare is responsible for the financial administration of three Votes — the Minister's office, Social Insurance and Social Assistance. The total of the three Votes (£25.3m.) represents 25 per cent. of the amount provided for all the other public services excluding capital services. The main function of the Department may be said to help the needy, and that help is given in two ways: (a) by means of Social Insurance Schemes where there is a title to relief, irrespective of means, by virtue of contributions to a fund; and (b) by means of Social Assistance Schemes where in all cases, except Children's Allowance, the relief afforded is dependent on the means of the person concerned, either because there have been no contributions to the fund, or because the insurance benefit dependent on contributions has been exhausted.

93A. *Social Insurance.* This covers Disability, Unemployment, Marriage, Maternity, Widows, Orphans, and Treatment (Dental and Optical). Insurance is compulsory for all employees between the ages of 16 and 70, whose earnings do not exceed £800 a year. There are three separate parties to the scheme, the employer, the employee, and the State. Notionally, each party is considered to contribute an equal share to the formation of the fund, but the legal position under the Social Welfare Act, 1952, is that the State must contribute the amount by which the income of the fund in any financial year is less than its expenditure. Thus, for 1959/60 the expenditure of the fund is estimated at £10.8m. and the income from contributions by employers and employees and from investments at £6.5m., so that the estimated cost of the State contribution is £4.3m. as provided in the Vote.

Formerly, the National Health Insurance Fund, the Unemployment Fund and the Widows and Orphans Pensions Fund were separate entities, but under the Act of 1952 they were merged into the Social Insurance Fund which carries the expenditure not only of Social Insurance but also of Social Assistance Schemes.

Some persons are not insured for all the benefits mentioned above and pay reduced rates of insurance. Domestic servants, for instance, are not insured against unemployment, and civil servants are insured only for widows and orphans pensions. Manual workers in certain trades are insured against working time lost owing to bad weather, and both employers and employees contribute, but there is no State subsidy; but the cost of administration is borne by the Department. Beyond promoting legislation to extend or amend the Acts, and beyond making Statutory Instruments under the Workmen's Compensation Acts, 1934-55, the Minister for Social Welfare is not responsible for death, injuries or occupational diseases arising out of and in the course of employment. These risks are outside the ambit of the Insurance and Assistance Schemes, and the onus for compensation falls on employers, or, in the last resort, in cases of dispute, on the Courts.

93B. *Social Assistance.* The assistance provided under this heading, entirely at the expense of the Exchequer, covers Children's Allowances (£7m.) for the second and each subsequent child under 16 years without any means test; Old Age Pensions (£10m.) payable at 70 but subject to a means and residence test; Blind Pensions payable at 21, also subject to the tests; Widows and Orphans (Non-Contributory) Pensions (£1.6m.) subject to the tests for those who fail to qualify for the Contributory Pension; and Unemployment Assistance (£1.4m.) for those not entitled to the Insurance Benefit, with the same tests.

The gross vote for Social Assistance is £20.8m. with appropriations-in-aid of £306,000 of which about £300,000 consist of statutory contributions from certain Local Authorities towards the cost of Unemployment Assistance. Of the gross vote, Old Age Pensions absorbs about one-half, and Chrildren's Allowances about one-third.

93C. *Other Schemes.* Under this heading are included a number of schemes administered by Local Authorities under the general supervision of the Minister for Social Welfare. They comprise (i) Home Assistance entirely financed by Local Authorities for persons incapable of providing for themselves the necessaries of life; (ii) School Meals for Children attending National Schools in certain areas and to the cost of which the State contributes one-half. In certain areas of the Gaeltacht, County Councils are given part of their expenditure out of a special grant; (iii) Cheap Fuel for necessitous householders, the net cost of which — that is, after deducting local administrative expenses and payments made by the recipients — is borne by the State; (iv) Cheap Footwear for poor children, free for recipients of home assistance, but otherwise dependent on the means of recipients. Fifty per cent. of the cost is paid by the State subject to a limit of £37,500.

93D. From the point of view of the ordinary supply services there are certain features peculiar to this Vote which should be noted. The first is that the Social Insurance Fund bears the cost of administering the Social Insurance as distinct from the Social Assistance scheme. The gross vote (£1.4m.) for the Minister's Office covers the administrative cost both of social insurance and of social assistance, but a sum of £.9m. is appropriated-in-aid and that represents the cost of administering social insurance, so that the net sum (£.5m.) is the cost of administering social assistance. Secondly, the Fund bears the cost of the services rendered by the Common Service Departments to the administration of Social Insurance—again as distinct from Social Assistance—and this in 1959/60 amounts to £312,000. This is used as an appropriation-in-aid to the different votes concerned, just as the £.9m. is used in that way by the Office of the Minister for Social Welfare. The cost of the Allied Services, estimated at £284,000 in respect of Social Assistance is treated in the ordinary way and is borne by the departments. Finally in the total £.6m. for Investments, there is included a statutory Exchequer contribution of £38,000 in respect of interest on the money expended from the Fund on the acquisition, completion and equipment of the Headquarters (Áras Mhic Dhiarmada) of the Department. Hence, as far as Social Insurance is concerned, the Department is—like any insurance business, and unlike the ordinary department of State—to a large extent an independent entity.

DEPARTMENT OF HEALTH

94. The Department of Health administers either directly or indirectly two votes, that for Health and that for Dundrum Asylum. The latter represents the entire cost of administering the Asylum and calls for no comment or explanation.

The Vote for Health includes the expenses of the Registrar General's Office—but the main service in it is the item or subhead, " Grants to Health Authorities, £8.2m." It is with these grants that we are concerned here. They are annual State grants to the funds of Local Authorities to recoup their expenditure on health services.

94A. To integrate the mental and other health services of the State, the Health Authorities Bill, 1959, proposes to set up a unified Health Authority in the Cork, Dublin, Limerick and Waterford areas consisting of members of the County Councils and Borough Corporations. Outside these centres the County Councils will be the Health Authorities, but where at present there exist Joint Mental Hospital Boards, new Boards will be established to act jointly with the County Councils. The Health Authorities will administer all the services outlined below and will be financed from the rates and the Exchequer.

94B. Under the Health Services (Financial Provisions) Act, 1947, each Health Authority receives annually a State grant equal to the amount by which its total expenditure on the approved health services exceeds the total net expenditure on such services for 1947/48 (The Standard Year) up to the point at which current expenditure is equal to twice the Standard Year's expenditure. Beyond that point expenditure is recouped to the extent of 50 per cent. In 1947/48, for instance, the local expenditure was £4.8m. and the State grant £.9m., but five years later the expenditure of all Health Authorities exceeded the equivalent of twice the appropriate figure for the Standard Year, and, therefore, the grants have been at the rate of 50 per cent. of current expenditure in all cases since 1952/53. Hence, in accordance with that statutory provision the Estimate for grants to Health Authorities may be summarised thus:—

	£	£
(i) Grants outstanding for years prior to 1959/60		370,000
(ii) Grants for 1959/60—Estimated Expenditure by Health Authorities on:		
(a) Institutional Services	11,610,000	
(b) Other Services	5,030,000	
Total	16,640,000	
50 per cent. of Total	8,320,000	
95 per cent. to be recouped within the year 1959/60	7,900,000	7,900,000
Total 1959/60		£8,270,000

94C. *Institutional Services.* By these are meant services provided for in-patients in a hospital, convalescent home, or home for persons suffering from physical or mental disability or mental deficiency, and they include the services of doctors and specialists within the institution together with maintenance, diagnosis, advice, treatment, specified appliances, medicines and special apparatus. The Health Authority may provide the services either in its own institutions, or in that of another Authority, or, by special arrangement, in a voluntary or proprietary institution. Insured persons— other than those entitled to general medical services and certain school children—are liable to a charge which varies from time to time for the institutional services.

94D. The services and the estimated net cost of each for 1959/60 are given as (i) General Hospitals (including Maternity and Special Hospitals), £5m.; (ii) Tuberculosis Hospitals, £1.4m.; (iii) Mental Hospitals, £3.7m.; (iv) Hospitals and Homes for Chronic Sick, Mental Defectives, etc., £1.5m. Those eligible for the services are (a) Insured Persons, provided that the necessary contributions have been paid, but under recent Health Acts virtually all insured persons (including voluntary contributors and persons insured for Widows' and Orphans' Pensions only) and their dependants are entitled to Hospital and Specialist Services, to a free maternity care service and to infant welfare service with a choice of doctor and midwife and if necessary to a free hospital service. In those cases the only condition is that a contribution under the Social Welfare Acts was paid, payable or credited since the beginning of the last but one contribution year before the date of application for the services; (b) Adults with yearly means of less than £800; (c) Adults engaged mainly or wholly in farming with a rateable valuation of £50 or less; (d) Pupils of National Schools for defects discovered at school health examinations; (e) Persons who in the opinion of the Authority are unable without undue hardship to provide the services for themselves or their dependants. They are also entitled to be treated as out-patients of the institutions, but, except persons in the General Medical Services class, they are subject to charges for such specialist services as X-ray examinations, etc.

94E. *Other Services.* These include (a) *General Medical Service* (£1m.) based on about 670 dispensary districts spread throughout the State. For persons unable to provide such services and appliances at their own expense or by other means, the Health Authorities under section 14 of the Health Act, 1952, are bound to provide, free of charge, a general practitioner to render ordinary medical and surgical assistance, treatment for eyes, ears and teeth, and medicines together with any necessary appliances. The names of eligible persons are entered on a Register which is renewed annually, and they are given a Medical Card indicating their eligibility. About 28 per cent of the population is registered.

(b) *Maternity and Child Service* (*including Maternity Cash Grants*)—£1m.) The groups mentioned above as eligible for institutional services are also eligible here. Briefly, the service consists of a General Medical Care for Mothers and Infants. An expectant mother, intending to be confined at home or in a maternity home, may choose any doctor provided by the Authority to render any necessary maternity services during her pregnancy and for six weeks after confinement both for herself and her child. She may also choose the midwife. Hospitals and Specialist Service are also provided. Under section 23 of the Act of 1953 a cash grant is payable to women in the lower income group in respect of each confinement.

(c) *Allowance to Disabled Persons and Rehabilitation Services* (£.7m.). The Disabled Persons (Maintenance Allowance) Regulations made under the Health Act, 1953, allows Local Authorities to pay allowances not exceeding £1 a week to chronically disabled persons over 16 years of age, who are not maintained in an institution, who are not able to provide their own maintenance, and whose near relatives are unable to support them. Rehabilitation Centres have been established in Dublin, Cork, Limerick and Tuam for training ex-patients of sanatoria and other institutions so as to fit them to take up suitable occupations in ordinary life.

(d) *Infectious Diseases Services and Maintenance of Persons with Infectious Diseases* (£.9m.). The services referred to here are chiefly preventive measures against infectious diseases such as B.C.G. vaccination and X-ray (including mass radiography) examinations against tuberculosis, immunisation against diphtheria and vaccination against poliomyelitis, typhoid and smallpox. There is in operation a scheme of Infectious Diseases Maintenance Allowances to help persons with such diseases, but the main beneficiaries are persons suffering from tuberculosis.

(e) *Other Services, e.g., Dental, Ophthalmic, Aural Services, etc.* (£1.3m.). Health Authorities are bound under statute to provide Dental and Ophthalmic Services for persons in the lower income groups, for children under six for defects discovered at child welfare clinics, and for pupils in National Schools for defects found at school health examinations. The services are free, but a charge is liable for replacement of dental appliances. Contact lenses and hearing aids are supplied on the condition that 156 contributions have been paid to the Social Insurance Fund, and that at least 26 have been paid or credited in the governing contribution year. Ear, Nose and Throat services are available in certain centres and are being expanded. The cost of the Other Services also includes Ambulance Services, administrative expenses and retiring allowances.

94F. In connection with hospitals one should not overlook the contribution made by the Hospitals Trust Fund. Originally sweepstakes for the support of public charitable hospitals and sanatoria were legalised by the Public Charitable Hospitals (Temporary Provisions) Act, 1930, but it was superseded by the

Public Hospitals Act, 1933. Briefly, that Act established: (a) The Associated Hospitals Sweepstakes Committee consisting of the representatives of participating hospitals to organise the Sweepstakes, but the Committee entrusts that work to Hospitals Trust Ltd.; (b) The Hospitals Trust Board (replacing by an amendment in 1938 The National Hospitals Trustees), which manages the Hospitals Trust Fund, and (c) the Hospitals Commission which surveys hospital services and reports thereon to the Minister either at his request or on their own initiative.

The net proceeds of the sweepstakes are paid into the Fund and the Minister makes grants therefrom for the benefit of any new or existing hospital or nursing organisation. By "hospital" is meant any institution or organisation which is not run for profit and which treats human ailments or defects or carries out medical research. The grants cover the purchase of lands, buildings or equipment, the construction and repair of hospitals and their maintenance expenses. It also covers the revenue deficits of Voluntary Hospitals which have increased from £.3m. in 1947 to £.9m. in 1958. All applications for grants are examined by the Commission which reports to the Minister.

Up to April, 1960, the Fund contributed £49.4m. to the hospitals, but as in recent years the Fund was not sufficient to meet demands, Exchequer contributions had to be made. Between 1953 and 1958 they totalled over £6m. Up to October, 1958, payments of £6.8m. were made in respect of revenue defects, and £23m. for capital expenditure.

DEPARTMENT OF LANDS AND FISHERIES

95. The Department of Lands is financially responsible for the administration of three Votes — Lands, Forestry and Fisheries. Under Lands there are three main items:—

Payments under Section 11 (7) *of the Land Act,* 1923. Before 1923 land purchase depended on agreement between landlord and tenant, and at that time there were 110,000 tenants remaining unpurchased. The Land Act of 1923, however, as amended by that of 1925, vested all tenanted land in the Land Commission for the purpose of subsequently revesting it in the tenants subject to appropriate annuities calculated to repay the purchase price paid to the landlord. This was derived by a formula from the rents being paid and was made payable in Land Bonds. A system of standard prices was prescribed, and the State provided the landlord with a contribution equal to 10 per cent. of the standard price together with a further amount for legal costs. The price, including the

61

State contribution, was paid in $4\frac{1}{2}$ per cent. Land Bonds guaranteed both by the Irish and the British Governments. Untenanted land in the congested districts was automatically vested in the Commission, and similar land outside the districts was, with certain exceptions, also vested in it, if requred to relieve congestion or to facilitate the sale of tenanted land. The price paid was the same but there was no State contribution. Under the Acts, Bonds at $4\frac{1}{2}$ per cent. totalling about £21m. were issued, and a Land Bond Fund was established under the control of the Minister of Finance out of which was paid the interest on the Bonds and sums required for their redemption. The Land Commission was required by the Act to pay into the Fund interest at $4\frac{1}{2}$ per cent. p.a. on the nominal amount of all bonds issued, 5/- per cent. p.a. in respect of Sinking Fund, together with all sums received for the redemption of purchase annuities, and all sums paid in cash on the sale of land vested in it. Hence, Land Bonds are primarily secured on the receipts of the Land Bond Fund established in 1923, and are repayable by means of their Sinking Funds operating by annual drawings at par, but after 1962 the Land Bonds created in 1923 may be repaid at par at the option of the Minister for Finance. Section 11 (7) of the Act of 1923 prescribes that " a sum sufficient to pay the interest and sinking fund on the Bonds issued under the Act for contribution to price and for the Costs Fund shall be paid each year to the Land Commission out of moneys provided by the Oireachtas."

The position as regards land purchase is briefly as follows: Under various Acts passed before 1923, some 300,000 tenants were assisted in purchasing 11,000,000 acres at a cost of £100m. Since 1923 a further 112,000 tenancies covering about 3,000,000 acres have been bought at a cost of about £21m. There now remain about 13,000 holdings outstanding for vesting in the tenants together with some 5,000 other holdings in the congested districts.

95A. *Payments under Section 27 (2) of the Land Act, 1933, and Section 6 (4) of 1953 (£7m.).* The Land Act of 1933 reconstituted the Land Commission, extended its powers for acquiring land for the relief of congestion especially for disemployed agricultural workers and former evicted tenants, and it curtailed the right of a dispossessed owner to claim an alternative holding. Financially, the Act remitted annuities in arrear to the extent of £254,247, and it funded the main amount, £4.7m., by making it repayable at the rate of $4\frac{1}{2}$ per cent. interest over a period of 50 years. Finally, as from the second gale day in 1933, it provided that all land purchase annuities should be reduced by about 50 per cent., the State contributing the other half during the whole currency of the annuities. Section 27 (2) of the Act of 1933 prescribes that "all deficiencies in the Land Bond Fund from the revision of annuities and from reductions made in this part of the Act in the amounts payable in respect of the annual payments shall, to such extent and at such time or times as the Minister for Finance direct, be made good to the said Fund out of moneys provided by the Oireachtas," and section 6 (4) of the 1953 Act, that "such sums as may from time to time be required to pay the interest and sinking fund on the additional bonds issued in pursuance of this section shall, subject to the approval of the Minister for Finance be paid to the Land Commission out of moneys provided by the Oireachtas." On the 31st March, 1960, advances for Costs Fund and State Contribution to Price (including deficiencies in Land Bond Fund arising from revision of annuities) formed a capital liability of £16m.

95B. *Improvement of Estates, etc.* (£639,605). The annual expenditure under this heading is incurred in connection with land division schemes — on the erection of dwelling-houses and out-offices, on the provision and repair of access roads, fencing, drainage, turbary development and on well-sinking. The bulk of the expenditure is on buildings including the construction and renovation of dwelling-houses. Before 1923 about £3m. was spent on these improvements and since 1923 about another £12m.

96. Forestry (£2m.) is an important division of the Department of Lands. Although the soil and climate of Ireland is most favourable for the cultivation of a large variety of trees, Forestry is for the most part and for some years past almost exclusively a State industry. For this there are several reasons. Psychologically there was no forest tradition except in one or two counties, and economically the system of land tenure led to an agrarian economy which militated against any large-scale afforestation. Indeed, at the beginning of the present century Ireland was almost completely denuded of trees, and was almost entirely dependent on foreign resources for its requirements of timber. Even in 1956 the net import excess was £10m. and in 1957 £7.7m.

In order to rectify this state of things, and in time to meet home requirements, especially for soft wood, the State about 30 years ago embarked on large-scale afforestation, and in the interval about 270,000 acres have been planted, mainly hitherto on waste land. The annual rate of planting has increased from 12,500 acres in 1952/53 to 25,000 in 1958/59, and as it is intended to continue that rate in future years it means that in ten years' time there will be another 250,000 acres planted. On the basis of a 50-year crop for sawlog crops, it is clear that the State forests have as yet produced little saw timber size. Meanwhile, thinnings—usual after 20 years to provide growing space for the remaining crops—are being used for fencing, rough farm buildings, pit props in mines, small size boards for boxes, etc. To provide for the absorption of the thinnings which must accumulate with the passage of time, there are many openings for subsidiary industries using small timber and its products. In order to induce private planting a grant—not applicable to poplar cultivation—of £20 an acre is now given, but up to the present only about 90,000 acres have been planted, the average annual rate being now about 420 acres.

96A. It is in the light of these general observations that the Estimate for Forestry is to be taken. It provides a grant-in-aid of £170,000 for the acquisition of land; £1.7m. for forest development and management—including £151,800 for nurseries; £.5m. for the establishment of plantations; £.3m. for new roads and buildings; £.5m. for general forest management; £94,500 for timber conversion, and £170,400 for mechanical equipment. All the items, except the management and timber conversion, are treated as voted capital expenditure. There are two State-owned sawmills, one in Co. Tipperary and the other in Co. Mayo, with modern equipment for drying and sawing and they are producing timber of first-class quality.

Taking into consideration the present estimate there has now been invested in State Forestry a capital sum of about £8.8m., and the sale of timber during 1959/60 is expected to reach about £250,000.

97. Another important public service for which the Department of Lands is financially responsible is that of Fisheries for which the estimate in 1959/60 provides £351,520. Apart from administrative expenses, the estimate falls into two parts according as it deals with Sea Fisheries or with Inland Fisheries. As to the former the two main items are a grant-in-aid of £180,000 for the administration and development of the Sea Fisheries Board (An Bord Iascaigh Mhara) which, being a State-sponsored body, is to a large extent independent of the Department, and will be dealt with in a subsequent chapter. The other item is "Provisions of Exploratory Fishing Vessel," £45,000, which is treated as voted capital expenditure. Of the grant-in-aid £101,800 is similarly treated. A contract has been placed for the vessel which is to carry out a scientific investigation of fish stocks around the Irish coast by carrying out such experiments as the freezing, smoking, and curing of fish at sea.

97A. As regards Inland Fisheries, there is an amount of £25,000 for Local Authorities under Section 13 of the Fisheries Act, 1925. That Act abolished the then existing Board of Conservators and established new Boards in each electoral district. They were empowered to issue on payment fixed by statute, licences for single salmon rods, and long lines for fishing, and to levy a rate on all fisheries within their districts. Any person so rated by the Conservators could claim exemption from rates struck on his property by the Local Authorities, but if the Minister for Local Government certified that by reason of the exemption the amount of the rate had been increased by an amount greater than one penny in the pound, the Minister for Fisheries may, out of moneys provided by the Oireachtas, pay to the Local Authority an amount equal to the sum which would be produced by a rate equivalent to the amount in the pound by which such increase exceeds one penny in the pound. In addition to this sum provided for Local Authorities, there is a further sum of £3,000 paid to the Conservators.

97B.   Another item of £14,000 is provided as a " Contribution to the Salmon Conservancy Fund " of which £12,000 is a grant and £2,000 a repayable advance.   The Fund also receives most of the fees for rod licences and the levy—about £9,000 a year—on the export of about £.5m. a year of salmon. From all sources it is estimated that during 1959/60 about £85,000 will be available for salmon fisheries and the money will be allocated to the Conservators according to their needs, efficiency and initiative, especially in such matters as protection, improvement and restocking.   Of the £14,000 contribution £4,000 is treated as voted capital expenditure and another item of £4,000 so treated is for the construction and operation of Fish Ponds for the culture of fish.

97C.   Apart from the Boards of Conservators, there is the Inland Fisheries Trust for which a grant-in-aid of £25,000 is provided. The Trust owns, or holds on lease, certain waters throughout the State, and one of its chief objects is to clear coarse fish from lakes, salmon and trout rivers and then to restock them with suitable fish. Thus it has cleared 33,000 pike from the River Lee, and predatory reduction has been effected in 19 lakes and many have been restocked.   Its main object is to improve brown trout fishing in its own waters, and to this end it operates a fish farm at Roscrea for the propagation of trout, etc., for the restocking of suitable waters.

DEPARTMENT OF THE GAELTACHT

98.   This Department deals with the special problem of preserving and developing the Irish-speaking districts of the Gaeltacht, that is, certain parts of Donegal, Mayo, Sligo, Galway, Clare, Kerry, Cork, Waterford and Meath in which the number of persons of three years or over speaking either Irish only, or

Irish and English numbered about 190,000 in 1946. Apart from a grant-in-aid of £110,000 to a Board (Bord Gaeltarra Éireann) set up in 1957 for the purpose of fostering and expanding the industries of the area, the main items in the Vote are: —

(1) *Housing.* Up to the present about 5,000 new houses have been built, and the same number repaired or improved at a cost of £1m. in grants and £250,000 in loans, but there are still required 3,000 new houses, and 5,000 need to be improved. It is also intended by means of grants to help the inhabitants to build chalets for renting to holiday visitors and hostels for approved bodies such as students.

(2) *Improvement Schemes.* These cover roads, water supplies, minor marine works, amenities, soil distribution, tomato houses and secondary education. Grants-in-aid are made available for the parents and guardians of Irish-speaking children between the ages of 6 and 16.

(4) *Technical Assistance.* Grants were provided for training courses in Ireland and elsewhere for technicians and entrants employed in rural industries.

(5) *Marine Industries.* A sum is provided to buy from the inhabitants kelp, carrageen and seaweed. Hitherto, the carrageen and seaweed—especially sea-rods—were purchased by the Department and sold to a State-sponsored body, Arramara Teo, for the purpose of being processed. It is now intended that the Company will itself arrange for its own buying, handling and transport.

(6) *Gaeltarra Éireann.* This is a body corporate created by the Gaeltacht Act of 1957. It consists of a Chairman, a Managing Director and three other members appointed by the Minister for a period of five years. Its functions are to control and manage the existing rural industries, to provide other industries and productive schemes of employment, and to encourage and extend the use of Irish. It has power to discontinue any unproductive industry. It operates factories for tweed and toys; it organises cottage knitwear industries, and markets the various products. When established it took over the assets and liabilities of the existing industries. It appoints its own officers and servants who must be capable of conducting business in Irish. The Board is entitled to an annual grant from the Oireachtas, and may receive advances repayable with interest up to £500,000. It has power to borrow temporarily with the consent of the Minister for Finance. Its accounts and report, which must be submitted annually to the Minister, are tabled in the Oireachtas.

DEPARTMENT OF INDUSTRY AND COMMERCE (INCLUDING DEPARTMENT OF TRANSPORT AND POWER)

99. According to the Estimates for the Public Services, 1959/60, this Department is responsible for the financial administration of six votes—the Minister's Office, etc., Transport and Marine Services, Aviation and Meteorological Services, Industrial and Commercial Property Registration Office, Tourism and Repayment of Trade Loans Advances. Since the publication of the Estimates, however, it has been decided to create a new *Department of Transport and Power* under the Ministers and Secretaries (Amendment) Act, 1959, and to transfer to it the following services hitherto administered by the Department of Industry and Commerce: Marine Services—shipping policy and development, the administration of various Acts dealing with shipping and marine services, coast life-saving, the foreshore, and Irish Shipping Ltd.; Harbours—administration of Harbour Acts and the general control of harbour authorities, administration of grants for harbour improvement work and Pilotage Acts; Inland Transport—transport policy generally, administration of Acts dealing with all forms of internal transport and C.I.E.; Civil Aviation—policy and development, administration of Air Navigation Acts and the Customs Fee Airport Acts, other Acts dealing with Air Traffic Control, tellcommunications services, and meteorological services, construction and maintenance of airports and the management of Shannon Airport; Power—all matters relating to the procurement and distribution of all types of fuel, the Gas Acts, the E.S.B. and Bord na Móna.

100. Taking the Estimates as published the major provisions are:—*Fuel Subsidy*. During the Emergency arrangements were made by the Department with a State-sponsored body, Fuel Importers (Éire) Ltd., whereby losses incurred by the Company in the marketing of turf, coal and timber fuel were borne by the Company in the first instance, but were subsequently recouped from moneys voted by the Oireachtas. Payments for such losses have continued since about 1947/48. Payments of nearly £11m. had been made up to the 31st March, 1957, and at that time the accounts of the Company showed that a balance of about 90,000 tons of coal, costing £800,000, remained unsold. In each of the years 1958/59 and 1959/60, provision was made for a further subsidy of £200,000. The Company was wound up in 1959/60.

100A. *Institute for Industrial Research and Standards.* An Industrial Research Council was appointed by the Minister in March, 1934, but was dissolved in October, 1946, and the Institute was established under section 4 of the Industrial Research and Standards

Act, 1946. Under that Act the Institute became a body corporate with all the legal properties inherent in such a body. Its functions were (i) to carry out scientific research for the purpose of utilising the natural resources of the State, improving the technical processes used in industry and for discovering new processes for new industries; (ii) to formulate standard specifications for commodities, processes and practices providing standard marks for them; (iii) to analyse goods for sale to the public, so as to facilitate scientific research and to ensure conformity with standard specifications; (iv) to ensure conformity with such specifications and to encourage the standardisation of products for the benefit of the public.

The Act set up a Council to assist in the administration of the Institute. It consisted of ex-officio members and not more than 50 others chosen for their scientific attainments in industrial research, or for their support to scientific research, or for their ability to promote the adoption of industrial standard specifications. There are two Committees—one of 9 members appointed every 5 years for Industrial Research, and the other of 7 members, including 3 of the Research Committee, appointed every 3 years for Standard Research. Members of both Committees are ex-officio members of the Council, and a Director of Industrial Research and Standards, appointed by the Minister, manages the Institute.

By an amending Act of 1954, the Minister, with the consent of the Minister for Finance, provides annually out of moneys voted by the Oireachtas a grant not exceeding £35,000 to meet the administrative expenses of the Institute. The Estimate 1959/60 is made up of Administration, £30,000; Buildings and Equipment, £500; Laboratories and Equipment for three additional laboratories, £53,000. Towards their total cost a sum of £130,000 will by agreement be made available from the Counterpart Reserve Fund.

At present a complete review of the Act of 1946 is in progress to determine what changes in the functions and powers of the Institute should be made so as to enable it to operate more effectively and give more active attention to the problems facing industry. It is also expected that the present statutory limit of the grant-in-aid will have to be raised to cover the operation of the new laboratories.

100B. *Industrial Development Authority* (£285,979). The Estimate includes a grant-in-aid for Industrial Development of £200,000. The Authority was established and its first members were appointed by warrants dated 26th May, 1949, made by the Minister with the approval of the Minister for Finance, and the establishment was confirmed by the Industrial Development Authority Act, 1950. Under the Act the Authority, a corporate body, consists of a

Chairman and not more than 4 other members appointed by the Minister for 5 years in a whole, or part-time capacity. Its officers and servants are also appointed by the Minister.

Its functions are to initiate proposals and schemes for the creation and development of industry; to survey possibilities of industrial development; to advise on and to assist persons contemplating the establishment of new or the expansion of existing industries; and to investigate the effect of protective measures. It has power to summon witnesses and to take evidence on oath. The Act also provides for an annual grant for administrative expenses and the audit of accounts by the Auditor General.

The Industrial Grants Act, 1956, provides that if the Authority considers that the manufacture of a particular commodity would be in the interest of the national economy or would provide substantial employment, or aid substantially in the development of exports, it may make grants towards the acquisition, construction and adaptation of buildings and other works for the purpose of the undertaking. The grants may not exceed two-thirds of the cost or £50,000, whichever is the less, they are not to exceed £2m., and may not be made for undertakings in an area to which the Under-developed Areas Act of 1952 applies.

In 1959 the Department and the Authority had before them 180 proposals for industrial projects and the members of the Authority had visited continental countries to show industrialists the advantages offered by Ireland for the establishment of undertakings. Grants totalling £439,350 under the Industrial Grants Act have been made to 17 new projects and £145,115 have been paid.

100C. *An Foras Tionscal.* This Board, a corporate body, was set up by the Undeveloped Areas Act, 1952, and consists of a Chairman and two other members appointed by the Minister for 5 years at rates determined by him out of the grants-in-aid voted by the Oireachtas. The areas to which the Act applies are the congested areas or any other area declared by the Minister to be congested. The congested areas are the Counties of Donegal, Sligo, Leitrim, Roscommon, Galway, Kerry and the former rural districts in County Clare and County Cork, such as Bantry, Schull and Skibbereen. If the Board considers that an undertaking will provide or maintain employment, that financial assistance is necessary, and that the work is of a permanent nature, it may acquire land and construct or adapt buildings. It may make grants for machinery and equipment, for training workers in Ireland or elsewhere, for roads, bridges, harbour works, railway lines, housing and canteens. The Local Authority may remit two-thirds of the rates. The Board is financed (Section 12) by an annual grant-in-aid voted by the Oireachtas which may not in the aggregate exceed £2m. The total of the grants approved so far amounts to £2.2m., of which £1.1m. has been paid. Thirty-eight projects are in production—many concerned with the export market —and 22 others have been promised financial assistance.

Hence, the Authority was to deal with developed and the Board with undeveloped areas, but a new Act, the Industrial Grants Act, 1959, provides for the making of grants-in-aid for industrial development in areas other than areas to which the Undeveloped Areas Acts, 1952 and 1957, apply. In effect, it transfers to the Board the functions covered by the Industrial Grants Act, 1956, so as to allow the Authority to concentrate on promotional activities.[1] If the Board considers that an undertaking of a nature, outlined above when dealing with the Authority, cannot reasonably be established or expanded in the undeveloped areas, it may provide the facilities hitherto afforded by the Authority. For the acquisition of land, the construction and adaptation of buildings and other facilities connected with land, the grants may not exceed two-thirds of the cost, and for machinery and equipment one-third within a limit of £250,000 unless the Government, having regard to the amount of employment likely to be afforded by the undertaking, decides on a grant beyond that limit. The Board may also contribute towards, or guarantee one-half of, the capital cost of installing electricity. It takes over all the assets and liabilities created by the Authority under the Industrial Grants Act, 1956. The aggregate amount of grants (other than those made under Section 12 of the Undeveloped Areas Act, 1952) made by the Authority under the Act of 1956, and by the Board and the Minister on foot of guarantees under the Undeveloped Areas Acts may not exceed £10m. The main financial sections of the Act remain in force until 31st December, 1963.

100D. *Technical Assistance.* This includes grants to industrial firms for the employment of technical experts to advise on how to improve efficiency and productivity. One-third of the cost of each project is borne by the State.

100E. *Fair Trade Commission.* This Commission was established by the Restrictive Trade Practices Act, 1953, and consists of a Chairman and from two to four other members appointed for a term of 5 years by the Minister, who may also appoint temporary members. It may, on its own initiative or on request, prepare and publish rules of fair trade conditions relating to the supply and distribution of goods and the rendering of services. Notice of the intention to make rules must be given, inquiries must be in public

---

1. See para. 363.

unless confidential information is involved, and witnesses may be summoned and examined on oath.

By "unfair trade practices" is meant any measure, rule, agreement or act by a person, alone or in combination, or any agreement, express or implied, with others or through a merger, trust, cartel, monopoly, or other means or devices, which limits or restrains unreasonably free and fair competition, or which is an unreasonable restraint of trade, or which unjustly eliminates a trade competitor, or which unjustly enhances the price of goods, or which unfairly promotes the advantages of suppliers or distributors at the expense of the public, or which secures a substantial control of the supply and distribution of goods contrary to the public interest, or which without good cause prohibits or restricts the supply of goods to any person, or which unjustly restricts the freedom of choice as to what goods will be distributed to a person or area, or which imposes unreasonable conditions regarding the supply or distribution of goods, or which in any way operates against the public interest.

The Commission's reports are sent to the Minister, who makes an order relating to the restrictive practices, but the order must be confirmed by an Act of the Oireachtas. The Commission has made to date 19 sets of Fair Trading Rules, and has held six public inquiries relating to the supply and distribution of radio sets, building materials, motor vehicles, grocery goods, chemists' preparations, and carpets. Hitherto, public inquiries had to deal with all the conditions and restrictive practices in the supply and distribution of goods, but the Restrictive Trade Practices (Amendment) Act, 1959, enables the Commission to hold an inquiry of limited scope into one or more aspects of restrictive practices (Section 2). Again, hitherto if an order had to be amended, another public inquiry had to be held, but Section 6 empowers the Commission to hold a special review of the operation of an order either in whole or in part. Finally under Section 4 it may investigate restrictive practices imposed by employees or employers or by both in combination if they refuse to use particular methods or materials for manufacturing or constructive purposes.

100F. *Córas Tráchtála Teoranta.* This includes a grant-in-aid of £145,000 for administration and general expenses, and £80,000 for promoting whiskey exports. Formerly a limited company, Córas Tráchtála has been constituted a body corporate by the Export Promotion Act, 1959. It consists of not fewer than 5 and not more than 7 members (including the Chairman) appointed by the Minister who also determines with the Minister for Finance the tenure and the terms of office. Remuneration and allowances are to be paid out of the Board's money. The assets and liabilities of the Company are to be transferred to the Board.

The functions of the Board are generally to promote, assist and develop exports and to advise the Minister thereon, but in particular it may purchase, lease or exchange or otherwise acquire lands or buildings in the State or elsewhere; it may apply in the State or elsewhere for any trade marks, licences, protections or concessions, and it may dispose of any of its lands or buildings. It is to receive out of voted moneys from time to time any sums which it may require within a limit of £1m., and such sums will not be repayable. Annual Accounts are to be audited by the Comptroller and Auditor General and with the report submitted to the Minister and tabled in the Oireachtas. The Board may with the consent of the Minister and of the Minister for Finance borrow from Bankers for current expenditure.

100G. *Labour Court* (£30,533). Constituted by the Industrial Relations Act, 1946, the Court consists of a whole-time Chairman and four ordinary members, two of whom represent workers and two employers. The Minister designates organs representing Trade Unions and Employers to nominate members who are then appointed by the Minister. A Deputy Chairman may be appointed, and the Court may act by divisions to expedite its work. It may appoint assessors to assist its proceedings or one of its officers to act as Conciliation Officer. It has a Registrar appointed by the Minister, and he must be a solicitor or barrister of at least ten years standing. A Register of Employment Agreements is kept. The Court has an official seal which must be judicially noticed: it may summon witnesses and examine them on oath, and it is master of its own procedure. Its decisions are not binding on the parties to a dispute, but no appeal lies to a law court from the Court's decision on a matter within its jurisdiction.

On the 31st December, 1958, there were 24 Employment Agreements on the Register, and the effect of the registration is to make them legally enforceable on both the employers and employees concerned.

Since its inception in 1946 to the end of 1958, the Court has dealt with 2,718 disputes including 280 in 1958. Conciliation Conferences were held in 226 of those 280 cases and 136 were settled at conciliation level. Of the remaining 144 disputes, the Court itself dealt with 137 and its recommendations were accepted in 104 cases by both parties.

The Act also provides for Joint Labour Committees which deal with rates of wages and conditions of employment. There are 21 such bodies for the same number of different trades, and they consist of two or three members appointed by the Minister, and a varying but equal number of representatives of employers and employees. Employment Regulation Orders made by the Court on the recommendations of the Committees are legally enforceable.

Only one Joint Industrial Council is registered under the Act, but there are also functioning several unregistered bodies acting as councils. All councils, whether registered or not, are assisted by the officers of the Court.

101. Apart from a provision for harbour improvement, constructional work and incidental expenses, the chief item in the Vote for Transport and Marine Service is the grant of £1.5m. to C.I.E. which includes £324,000 as Redundancy Compensation. Under Section 10 of the Transport Act, 1958, the Board was entitled to £1m. a year for 5 years beginning on the 1st April, 1959, for payment of interest on Transport Stock and other expenses of the undertaking, but Section 23 of the Great Northern Railway Act, 1958, increased this figure to £1,175,000. The Redundancy Compensation is for employees of both railways whose services are dispensed with or conditions of employment worsened for any reason connected with the reorganisation of the railway system within the State.

102. *Aviation and Meteorological Services.* As regards Aviation Services the Vote provides £1m. for the acquisition of lands and buildings, for constructional works (including furnishings), at Shannon, Dublin and Cork, and £115,800 for their maintenance. The provision for the Meteorological Services includes £71,460 for equipment, stores and maintenance.

The State maintained at Montreal a permanent representative on the Council of the International Civil Aviation Organisation. The cost of the representative was estimated at £74,023 including a contribution of £57,000 to the Organisation.*

103. The Vote for *Tourism* consists of three grants-in-aid, one (450,000) for the administrative expenses of Bord Fáilte Éireann, the second (£100,000) for schemes designed to improve major tourist resorts, and the third (£50,000) to encourage the provision of additional bedroom accommodation at tourist resorts. The functions of the Board will be dealt with in a later chapter.

DEPARTMENT OF POSTS AND TELEGRAPHS

104. This Department administers two votes — Posts and Telegraphs £10m., and Wireless Broadcasting £436,500. Though run on commercial lines, the Department is essentially a department of State, and like any other department is administered by a Minister,

---

* In the Estimates for 1960/61 no provision is made for the representative but £30,655 is provided for Contributions to the Organisation.

and a Secretary as Principal and Accounting Officer. At the Headquarters in Dublin there are different Branches dealing with Personnel, with Telephone, Wireless, and Telephone Communications, with Mails, with Savings (including the Post Office and Trustee Savings Banks) and with Engineering. A Stores Branch deals with the purchase, storage and distribution of all material required for the Post Office, and the placing of contracts for the supply of certain goods, e.g., uniforms for the Army, the Gárdaí, and all other departments of State. A factory is operated for the manufacture and repair of telegraphs and telephone apparatus.

104A. In the provinces there are some 55 head offices with 89 postmasters administering 2,009 sub-offices, some of which provide money order facilities. A Postmaster is a civil servant, and is responsible for the collection, sorting and distribution of mail and for the operation of the telegraph and telephone services. Sub-postmasters are not civil servants and are paid on a unitary basis according to the amount of work transacted.

104B. As a Department of State, the Post Office renders renders annually an Appropriation Account to the Auditor General, and, like all such accounts, it is based on the cash transactions which have taken place during the year. But as a commercial undertaking it also renders an Income and Expenditure Account based on the revenue accrued and the expenditure incurred during the period covered by the account—taking credit for services rendered free to other departments and raising debits for services rendered to it. A surplus is regarded as surrendered to, and a deficit as made good by, the Exchequer, so that there is no carry forward of balances from one account to another. Over a period of 36 years, from 1922/23 to 1957/58, there were deficits in 20 and surpluses in 16 financial years. The surplus in 1957/58 was £293,820 — surpluses of £104,999 and £366,377 on the Postal and Telephone services respectively and a deficit of £177,556 on the Telegraph services. A small surplus is also expected for 1958/59.

104C. The expenditure of the Department, like all other departments, is met out of the annual grant of the Oireachtas, and its revenue is surrendered to the Exchequer. Money for telephone development is borrowed from the Central Fund within limits prescribed by statute, and repayment is made by means of terminable annuities voted by the Oireachtas and charged in the Department's Vote. For 1959/60 the amount voted is £1.3m. The rate of interest charged varies with fluctuations in the money market. Capital authorised under British and Irish Acts for capital development of the telephone service up to 31st March, 1958, amounts to £24m., and the total sum raised was £20m.

No portion of the revenue is appropriated in aid of the Vote, and the actual appropriations consist mainly of Agency Services, such as receipts from Savings Bank Funds (£196,700) and from the Insurance Fund (£152,000).

104D. Under the Ministers and Secretaries Act, 1924, the Minister for Finance is responsible for the investments of the Post Office Savings Bank, and the Minister for Posts and Telegraphs for the actual business with depositors. Surplus income may, under the Finance Act, 1930, be transferred to the Exchequer. All deposits carry a State guarantee. Interest has always been at $2\frac{1}{2}$ per cent. per annum on the deposits — which may be as low as 1/-, and as high as £500 net — despite their ability to earn more on investment because, being payable on demand, they have to be protected by liquid assets. At the end of the financial year 1958/59 they totalled £79m. The Post Office also receives the funds and supervises the operations of the five Trustee Banks situated in Cork, Dublin, Limerick, Waterford and Monaghan. These Banks date from 1817 and were formerly supervised by the National Debt Commissioners. Deposits at those banks at the end of 1958/59 totalled £12$\frac{1}{2}$m.

104E. Wireless Broadcasting in Ireland is not in the hands of a private company as in the United States of America, nor is it operated by a Corporation established by charter or statute as in Great Britain. It was established under the Wireless Telegraphy Act of 1926 which entrusted to the Post Office the establishment and maintenance of broadcasting stations throughout the State. It is, in effect, at least at present and until a Television Service has been established, another of the many branches of the Department of Posts and Telegraphs.[2]

Radio Éireann is a simple organisation consisting of a Director, an Administration Officer, a Controller of Programmes and a Chief Engineer who control the whole operational staff. A certain degree of autonomy or independence has been secured by a delegation of powers to the Director who is in close touch with both the Secretary and the Minister. He is also assisted by an Advisory Committee consisting of a Chairman and four members chosen for their interest in cultural, agricultural and industrial matters.

It is financed by the annual vote of the Oireachtas and its appropriations-in-aid are mainly receipts from advertisements. Licence Fees, collected by the Post Office, are surrendered as Extra Exchequer Receipts, and the administrative expenses in collecting the fees and in other matters are charged not in the Appropriation, but in the Commercial Accounts of the Department.

---

2. See Appendix, para. 362.

Advertisements for sponsored programmes are confined to Irish industrial products, services or organisations, but those relating to patent medicines, cosmetics and alcohol are excluded.

DEPARTMENT OF DEFENCE

105. This Department administers two votes, one for the pay and maintenance of the different arms of the Forces, and the other for Army Pensions. The Arms of the Forces consist of a small whole-time Regular Army, a small Reserve of Officers and Men First Line, and a large Reserve Second Line (An Fóras Consanta Aicniúil and An Slua Muirí) of Officers and Men. The Reserves are part-time and are called up for training either annually in the case of the First Line, or both annually or at periods during the year in that of the Second Line. The Forces also include a small Air Corps and a small Naval Service. The Second Line has recently been integrated in the Regular Army.

The administration of matters not of a direct military nature (including that of Civil Defence) is in the hands of civil servants, and a large number of Civilian Employees are engaged in maintenance and minor new works throughout the different services of the Army.

About 75 per cent. of the Vote (£7m.) is absorbed by salaries, pay, wages and allowances, so that when the cost of the ordinary maintenance stores is taken into consideration only a small fraction is devoted to stores of a purely defensive nature.

The other Vote provides for the payment of various forms of Army Pensions — Military Service Pensions for Pre-Truce Service, that is, service before the Truce against the British Forces in 1921; Wounds and Disability Pensions for wounds or disease incurred or contracted in the course of service; Defence Forces Pensions for service in the Regular Army; and Special Allowances for the dependants of certain persons who were killed or died from wounds or disease attributable to service.

The Pensions Acts are administered by civil servants of the Department and the adjudication of claims under the Acts (other than the Defence Forces Pensions Act) is in the hands of the Army Pensions Board established under the Act of 1927.

DEPARTMENT OF EXTERNAL AFFAIRS

106. This Department administers two Votes — External Affairs and International Co-operation. Apart from a sum of £21,600 for miscellaneous items, the former Vote is taken up with the salaries, wages, allowances and expenses of the staff at Headquarters, and at the different representations abroad. Ambassadors

are maintained at the Holy See, in Great Britain, in the United States of America, in Spain, in Italy, in Canada, in Australia, in Belgium, in the Netherlands and at the United Nations. Envoys Extraordinary and Ministers Plenipotentiary represent the State in Switzerland, Sweden, and the Federal Republic of Germany, and Chargés d'Affaires in Portugal and in the Argentine. There are consular offices in New York, Chicago and San Francisco. A Counsellor is the representative at the Council of Europe.

Vote 60, International Co-operation, provides for Ireland's contribution to, and expenses connected with, various international organisations. These are dealt with in a later chapter.

CHAPTER V

Estimates of Receipts [1]

107. The White Paper summarises the Receipts for 1959/60 thus:—

	£
Tax Revenue (excluding Motor Vehicle Duties)	100,610,000
Motor Vehicle Duties	5,550,000
Non-Tax Revenue	23,034,000
Repayments of Capital and other Issues ...	1,242,000
Capital raised under Telephone Capital Acts ...	1,610,000
Additional amount to be found by Borrowing or Otherwise	28,038,000
Total	£160,084,000

TAX REVENUE

108. The following are details regarding Tax Revenue:

(1) *Customs (excluding Special Import Levy)* — (£48m.). These duties, levied on imported goods, either for revenue or protective purposes, are the largest factor in indirect taxation. They are Specific when charged by weight or quantity, and Ad Valorem when levied on the declared value of the goods. Soon after the arrival of a ship, its Captain lodges with the Customs Officer a report giving details of the ship, the voyage, the cargo and the ship's stores. If the goods be for immediate use, the importer declares on a form whether the goods are dutiable or free. If dutiable, payment is made at once. When the form is signed by the Customs Officer, it becomes a warrant for the discharge of the goods, and is passed to a transit shed where the goods are produced for examination. If the goods are to be warehoused, they must be placed in warehouses owned by the Revenue Commissioners. Duty is not paid on the goods while warehoused, but a bond is given for the amount of the duty, and the duty is paid on delivery being taken. The principal articles are Tobacco, Oils, Wines, Beer and Spirit, Motor Vehicles, Parts and Accessories.

(2) *Special Import Levy* — (£1.75m.). This levy was an extra tax or levy imposed in 1955 on a large variety of goods already subject to existing duties. Its object was to redress the

---

1. See Appendix, para. 359.

unfavourable balance of international payments then existing, and to use the product of the levy for capital purposes. Later, however, the levies were absorbed in the ordinary customs duties and treated as ordinary revenue. During 1958 the levy yielded £2.5m. net. The levies were imposed on such goods as Motor Vehicles, Parts and Accessories, Clocks, Watches, Jewellery, Newspapers, Periodicals, Refrigerators and Electric Apparatus.

(3) *Excise* — (£18m.). These are duties imposed (a) on certain goods manufactured within the State such as beer and spirits, (b) on liquor licences for dealing in and retailing beer, wines and spirits etc., (c) for licences on certain activities, such as auctioneering, bookmaking and pawnbroking, (d) on certain amenities such as betting and entertainments. In the manufacture of excisable commodities there is constant supervision by Excise Officers over both the process and product of the manufacture, and the same system of bonded warehouses is applied.

(4) *Estate etc. Duties* — (£3m.). These comprise (i) Estate Duty, a graduated ad valorem tax on the value of property passing on a person's death. It is levied on all property whether immovable (e.g. lands, house, etc.) or movable (e.g. furniture, stocks, shares, etc.) in the State so passing on the death of a person, and on movable property outside the State, if deceased was domiciled in Éire. Before probate or administration is granted an Inland Revenue affidavit must be sworn giving details of the deceased's property, and the duty must be paid thereon. (ii) Legacy and Succession duties payable on the acquiring of property by beneficiaries on a person's death, the percentage levied being dependent on the relationship of the beneficiary to be deceased. (iii) Corporation duty payable as annual compensation for non-liability to death duties on certain property vested in bodies corporate and incorporate, but not including limited liability companies.

(5) *Stamp Duties* — (£2m.). These are stamps impressed on certain documents requiring stamping for their validity or authenticity. They include Deeds, Bills of Exchange, Insurances and Cheques. Stamp Duties on Sweepstakes are also included.

(6) *Income Tax* — (£23m.). This is a direct tax on all income arising within the State, and is, therefore, payable even by persons resident outside the State, and also on all income arising outside the State by persons resident within the State. By a reciprocal arrangement between Ireland and Great Britain exemption from the Irish tax is granted to British nationals, and Irish nationals are similarly treated as regards the British tax. The tax is temporary and is re-enacted each year by the Finance Act. Assessments are made with the

79

exception of Schedule C by the Inspector of Taxes. The rules for assessing income tax are contained in five schedules according as they relate A to income from the ownership of lands or buildings; B to income from the occupation of lands; C to interest, etc., from any public revenue; D to profit from trades, professions, foreign securities, etc.; and E to income from employment. Irish Companies are charged income tax on the full amount of their trading profits but may deduct tax from dividends, etc., paid to shareholders.

(7) *Sur-Tax and Super-Tax* — (£2m.). Super-Tax has been merged in Sur-Tax since 1928 but the term is retained in respect of arrears which arise occasionally. Sur-Tax is a graduated tax levied in addition to income tax on incomes over £2,000 a year.

(8) *Corporation Profits Tax* — (£2.9m.). This is a tax on the net as distinct from the trading profits of limited liability companies; but public utility companies such as Railways, etc., are generally excluded from the tax. The first £2,500 is free but beyond that figure Irish concerns pay 10 per cent. and foreign 12½ per cent. on their profits. By " foreign " are meant companies which do not keep a register of their Irish shareholders in Ireland. The tax is allowed to be deducted in computing income tax.

NON-TAX REVENUE

109. The details of the Non-Tax Revenue are as follows:—

(1) *Postal* (£5m.), *Telegraph* (£38,300), and *Telephone* (£4m.) Services total £9m.

(2) *Land Annuities* — £2m. See para. 95A.

(3) *Interest on Exchequer Advances* — £7.2m. Advances made from the Exchequer to such bodies as the Electricity Supply Board and Bord na Móna are usually repayable at varying rates of interest, and the interest repayable is provided for here.

(4) *Central Bank Surplus Income* — £1.8m. See Chapter XV.

(5) *American Loan Counterpart Fund* — £1.6m., being payments to cover interest and principal of Dollar Borrowings repaid.

(6) *Wireless Licence Fees* — £440,000.

(7) *Fee Stamps* — £430,000. The stamps referred to previously are a form of duty, and are distinct from Fee Stamps which are for fees paid by means of stamps affixed to documents, e.g., Passports, Visas or Consular services, Censorship of Films, the Civil Service and Local Appointments Commission and the Registration of Deeds.

(8) *Miscellaneous*. This heading (£350,000) covers a wide variety of items, but they are arranged in two divisions:

(a) Receipts by Departments not appropriated in aid of their

Votes, such as refund of overpayments, salaries of loaned officers, compensation for services of officials injured in accidents, sales of property and stores, interest on accounts of sub-accountants, charges for collecting insurance premiums, and fees for weights and measures.

(b) Other Receipts. These include Dividends (net) on shares held by the Minister for Finance, Conscience Money, Forfeited Election Deposits and Savings on Supply Services surrendered in cash.

OTHER REVENUE

110. The Motor Vehicle Duties have already been explained (para. 68). The repayment of Capital Issues refers to the repayment of advances by the E.S.B., the Road Fund, Bord na Móna, the Sea Fisheries Board and of issues made under the Trade Loans (Guarantee Acts). The Capital raised under the Telephone Capital Acts has been dealt with in para. 72.

Chapter VI

The Form of the Supply Estimates:
The Vote on Account: The Central Fund Act.

FORM OF THE SUPPLY ESTIMATES

111. The Estimates presented to the Dáil are all of the same pattern. Some, naturally, are more complex than others, but are taken from the same mould. As an example we shall take that for the Comptroller and Auditor General for the year 1958/59, not because it has any special excellence or virtue, but simply because it is one of the shortest in the Book of Estimates, and will serve to bring out the principal features common to all the others.

5.
COMPTROLLER AND AUDITOR GENERAL

112. I.—Estimate of the Amount required in the year ending 31st March, 1959, for the Salaries and Expenses of the Office of the Comptroller and Auditor General (No. 1 of 1923).

THIRTY-FOUR THOUSAND NINE HUNDRED AND SIXTY POUNDS

II.—Subheads under which this Vote will be accounted for by the Office of the Comptroller and Auditor General.

		1958/59	1957/58	Increase	Decrease
		£	£	£	£
A	Salaries, Wages and Allowances	40,240	40,850	—	610
B	Travelling Expenses	600	420	180	—
C	Incidental Expenses	240	240	—	—
	Gross total £	41,080	41,510	180	610
Deduct:—					
D	Appropriations-in-Aid	6,120	5,980	—	140
	Net total £	34,960	35,530	180	750
				Net Decrease	£570

The total expenditure in connection with this Service is estimated as follows:—

	1958/59 £
Gross Estimate above	41,080
Estimated amounts included in other estimates in connection with this service:—	
Vote	
9 Public Works and Buildings	780
16 Superannuation and Retired allowances ...	11,000
22 Stationery Office	860
26 Rates on Government Property	175
55 Posts and Telegraphs	10
Central Fund — Comptroller and Auditor General's salary, and pensions of former Comptrollers and Auditors General	4,569
Total Expenditure £	58,474
The receipts in connection with the service are estimated as follows:—	
Appropriations-in-Aid above ... ... £	6,120

113.   III—Details of the foregoing

A.   Salaries, Wages and Allowances

Numbers			1958-59	1957-58
1957 1958	1958 1959		£	£
1	1	Secretary and Director of Audit	2,047	2,102
1	1	Deputy Director of Audit	1,367	2,102
4	4	Senior Auditors	5,412	5,442
10	10	Auditors	10,869	11,558
9	8	Assistant Auditors	4,237	4,321
7	7	Audit Clerks (1 temporary)	5,014	5,070
27	27	Clerical Officers (2 temporary)	9,872	9,406
—	—	Allowance to Private Secretary (a)	63	63
1	1	Typist	385	385
1	1	Messenger (with 9/4d. non-pensionable allowance)	396	396
1	1	Cleaner	184	184
—	—	Provision for Additional Assistance	300	300
—	—	Social Welfare Acts — Employer's Contributions	94	95
62	61	Total for Salaries etc. £	40,240	40,850

B. Travelling Expenses
    Travelling expenses and Subsistence Allowances £ | 600 | 420

C. Incidental Expenses
    Telephones (£210), Postage (stamps) (£2)
    Carriage (£1), Uniform (£9), Newspapers and
    Miscellaneous (£18)   £ | 240 | 240

D. Appropriations-in-Aid
    Audit Fees, etc.   £ | 6,120 | 5,980

(a) Private Secretary to Comptroller and Auditor General
    (Clerical Officer).

Appendix

Secretary and Director of Audit ...	Same as Assistant Secretary
Deputy Director of Audit	... Same as Assistant Principal (Scale 1)
Senior Auditor	... Same as Assistant Principal (Scale 2)
Auditor	... Same as Higher Executive Officer
Assistant Auditor	... A £285 x 20 — 665 B £285 x 28 — 425 x 30 — 830
Audit Clerk	Same as Staff Officer, Grade III

114. This example shows that the Estimate contains three parts numbered I, II and III, together with two appendices, one giving the total cost of the Service, and the other showing how the departmental grades of auditors are related to the General Service Grades. We shall now deal with each of these parts.

Part 1 gives (a) the number of the Vote (5); (b) the service generally covered by the Vote (Office of the Comptroller and Auditor General); (c) the statutory authority for the establishment of the service (No. 1 of 1923); and (d) the exact amount to be voted by the Dáil in respect of the service, and this, it will be noted, is not the gross or the total cost but the net cost of the service. In other words, from the gross cost are deducted the receipts or appropriations-in-aid which the Dáil authorises the department to appropriate in aid of its expenditure, so that in effect the Dáil grants the net total and approves the use of departmental receipts to meet expenses. Hence arises the dictum, " The Dáil approves the gross but votes the net."

Regarding this part of the Estimate, the following points are to be noted : —

(a) With the exception of the Appropriations-in-Aid, it is the only part to which statutory effect is given, because it alone is repeated in the Schedule to the annual Appropriation Act.

(b) The service or ambit of the Vote is described in general terms, but the amount to be voted is set out definitely.

(c) Though the service is thus described in general terms, its ambit is not indefinite, and any expenditure not falling fairly within that ambit cannot be met out of the amount voted.

(d) The service may be described by means of a general term, or by a general term qualified by reference to a statute or statutes. In the latter case the term used must, of course, be interpreted by reference to the qualifying statute or statutes.

(e) If a new service has been created or an old service extended either by statute or by administrative action, and if it has been added to the existing functions of the Department the ambit of the Vote as defined by Part 1 has to be correspondingly widened so as to embrace the new or extended service. Conversely if a service has for any reason ceased, the ambit as set out in Part 1 must be narrowed.

115. The service which is described generally in Part I is described specifically in Part II, which sets out the " Subheads under which the Vote will be accounted for " by the Department administering it. In other words, the service described generally in Part I is here divided into a number of specific services included within the ambit of the Vote. Each subhead is lettered and against it is set out the amount which it is anticipated the service will cost. The services described by means of these subheads will vary with the nature of each Vote. Some Votes have only 1 or 2 subheads while others have as many as 50 or 60. Regarding this part of the Estimate the following points should be noted: —

(a) The subheads as such have no legal effect.

(b) The subheads form the basis of the Appropriation Account —in fact, this is one of their primary functions.

(c) A second but important function is that by giving specific information as to the various services included in the ambit of the Vote, it facilitates the financial control of the Dáil when considering both the Estimates and the Appropriation Account.

(d) A third and also important function is that it enables the Department of Finance to exercise financial control over expenditure during the financial year.

(e) The amount set out against each subhead is definite, but unlike that set out in Part I it has no legal binding effect. The amounts are not considered to be absolutely accurate in detail, and the Dáil in voting Part I recognises that there will inevitably be savings on some and excesses on other subheads. How these may be offset will be considered later.[1]

---

1. See para. 189.

(f) These subheads are known as the Debit Subheads and the total of the amounts set out against each of them is known as the Gross Total. If the Estimate has no Credit Subhead — called Appropriations-in-Aid — then the Gross Total is that voted in Part I by the Dáil.

(g) If, on the other hand, a Department be allowed to appropriate in aid of its votes certain receipts for services rendered by it, these receipts constitute a Credit Subhead, the total amount of which is deducted from the Gross Total giving a Net Total, which is the amount voted by the Dáil in Part I. For receipts to be appropriated in aid of a vote the following conditions must be verified:—

(i) They must be regular both as to amount and as to time of receipt;

(ii) They must be germane to the vote;

(iii) They must be authorised by statute, or by a Minute of Finance;

(iv) They must be approved and voted by the Dáil. This is done in a schedule of the annual Appropriation Act.

116. The services which are described generally in Part I and specifically in Part II are, so to speak, individualised in Part III, which further subdivides the divisions of Part II and thus sets out in greater detail the services included in each subhead. In other words, just as Part II specifies the services included in the ambit of Part I, so Part III further specifies the services included in each subhead of Part II. With regard to this Part of the Estimate it is to be noted:—

(a) It is in itself purely explanatory and has no statutory effect.

(b) It is not a basis of accountancy as far as the final appropriation account is concerned.

(c) It may and frequently does form the basis for the departmental internal accounting, and Finance may in fact direct a department to keep its accounts on that basis.

(d) If no information, additional to that given by the subhead in Part II, can be given in Part III, then mention of the subhead is omitted in Part III.

117. The "Total Cost Statement" appended to Part II of each vote is compiled not by the service department but by Finance — in fact, the former may not see it until it appears in the Book of Estimates. Finance in its "Standing Instructions to Accounting Officers" says:—

"As it is desirable to show in respect of each vote the total cost of the service, it is necessary for the Department of Finance to be in possession of a complete statement of the allied services for the purpose of compiling the 'Total Cost' tables which appear at the end of Part II of every Estimate. Each Estimate should accordingly be accompanied by a statement indicating what portion, if any, of the expenditure proposed to be incurred is in respect of allied services rendered on behalf of other Departments."

The aim of the Statement is to assess the total cost of the department by adding to its own administrative expenses the estimated cost of other services or supplies rendered to it by any other department, but usually and mainly by what are called Common Service Departments, that is departments which serve the common needs of all other civil departments, and the services of which are called " allied ". By this term is meant services allied or connected with the normal business of the departments. In our example are listed five Common Service Departments or Offices — the Office of Public Works for the maintenance of buildings, furniture, fuel, light and water; the Paymaster General's Office for the payment of pensions and retired allowances; the Stationery Office for paper, binding and other similar requisites; the General Valuation Office for rates on public buildings; and the Post Office for postal and telephone facilities, etc. For reasons of convenience and economy, the allied services and supplies must be obtained from the Common Service Departments, and the cost borne on their Votes, irrespective of any question as to which department benefits by the outlay. Any other arrangement would involve a duplicate charge, one on the administering and the other on the receiving department, and would mean a payment from one department to another.

Departments, other than Common Service Departments, may also render services and the cost thereof is included in the Total Cost Statement. Thus the Revenue Commissioners render certain services to the Stationery Office and the Department of Justice, and the Department of Defence supplies military aides to the President and the Taoiseach and the expenses are included in the Statement.

118. The Allied services are concerned only with the ordinary needs of the departments so that if anything of a special nature is required its cost must be borne on the departmental votes. Thus in our example, Subhead C carries the cost of special telephone calls, postage stamps—as distinct from the ordinary franked official correspondence—and a uniform which are not included in the ordinary services rended by the Post Office. Again in the Army and the Gárdaí the cost of clothing, fuel, light, water, telegrams and telephones are borne on the relevant votes. In these cases direct purchases may be made, with the assent of the Minister for Finance represented by the Government Contracts Committee, and the Common Service Departments may then act not as principals but

as agents. We must, therefore, distinguish between Principal or Allied Services and Agency Services. In the former the Common Service Departments administer, execute and pay for the supplies, but in the latter they neither administer nor pay for them, but as a matter of convenience merely execute them on behalf of the other departments. Again, in the matter of services the Post Office, for instance, with branches distributed throughout the entire State, is in a much more favourable position to pay the Old Age Pensions than the administering Department of Social Welfare, and it, there-fore, acts as agent for the latter. The agent may not have sufficient funds of its own to meet the disbursements, and in that case an advance is made by the principal, but all payments made by the former, whether out of the advance or not, must be charged against the Vote of the latter according to the date of payment made by the agent, provided, of course, that its appropriation account be still open.

119. The Notes added by way of an Appendix to Part III of the Estimate are used for a variety of purposes but mainly to give information, either special or general, about the salaries of the staff. Thus, in Part III above we have an example of the bewildering variety—said to number over 1,000—of departmental as distinct from general service grades in the Civil Service, the salaries of which are given in the early pages of the Book of Estimates, and the aim of the Appendix is to bring out the relation between the two. Thus, " Same as Assistant Secretary " means that the salary is either A £1,380 x 50 — 1,630 or B £1,550 x 50 — 1,800.

A applies either to a woman or an unmarried man whose remuneration is governed by differentiation on a married basis, and B either to a married man, or an unmarried man whose remuneration is not governed by the differentiation.

COMMITTEE ON ESTIMATES

120. The Estimates, as presented to the Oireachtas, represent as we have seen, a joint effort at departmental and even at ministerial level to produce a document containing the minimum financial needs of the Supply Services for the year. In the end, however, it is the financial policy of the Executive which must stand or fall by it. Seeing that it will be the task of the Government to impose taxation to meet these requirements, it is a sound principle of economical administration that it alone should be responsible for the Estimates, and that though the Dáil may reduce the amounts required, it cannot increase them. The right of the executive to seek supply on the one hand, and that of the Dáil to refuse it on the other, produce a balance of interest which is a vital factor in the control of expenditure.

On three occasions each year, the Dáil is confronted with one aspect or another of the Estimates of Expenditure. It meets them first in a general way when it discusses the Vote on Account issuing in the annual Central Fund Bill. It meets them a second time, again in a general way, when dealing with the Budget resulting in the annual Finance Bill; and it debates them in a special way when it deals with the Financial Resolutions for each Vote in preparation for the annual Appropriation Bill. But on any of these occasions the Dáil does not conduct a detailed examination of any particular Estimate or group of Estimates. Hence, although the Irish system of financial control and procedure follows almost rigidly that of Great Britain, it has not, unlike the latter, any Select Committee on Estimates.

121. That Committee in Great Britain was first appointed in 1912 by the House of Commons "to examine such of the Estimates presented to this House as may have been put to the Committee, and to suggest the form in which the Estimates shall be presented for examination, and to report what, if any, economies consistent with the policy implied in these Estimates may be effected therein." It cannot, therefore, deal with the Government's policy, but only with the administrative methods in carrying it out. The Committee consists of 36 members drawn from all parties, and is presided over by a member who is usually a prominent member of the Government in power. During the two World Wars the Committee was suspended and gave way to a Select Committee of National Expenditure, but when the second war ceased, the Estimates Committee was again rivived.

The Committee generally selects for examination a group of estimates and in its Reports has dealt with the methods used in framing estimates, with the causes of increased amounts for the same estimates over a number of years, and with the Treasury control over them. In 1959 it issued a report on the Treasury itself and criticised its lack of long-term financial planning, stressing that too much attention was paid to unimportant details. It considered that the Treasury's proper role in modern circumstances was not to sit on the tails of departments, but to instil into them a finer sense of financial control and that the Treasury itself should exert more financial control when policy was being formulated.

The Committee has no executive power, and its effectiveness is further hampered by the fact that it cannot deal with the estimates until they are presented to Parliament, that it cannot deal with questions of policy, and that it has no official comparable in status to the Comptroller and Auditor General to help it in its deliberations.

Its influence is mainly in the publicity given to its reports by the Press and Radio.

THE VOTE ON ACCOUNT

122. Although the Estimates are in the hands of the Dail some time in March, the Votes on each one of them will not have been discussed and passed until the following July or August. Now, as, on the Principle of Annuality, grants made in one financial year in respect of Supply, as distinct from Central Fund and Capital, Services, cannot be used to defray the expenditure of a subsequent year, the problem arises, how are the public services to be financed until the Annual Appropriation Bill has been enacted ? The same problem has to be solved in every democratic state following the same principle, and each has its own way of meeting it. Some, as for instance Switzerland, are empowered to re-apply the old estimates until the new are approved; others, like Norway, are empowered to carry on until the new estimates have been passed; but in most states, like Great Britain and Ireland, the situation is met by passing what is called a " Vote on Account ", taken before the end of the current financial year.

The Vote on Account may be defined as a temporarily unappropriated grant of supply to the Government to enable it to carry on all the supply services already approved, until the supply for each specific Vote has been passed. In effect, it is a temporary advance of money to enable the Government to meet its financial commitments after the end of the expiring financial year. It is " unappropriated ", because it is not for any special service but for all services generally, and it is " temporarily unappropriated " because the allocation or appropriation to each Vote does not take place until the Appropriation Bill has been enacted. In some countries the Vote is taken to cover only a month's supply, but in Great Britain and Ireland it is taken for four months, though the procedure followed is slightly different in each case.

The British Estimates are divided into two classes: those for the Civil Services (including the Revenue Department) and those for the Fighting Services. The Votes for the former are taken for each department, but the estimates for the latter proceed on different lines. A separate estimate is submitted for each service— Air, Army and Navy—but it is immediately divided not into subheads but into Votes. Thus the Army Estimate is divided into about 12 Votes—one relating to Numbers and the others to Pay, Clothing, General Stores, Warlike Stores, Pensions, etc. In the case, therefore, of those services it is the practice to pass Vote A (numbers) and some of the larger Votes for each service, the aggregate totals of which are sufficient to cover expenditure on all the Votes until the end of the Summer. A single Vote on Account is taken for all the civil services. In Ireland no distinction is made between the military and civil services, and the Vote on Account covers both.

The Irish Constitution makes no mention of the Vote on Account, and there is no statute authorising it. Constitutional lawyers have indeed cast doubts on its validity and on that of the Central Fund Act by which it is implemented. With an unwritten and, therefore, flexible Constitution and the British Parliament being supreme, no such doubts can be raised about the constitutional validity of the British practice, but with a written Constitution in Ireland, one would have expected some reference to the Vote on Account.

As regards the procedure followed in preparing and presenting the Vote, each department must first prepare its own statement in accordance with the following " Standing Instructions to Accounting Officers " : —

1. The Estimates Circular is accompanied each year by a form on which must be inserted the total requirements for each service for a period of four months from the 1st April. The form, duly completed, must be returned to the Department of Finance by 1st January if possible, and in no case later than 1st February.

2. A full explanation must be given in any case where it is considered necessary to ask for a Vote on Account exceeding one-third of the total Estimate.

3. Under no circumstances can provision for a new service be included in the Vote on Account.

When Finance has received the statements for each Vote, it prepares a comprehensive statement to be presented to the Dail, showing without details the total net estimate for each service, together with the amount required for the period of the Vote on Account.

The next stage is in the Dáil when the statement prepared by Finance is presented to it at the end of the current financial year, and the Dáil in Committee on Finance goes through the financial phases and legislative stages already described, the financial resolutions being embodied in the annual Central Fund Bill.

THE CENTRAL FUND ACT

123. The Central Fund Act is a very short statute, consisting almost invariable, apart from its long and short titles, of three Sections. Thus, Section 1 of the Act of 1959 runs: " The Minister for Finance may issue out of the Central Fund and apply towards making good the supply granted for the service of the year ending

on 31st day of March, 1959 the sum of £3,688,982." This Section deals with the Supplementary Estimates passed during the current financial year. On page xi of the Book of Estimates for 1959 thirteen of these estimates are listed totalling £2.6m., but a footnote warns that further supplementary estimates might arise. In fact, as the Act shows there were actually other such estimates and all totalled £3.6m. Although each of these supplementary estimates was taken in respect of a particular vote or service, the supply voted remains legally unappropriated until the passing of the annual Appropriation Act.

Section 2 of the Act is, " The Minister for Finance may issue out of the Central Fund and apply towards making good the supply granted for the service of the year ending on 31st March, 1960, the sum of £38m." This sum is approximately one-third of the total (£115,547,070) required for the Supply as distinct from the Central Fund and Capital Services, and refers to the Vote on Account. Here again no appropriation is effected. It should be noted that no provision is made in the Act for Central Fund or Capital Services, because they are provided for by permanent statutes—as opposed to the annual Central Fund and Appropriation Acts—which are deemed to give continuing grants to the Minister for Finance for their implementation.

Section 3 (1), " The Minister for Finance may borrow from any person and the Bank of Ireland may advance to the Minister for Finance any sum or sums not exceeding in the whole £41,688,982 and for the purpose of such borrowing the Minister for Finance may create and issue any securities bearing such rate of interest and subject to such conditions as to repayment, redemption or otherwise as he thinks fit." The total here is, of course, the total of the Supplementary Estimates and of the Vote on Account. It will be noted that, though the Central State Banks usually act as bankers for their governments, the Central Bank of Ireland—except for special purposes defined by statute—does not do so, because its main function is the management of currency by the issue of notes. The Irish Government's bank is the commercial privately-owned Bank of Ireland.

Section 3 (2), " The principal and interest of any securities issued under this Act and the expenses incurred in connection with the issue of such securities shall be charged on the Central Fund or the growing produce thereof." This last phrase is very old and frequently occurs in British and Irish financial statutes. All it means is that charges on the Central Fund are payments falling due at the end of a quarter, while payments due from day to day are charged on its growing produce.

Section 3 (3), "Any money raised by securities under this Act shall be placed to the credit of the account of the Exchequer and shall form part of the Central Fund and shall be available in any manner in which such Fund is available. Here it is to be noted that the account of the transactions of the Central Fund is called the Exchequer Account.

124. As regards the Vote on Account the following points should be noted: —

(a) As the Vote presented to the Dáil contains the totals of each Vote, no alteration can be made in the total of any Estimate after it has been so presented.

(b) Provision for any new service cannot be made in a Vote on Account, and by "any new service" is meant any service not previously approved by the Dáil. Hence, even if the Estimate itself includes provision for any such new service, it cannot be begun until the Vote making provision for it has been passed by the Dáil. In very exceptional cases, however, Finance may authorise the initiation of such a service pending the passing of the Vote authorising it.

(c) The Central Fund Act legalising the Vote on Account authorises the total amount as demanded without appropriating or allocating that amount for any definite or detailed purpose. In principle, therefore, it is objectionable in as much as it permits of temporary misapplication of the sum so voted.

(d) A Vote on Account must not be confused with a Vote of Credit. The latter is a grant by Parliament for services which are of such an indefinite character that the details cannot be estimated in advance. In granting such, Parliament waives its rights of detailed appropriation, and its control over it is simply limited to its control over the general policy of Government. (Strictly it is true that a Vote on Account likewise does not demand detailed appropriation, but, as we shall see, the sum so voted is subject to detailed appropriation when the total supply for the year is legalised by the Appropriations Act.) Yet, a Vote of Credit cannot be regarded as an unconditional grant, because it is subsequently accounted for in the usual way and as far as possible under the usual headings. In other words, the appropriation of the amount voted is not done by Parliament, but by the Department concerned, under the direction of Finance, and it receives the implicit consent of Parliament when the accounts are presented to and passed by it. This form of Vote has not been used in Ireland, but in Great Britain during both World Wars many departments were financed in that way so that valuable information might not be elicited by the enemy.

CHAPTER VII

The Central Fund: The Exchequer Account: Borrowing: The Public Debt.

THE CENTRAL FUND

125. The word "Fund" means a store or sum of money set apart for a particular purpose, and in that sense we speak of "The Road Fund", a "Sinking Fund" or the "Contingency Fund". The term "Central Fund" is not used either in the new or in the old Constitution, but both prescribe that all the revenues of the State from whatever source arising shall with certain exceptions form one fund. This fund we know as the Central Fund, the purpose of which is that "it shall be appropriated for the purposes and in the manner and subject to the charges and liabilities determined and imposed by law". The term is used for the first time in the Appropriation Act, 1922, but the Constitution (Consequential Provisions) Act, 1937, declares that the Fund mentioned in Article 11 of the Constitution shall be known as the Central Fund and for purposes of distinction as the Central Fund of Ireland or the Exchequer of Ireland. Hence, according to the Constitution, the Central Fund embraces all the receipts (including Borrowings) set out above in par. 107.

THE EXCHEQUER ACCOUNT

126. The account of the Central Fund is known as the Account of the Exchequer or Exchequer Account and from their close relationship, the Central Fund is commonly and officially referred to as the Exchequer. The account is, therefore, a record of all the transactions, credit and debit, on the Fund.

127. The Exchequer Account deals with cash transactions, and as other forms of account also deal with them, it will be useful at this stage to differentiate between them. Broadly speaking, accounts dealing with such transactions may take the form of (a) A Commercial Account, or (b) An Income and Expenditure Account, or (c) A Receipts and Payments Account.

(a) *A Commercial Account* may be said to contain three distinct parts — (i) a statement of the cash transactions during a period covering Personal Accounts and Real or Property Accounts; (ii) a

94

statement showing for a period the trading results and the net profit or loss thereon, and comprising what are called Nominal Accounts; and finally (iii) a statement—called technically a Balance Sheet—which records those financial transactions which have not during a period developed into cash transactions.

(b) *An Income and Expenditure Account,* on the other hand, comprises in practice two statements giving (i) the Income and Expenditure for the period; and (ii) a Balance Sheet. It includes all revenue belonging to the period, irrespective of the date of receipt, and all expenditure incurred during it, even though not paid till a later period. It, therefore, deals with all the income and expenditure of the current period whether actually received and paid or not, and consequently all income accruing and all liabilities outstanding must be included before the Balance Sheet is struck. Finally, the balance in this type of account will represent the surplus or deficit, as the case may be, for the period.

(c) *A Receipts and Payments Account* is simply a summarised statement of the cash transactions which have taken place within a given period. It deals only with the part of the income and expenditure which is actually received or actually paid. It may contain the cash in hand at the commencement and at the end of the period together with the cash received and paid during it. It is clear, therefore, that it may contain the receipts and payments not only for the current but also for the previous years. Moreover, its balance will not represent the surplus or deficit for the period, but merely the cash in hand at the close thereof. All assets and liabilities are ignored, until such time as they become cash transactions, so that the account records only the actual incomings and outgoings.

128. The elaborate system of commercial accounting is not suited for dealing with the finances of the State, because the chief consideration of the latter is the creation not of a monetary but of a social profit in carrying out the public services in accordance with legal and constitutional principles. State finance aims at a balance between income and expenditure so as to ensure a small surplus and thus avoid a deficit.

129. Setting aside, therefore, the commercial system as unsuitable, the only choice is between the Income and Expenditure and the Receipts and Payments systems. Some countries, such as France and Belgium, follow the former, and others, like Great Britain and Ireland, use the latter, and indeed ultimately the choice of one rather than the other would seem to depend on national outlook and character. For the reasons given the Income and

Expenditure type is more complete, but it is less simple and timely, and the countries which use it often take a year or more to close their accounts.

130. From time to time, the present system of Irish and British Government Accounting is adversely criticised, and writers conclude that it should be scrapped, and that a new system should be introduced with particular reference to the adoption of the income and expenditure basis. As a result of such criticism, a British Select Committee was set up in 1947 " to examine the existing systems of accounting in Departments in the light of modern accounting practice ". The Committee held 77 sessions, receiving oral and written evidence not only from the Treasury, but also from external organisations comprising accountants, economists, and statisticians, and among the main conclusions it reached in 1950 were the following:—

1. The main Exchequer Accounts, and the framework of both Estimates and Appropriation Accounts should remain on a cash basis.

2. The adoption of an income and expenditure basis would not result in staff economies, and it would involve the capitalisation and depreciation of fixed assets, which would encounter insuperable practical difficulties.

3. Apart from trading services no practical advantage would be secured from the adoption of the proposed basis.

EXAMPLE OF THE EXCHEQUER ACCOUNT

131. The Exchequer Account is published periodically in Iris Oifigiúil, and as an example we shall take that published for the whole year 1958/59, omitting the comparable figures for 1957/58. It is as in Table opposite.

The Account is thus divided into four parts—the first dealing with current revenue and expenditure; the second, mainly with capital receipts and expenditure; the third, with borrowings and repayments; and the fourth, with the balance.

132. As regards the first division, opposite the words " Total Revenue " on one side, and " Total Expenditure " on the other, the account is ruled off. The items above the ruling are known as " Above the Line ", and those beneath as " Below the Line " transactions. The original purpose of the division was no doubt to enable one to distinguish current revenue and expenditure above, from capital receipts and expenditure, below the line. But that no longer holds good. In the account above, for instance, it would appear at first glance as if the year ended with a deficit of

EXPENDITURE

	Total Issues out of the Exchequer to meet payments from April 1, 1958 to March 31, 1959
	£
Central Fund Services	26,417,740
Supply Services	111,836,032
TOTAL EXPENDITURE	138,253,772
OTHER ISSUES	
Issues under the following Acts:—	
Local Loans Fund Acts, 1935-56	4,600,000
Turf Development Acts, 1946-57	1,101,000
Telephone Capital Acts, 1924-56	1,450,000
Irish Shipping Ltd. Act, 1947	604,599
Transport Acts, 1950-55	
Industrial Credit Acts, 1933 and 1958	1,007,330
International Finance Corporation Act, 1958	118,548
Sea Fisheries Acts, 1952 and 1956	167,171
Trade Loans (Guarantee) Acts, 1939-54	34,938
Electricity (Supply) Acts, 1927-58	1,000,000
Finance Acts, 1953 (Sec. 16) and 1954 (Sec. 22)	179,500
Insurance Act, 1953 (Section 2 (4))	8,503
Road Fund (Advances) Acts, 1926 and 1948	—
Bretton Woods Agreements Act, 1957	407,500
	10,679,089
Issues for Redemption of Debt:—	
Ways and Means Advances	11,375,000
Exchequer Bills	67,500,000
Savings Certificates	1,809,000
Prize Bonds	1,168,000
Other Borrowings	5,195,000
	87,047,000
TOTAL ISSUES	235,979,861
Balance in Exchequer on 31st March, 1959	544,700
TOTAL	236,524,561

REVENUE

	Total Receipts into the Exchequer from April 1, 1958 to March 31, 1959
	£
Customs—excluding Special Import Levy	46,510,000
Customs—Special Import Levy	1,788,000
Excise	17,470,000
Estate etc., Duties	2,894,000
Stamps	2,122,000
Income Tax (including Sur-Tax)	25,016,000
Corporation Profits Tax, etc.	2,800,000
Motor Vehicle, etc., Duties	5,509,000
Post Office	8,650,000
Sundry Receipts	13,650,558
TOTAL REVENUE	126,409,558
OTHER RECEIPTS	
Repayments, etc.:—	
In respect of issues under:—	
Electricity (Supply) Acts, 1927-58	544,379
Turf Development Acts, 1946-57	180,178
Sea Fisheries Acts, 1952 and 1956	22,092
Insurance (Intermittent Unemployment) Act, 1942 (Section 47 (1))	2,000
Finance Act, 1941 (Section 49)	200,000
Trade Loans (Guarantee) Acts, 1939-54	18,347
Transport Acts, 1950-1955	793,300
Road Fund (Advances) Acts, 1926 and 1948	297,480
Insurance Act, 1953 (Section 2 (4))	56
Tourist Traffic Acts, 1939-55	
	2,057,832
Money raised by Creation of Debt:—	
Ways and Means Advances	16,550,000
Exchequer Bills	63,000,000
Savings Certificates	2,725,000
Telephone Capital Acts, 1924-56	1,450,000
Prize Bonds	3,430,405
6% National Loan, 1967	
5¼% Exchequer Stock, 1971/74	14,786,212
Other Borrowings	5,695,000
	107,636,617
TOTAL RECEIPTS	236,104,007
Balance in Exchequer on 1st April, 1958	420,554
TOTAL	236,524,561

£11,844,214, but in the figure (£111,836,032) for supply services there are included voted capital services to the extent of £12,003,806, which must be deducted to determine the balance on ordinary current account and we thus arrive at a modest surplus of £159,599. The account, therefore, may be summarised thus:

	£	£	£
Revenue			126,409,558
Expenditure—Central Fund			
Services		26,417,740	
Supply Services	111,836,032		
Less Voted Capital Services	12,003,806		
		99,832,226	
			126,249,966
Surplus			£159,952

The estimated expenditure for 1958/59 on Supply Services was £110,002,220 including £11,740,700 Voted Capital Services, and, as has been shown, the actual expenditure thereon was £111,836,032 including £12,003,806 capital. It is thus clear that if expenditure exceeds revenue, one cannot say whether the budget for current expenditure is balanced or not, until one knows how much voted capital expenditure is included in the figure for expenditure on the Supply Services. To that extent, therefore, the division as between current items above, and capital items below the line, is misleading, and indeed some of the items below would seem to be of a doubtful capital nature.

133. As regards the first below the line items, " Other Receipts " and " Other Issues ", it is obvious that apart from a reference to four Acts, the account deals mainly with the financing of certain State-sponsored Bodies coming within the purview of Ministers, which, with the Finance Acts, 1953 and 1954, and the Insurance Act, 1953, are dealt with elsewhere in this work. The Insurance (Intermittent Unemployment) Act, 1943, Sec. 47 (1) refers to the Supplementary Unemployment Fund providing insurance for certain workers against unemployment due to bad weather. Section 49 of the Finance Act, 1941, refers to the Foreign Exchange Account for the purchase of gold, foreign exchange or foreign securities.

SOURCES OF BORROWING

134. The figures for Other Receipts and Issues show that during the year the State expended on capital projects £8,621,257

more than it received, or £20,625,063, if the amount £12,003,806 for voted capital services be taken into consideration. From what has already been said about items above the line, it is clear that the ordinary revenue is stretched to the limit to meet the recurring expenditure on the Supply and Central Fund services, so that expenditure on capital projects must be met by borrowing. That, indeed, seems to be the settled policy of the State.

In its "Programme for Economic Expansion" over five years beginning in 1959/60, the Government proposes to spend £167m. to finance its capital projects on the basis of present policies, and a further £53m. on new development proposals, and of the total £220m. public bodies are expected to find £19m. from internal sources. Hence the net amount to be financed from Exchequer and non-Exchequer sources is £201m., an average of about £40m. for each of the five years. The resources available to finance the proposals are, according to the Programme, the following:

(1) *Current Savings.* These include private savings, the undistributed profits of industrial companies, and increases in the life funds of insurance companies. It is hoped that the yearly average savings for the five years will reach £45m., although those from 1953 to 1958 was about £43m.

(2) *External Assets.* These consist of (a) *External Investments* held abroad by private individuals, the income from which in 1958 came to £13.2m. The Programme rightly does not regard these as a likely source of help, unless they are voluntarily sold by their owners, or used by them for the purchase of exports. (b) *External Reserves.* At the end of 1958 these amounted to nearly £206m. of which about 25 per cent. were not of a liquid nature. The Central Bank held £87m., the Commercial Banks £105m., and the Minister for Finance £14m. But they were all held for specific and well-defined purposes. The Central Bank required about 90 per cent. of its holding to support its Legal Tender Issue of Notes in order to maintain the exchange value of Irish currency. The reserves of the Commercial Banks represent only about 30 per cent. of their deposits within the State, and are the minimum necessary to meet fluctuations in international trade. Any undue reduction in them might well upset the banking system. The funds held in trust by the Minister for Finance constitute only a small liquid reserve to meet calls on deposits in the Post Office and Trustee Savings Banks, Saving Certificates and Prize Bonds.

(3) *External Borrowing.* Should the sources just outlined be insufficient to finance the Government's projects, the Programme proposes to borrow from the specialised international institutions of

which Ireland is a member, or to encourage foreigners to invest directly in new industrial projects. But borrowing from the institutions is not an easy matter and the terms of repayment, usually in their own currency, are relatively high, thus imposing a severe strain on the balance of payments.

MODES OF BORROWING

135. Savings, whether intern or extern, are channelled in various ways and placed at the disposal of the Government. The principal ways are indicated in the account above and are briefly as follows: —

(1) *Ways and Means Advances.* These are temporary borrowings to meet immediate expenditure and are usually said to embrace: (a) Day-to-day Borrowings at an agreed or daily rate from the Bank to meet a possible overdraft and they are secured by the phrase in the various financial Acts that " The Bank may make advances ". Nowadays, this method is rarely used*, and ordinarily reliance is had on (b) Internal Borrowings from Funds held by Departments for specific purposes but not immediately needed for those purposes, such as Insurance Funds, Savings Banks Funds, or Suitor Funds held by the Courts. At the end of 1959 the outstanding advances (including the Counterpart and National Development Funds) were £95m. In the Capital Services Redemption Account, 1958/59, a sum of £2.6m. is applied for meeting interest on the Advances.

(2) *Exchequer Bills.* These are another form of short-term borrowings usually for a period of three months open to competitive tender and subject to a minimum subscription of £10,000. Until quite recently, these Bills were confined to the Banks, but of late a small money market has been created by throwing the amount required open to tender by the public. During 1958/59 the public took £3m. The Bills, like Bills of Exchange, are discounted by the Commercial Banks, and are re-discounted by the Central Bank, at a rate which varies with the Bank Rate. At the end of 1959 the amount of the Bills outstanding was £13m., and during the year a net repayment of £8m. was made to the Banks.

(3) *Saving Certificates and Prize Bonds.* Designed to attract the savings of the ordinary citizen these are another form of short-term borrowing, being repayable on demand with or without interest according to the terms of issue. At the end of 1959 the Bonds outstanding totalled £10m. The principal of the Certificates outstanding in 1959 amounted to £23m. The interest due on the

---

* In the Account for 1959/60 there is an item " Bank Advances £9.8m." which were received and repaid during the year.

Certificates in 1959 was about £5.3 m. and was safeguarded by a
reserve of £4.5m.

(4) *Loans* (including Exchequer Bonds and Exchequer Stock).
Loans are long-term borrowings at varying rates of interest,
dependant to a large extent on the Bank Rate obtaining at the time
of issue and repayable at par within a certain stated period. At the
end of March, 1959, there were eleven loans outstanding carrying
rates of interest varrying between 3 and 6 per cent. and totalling
approximately £172m.

(5) *Other Borrowings.* These include (a) a Terminable
Annuity of about £3.7m. for certain compensation claims payable
to Great Britain. Under Section 6 of the Damage to Property
(Compensation) (Amendment) Act, 1926, the Irish Government
agreed to pay at once a lump sum of £150,000 and thereafter for
60 years an annual sum of £250,000; (b) Dollar Borrowings under
U.S. Loan Agreements of about £40m.; and (c) Temporary Borrowings under Central Fund and Appropriation Acts of about £3.6m.
Direct Borrowings amounted, therefore, to £360m.

THE PUBLIC DEBT [1]

136. *Direct Liabilities.* The term " Public Debt " is used in
preference to " National Debt " in order to distinguish it from the
indebtedness of Local Authorities, which itself, at the end of 1958,
stood at £137m. In the direct borrowings of £360m. there is,
however, included a double reckoning of £42m. in respect of Dollar
Borrowings on the one hand, and, on the other, investment in Ways
and Means Advances of balances in the Counterpart and National
Development Funds. To offset the duplication there is included in
the Assets Statement a sum of £42m. in respect of the balances.

137. *Indirect Liabilities.* In addition to those direct borrowings, the State has other liabilities of a capital nature, which must
be considered in determining its gross indebtedness. At the end of
March, 1959, they totalled £68m., made up of liabilities under the
Telephone Capital Acts (£15m.), the Land Acts (£16m.), Housing
Acts (£33m.), and Sanitary Services (£4m.). Hence, the State's
gross indebtedness at the end of March, 1959, was £428m. The
National Income in 1958 was estimated at £480m., so that it would
appear as if the gross liabilities of the State were gradually approaching the size of the National Income.

PUBLIC ASSETS [2]

138. Against those liabilities, the State holds certain Assets
estimated at £236m. which are grouped under three headings: (a)

1. See Appendix, para. 360.
2. See Appendix, para. 361.

Repayable Advances of £171m. made to Other Funds (e.g., The Local Loans Fund) and to State-sponsored Bodies; (b) Shares of Sundry Undertakings—these are shares valued at £14m., held by the State in State-sponsored Bodies and include payments under the Bretton Woods Agreements and International Finance Corporation Acts amounting to £2.6m.; (c) Liquid Assets, being balances held on Sundry Funds and Accounts such as Sinking Funds, and the National Development Fund (Winding-up) Account. They totalled £51m., including £41m. balance on the American Counterpart Fund.

139. The Assets of the State, like those of the ordinary citizen, are its property and its possessions—land, buildings, stores, equipment, book debts, etc.—and it would appear that the assets set out above are mainly book debts or cash transactions between Funds or with certain Bodies. They vary in value and it has been held that at least some of them are not realisable. In dealing, for instance, with an asset, £793,300 for Repayable Advances under the Transport Acts, 1950 and 1953, a footnote adds that " the advances under the Acts amounted to £5.6m., of which £4.8m. has been repaid from voted moneys. Córas Iompair Éireann remains liable for the repayment of the total amount advanced ". But the Transport Act of 1958 wrote off the whole amount as an irrecoverable debt. Similarly, in the accounts for 1957 there is an asset or repayable advance due by Mianrai Teo of £145,477, but the Auditor General reported in 1957/58 that the Company could not discharge a liability of £196,320 and it was written off by a Supplementary Estimate.

140. As regards the shares held by the Government, it would be difficult to assess their value as tangible assets. Again and again in his treatise, Mr. Whitaker lays emphasis on *productive* development and *productive* projects, and the Government's Programme lays down the principle that productive capital expenditure—productive in the sense of yielding an adequate return to the community in competitive goods and services—must receive a greater priority than at present in the public capital programme. On the other hand, the Capital Investment Advisory Committee in its Third Report said that only parts of the State capital programme had been wholly productive and had resulted in the creation of assets which yielded an enhanced flow of goods and services at competitive prices. The rest of the public capital programme had been in varying degrees redistributive. Once the redistributive investments had been made, the assets could only be fully maintained if there was a continuous redistribution of real income.

What the Banking Commission said in 1938 of the Assets is

equally true in 1959. Para. 586 runs: " The Finance Accounts regularly contain a statement of the Assets of the State to which reference is often made in relation to discussions of the net amount of the public debt. It may be well to observe that the selection of the items appearing in the statement does not rest on any definite accounting basis, and that the statement merely provides a convenient list of certain important assets which are not elsewhere assembled in the public accounts. The statement in no way purports to be a complete inventory of State assets, and obviously does not comprise such items as the value of public buildings which would be proper to such an inventory. It does not appear to be feasible to apply a strictly objective test in the selection of items, but in general the scope of the statement is limited to claims of a financial character. The quality of the items is not uniform, and many are merely claims of one State fund, viz. the Exchequer against another State fund, e.g., the Local Loans Fund, so that the ultimate value as State assets may not be determinable without examination of the position of the funds against which the claims lie. For instance, the Exchequer claim against the Road Fund is merely a claim against future taxation, and is accordingly of no value as a State asset considered as an offset against public debt ".

Chapter VIII

The Operation of the Exchequer Account

141. Having described how the Central Fund is built up, and how its transactions are recorded in the Exchequer Account, it is now necessary to show how that Account is controlled and operated.

Revenue reaches the Central Fund through various subsidiary channels — such as the Revenue Commissioners, the Post Office, the Motor Tax Account, etc. — through which transfers are effected at daily or other intervals to the credit of the Exchequer Account. In like manner Issues out of the Exchequer reach the various departments, not directly but through the intermediate accounts of the Paymaster General, the Revenue Commissioners, the Post Office and the Bank of Ireland in connection with the servicing of the Public Debt.

THE COURSE OF THE EXCHEQUER

142. The stages of administrative action by which money for the various services — Central Fund, Supply and Capital — is released from the Exchequer is called the " Course of the Exchequer," and it is, therefore, necessary to describe briefly what takes place:

(1) The initiative comes from the Minister for Finance who, under his own hand, requests the Comptroller and Auditor General to grant in respect of the services set out in his requisition a credit for a stated sum on the Exchequer Account. This step is necessary because the Comptroller and Auditor General in his capacity as Comptroller has " to control on behalf of the State all disbursements of moneys administered by or under the authority of the State " (Art. 38.1 Cons.). This function was originally prescribed by Section 13 of the Exchequer and Audit Act, 1866-1921, and is repeated in Section 7 of the Comptroller and Auditor General Act, 1923.

(2) The next step is with the Comptroller General. If he is satisfied that the sum requested together with other sums already granted is within the limits prescribed by the Statutes — e.g., the Central Fund and Appropriation Acts in the case of the Supply Services — he informs the Bank that he has granted the credits requested. The Bank is precluded by law from allowing the Minister to draw beyond the limit of the credits granted.

As the Department of Finance alone is concerned with the

104

credits granted for the Central Fund and Capital Services, it is not necessary to pursue the expenditure of those credits further, so that in what follows attention is confined to those supply departments for which the Paymaster General acts as banker.

(3) Next, the Secretary of the Department requests the Bank by letter to transfer a stated sum to the credit of the Supply Account of the Paymaster General, and the letter also sets out the Votes for which the issue is required and the amounts to be issued. Having effected the necessary transfer, the Bank transmits the letter to the Comptroller and Auditor General, who is thus able to see that the particular issue made to the Minister is within the net total of the Vote passed by the Oireachtas for the service in question. In the case of the Post Office and the Revenue Department the issue from the Exchequer is made direct to their own accounts and not to the Paymaster General. It must be noted that, although the letter from the Secretary of Finance specifies the Votes for which the transfer is made, there is not, however, any earmarking of the credit as issued for that purpose. It becomes, in fact, a single general cash balance, and is available for any purpose for which the Paymaster General is authorised to make payments. The practice of keeping one and not many balances by the Paymaster General is governed by Section 11 of the Exchequer and Audit Departments Act, 1866.

The credit issued from the Exchequer in respect of the Supply Services for the Departments is now available in the Supply Account of the Paymaster General, and their Payable Orders are drawn on the Paymaster General who meets them on presentation in the same manner as a Bank.

(4) The Paymaster General, however, does not meet departmental orders directly from his Supply but from another Account, which he also keeps at the Bank of Ireland and which is known as the " Drawing Account." Each day this is fed from the Supply Account, and through it the Paymaster General makes payments by cash, by cheque or by " writes off."

143. Departments issue drafts daily to their creditors, and at the same time they transmit to the Paymaster General a Schedule of all drafts issued. The drafts are signed by an officer of the department specially deputed for that purpose, and the schedules are signed by two other officers. The Schedule runs: " The Paymaster General, Dublin, is authorised to make the following payments chargeable to the above account " (e.g., Army Vote). Then follows the date on which the Payable Order was issued, its number, the Payee and the amount payable. The drafts are crossed and bear either the simple inscription " Payable at the Paymaster General's Office,

Dublin," or they may state more fully "The Paymaster General has been authorised to pay to you the sum of £......... for (service). Payment will be made at the Paymaster General's Office, Dublin, on presentation of this notification with the form of receipt herunder duly signed by you. This document must be presented through a Bank." The authorisation referred to consists of the schedule sent to the Paymaster General. That, and not the draft itself is the effective authority for payment.

Drafts issued by departments are generally crossed and must, therefore, be presented and cleared through a personal account in a bank. All drafts received by each bank from their customers are daily presented to the Pay Office for clearance. There they are compared with the departmental schedules, and if found correct a draft for the total due to each bank is issued on the Drawing Account.

144. In addition to the exchequer issues, the Supply Account is also fed by moneys, appropriations-in-aid received by departments for services rendered in the course of their business. Some of these receipts reach departments in cash, but generally they are collected by means of Receivable Orders — that is, orders requesting the Paymaster General or the Bank of Ireland to receive from the debtors a certain sum to be placed to the credit of the Supply Account. The order and money may be lodged at any bank for advice at the Bank of Ireland. The latter lodges the amounts to the credit of the account and transmits the order to the Paymaster General who in turn notifies the departments of the receipts. If the money be received in cash, the department makes out an Order and lodges it with the cash at the Bank for the credit of the Supply Account. If the net supply voted by Parliament has been expended, a department may rely on these receipts to meet its expenditure up to the amount approved by Parliament.

145. Independently of the Accounts kept at the Bank, the Paymaster General keeps his own accounts for each department. In them are recorded the grants made by Parliament, and, when Finance issues a credit from the Exchequer to the Supply Account, the portion of it allotted for each department. Against the Exchequer issues are debited the departments' drafts cleared by the Pay Office. At the end of each month each vote account is balanced, so that if a department is spending more than its exchequer issues, the Paymaster can inform Finance and ask to have the discrepancy adjusted.

146. The Paymaster General's accounts are closed on 31st March, but any balance on hands is carried forward and treated as an exchequer issue for the new year. Hence, once Supply has been

voted, departments may begin their expenditure at once out of the general cash balance brought forward from the previous year. Similarly treated are departmental balances of grants held by the Pay Office, although from a department's viewpoint they must be regarded as cancelled or surrendered.

147. The grant voted by Parliament is issued in instalments throughout the year. How then does Finance know how much to issue to each department ? It has three checks. The first is the monthly check through the Paymaster General's departmental accounts. A second takes place in October when Finance requests each department to furnish a statment of the probable savings or excesses on each vote as a whole, and a third in December when in a circular on " Savings and Supplementary Estimates," each department has to show by subheads its anticipated savings or excesses for the whole year as compared with the estimate. Finance is thus in a position, before the end of the financial year, to gauge with reasonable accuracy the amount which it will have to issue from the Excequer.

PAYABLE ORDERS

148. Throughout the foregoing there has been frequent use of the word " Drafts " and " Payable Orders," and it is now necessary to see how they differ from Cheques. If we take the word " Draft " to mean the drawing of money by an order in due form, it will apply equally to cheques, bills of exchange and payable orders. But a cheque is a written unconditional order by the drawer to a banker directing him to pay the sum stated therein, and a bill of exchange is a written unconditional order by the drawer to the drawee, or to the payee. Both are negotiable instruments. The payable order, however, is not an order to pay, for, as we have seen, the schedule of payable orders sent daily to the Paymaster General is the order to pay, and it is not unconditional, because payment is conditioned on the signature of the payee. In fine, a payable order is a fiduciary instrument addressed to a person informing him that the Paymaster General has been authorised to pay him on presentation the sum set out therein. It is not a negotiable instrument.

Hitherto, the legal position of the Payable Order was regulated by Section 17 of the Revenue Act, 1883, which applied Section 82 of the Bills of Exchange Act, 1882. But both these sections have now been repealed by the Cheques Act, 1959, the provisions of which are briefly as follows :

(1) A banker incurs no liability if, in good faith and in the

ordinary course of business, he pays without endorsement or with irregular endorsement:

(a) a cheque drawn on him, or

(b) a customer's document, which, though not a bill of exchange, is intended to enable a person to obtain payment from him of the sum stated in the document, or

(c) a draft payable on demand by him upon himself, whether payable at the head office or some other office of his bank.

(2) If in good faith and without negligence — including absence of, or irregularity in, endorsement — the banker receives payment either for a customer, or—having credited a customer's account—for himself, and if the customer has no title or a defective title to the instrument, the banker is not liable to the true owner by having received payment thereof. This applies to the instruments mentioned in para. (1) and also " to any document issued by a public officer which is intended to enable a person to obtain payment from the Paymaster General of the sum mentioned in the document but is not a bill of exchange." Further, " the provisions of the Bill of Exchange Act, 1882 — and the new Act is construed as one with that Act — relating to crossed cheques, shall, so far as applicable, have effect in relation to the instruments (other than cheques) as they have effect in relation to cheques." The Act does not make negotiable any instrument which, apart from them, is not negotiable.

(3) A Banker who gives value for, or has a lien on, a cheque payable to order which the holder delivers to him for collection without endorsing it, has such (if any) rights as he would have had, if upon delivery the holder had endorsed it in blank.

(4) An unendorsed cheque which appears to have been paid by the banker on whom it is drawn is evidence of the receipt by the payee of the sum payable by the cheque.

CHAPTER IX

The Annual Budget: The Finance Act:
The Appropriation Act.

BUDGETS GENERALLY

149. The next important event in the Financial Year occurs towards the end of April, when the annual Budget is introduced in the Dáil. It is, of course, of special importance to the ordinary citizen, because on it will depend his personal finances for the remainder of the year. There is, indeed, this fundamental difference between the economy of the State and that of its citizens, that whereas the former regulates its revenue according to its expenditure, the latter must order their personal expenses according to the measure of their incomes.

The term " Budget " here means a statement giving the actual revenue and expenditure of the previous year, the estimated revenue and expenditure for the new year, and the amount of revenue from taxation and other resources which must be levied to meet that expenditure.

150. Taxation to-day covers practically the whole field of human endeavour. Direct taxation is levied on income and sometimes on capital, and even if the citizen is not liable to direct, he cannot escape indirect taxation which is imposed not only on certain activities, but also on a wide range of commodities or goods in ordinary everyday use. The taxes so imposed may be permanent, when they last for an indefinite period, or temporary when their duration is limited to a year.

151. The expenditure on current account for the year has already been determined by the amount needed to carry on the Central Fund and Supply Services, and the problem now confronting the Minister for Finance is to explore the various sources of taxation to see how that expenditure can be met. The estimation of expenditure is difficult enough, and the work of pruning departmental proposals is not easy, but these difficulties are relatively light compared with the task of estimating the probable revenue. So many things have to be taken into consideration such as the law of diminishing returns, and changes in the way of life of the citizens which are not amenable to any form of law. Once, however, the task has been

completed the estimates of revenue and expenditure are brought together and form the basis of the Budget for the financial year. That is the purport of the Governmental White Paper already given above. The Budget is the work of the Minister for Finance, but in the end, when presented to the Dáil, it is not a report for the information of the legislature, but a definite declaration of the policy of the Government.

BUDGET STATEMENT

All budget statements follow much the same pattern, and, generally speaking, fall into three parts, an Economic Review of the Present, a Financial Review of the Immediate Past, and a Financial Statement on the Present Budget.

152. The Economic Review will deal with such subjects as the Balance of International Payments, Agricultural and Industrial Production, Employment and Unemployment. If the position regarding any of these matters be unsatisfactory, measures will be outlined to deal with them. If, for instance, there be an excess of imports over exports and the excess is disturbing the balance of the economy, steps will have to be taken to re-adjust the balance, either by curbing imports or by stimulating exports by incentives to increased productivity. All these problems have an important bearing on the current budget, for on their solution will depend the amount of taxation which must be raised.

153. The Financial Review will examine the results of the previous year's budget. On the current account were the estimates of expenditure sufficient, or did circumstances necessitate recourse to supplementaries ? Did the revenue hopes materialise ? Was there a surplus or deficit on the year's workings ? Similar questions will arise on the capital account. Did the actual expenditure exceed or fall short of that estimated and how was the expenditure financed ? Thus in the Budget for 1959/60 the Minister reported that despite large supplementary estimates to support wheat and butter prices, the estimate for the supply services was only £96,000 greater than the original figure, that revenue exceeded hopes, that the allowance for overestimation of £1½m. was fully justified, and that the budget had been balanced with a small surplus. On the capital side the actual was less than the estimated expenditure by about £2½m., mainly because Local Authorities needed about £4m. less than expected. During the year the Exchequer had to provide nearly £25m. to finance capital projects.

154. As regards the Financial Statement we may take as an example the Budget for 1959/60. The problem confronting the

Minister on the current account was already posed in the April White Paper. On the revenue side he expected £129,194,000 and on the expenditure side he had to provide for £129,105,000 spread over Central Fund Services, Road Fund and Non-Capital Supply Services, so that if the estimates were realised there would be a small surplus of £89,000.

Despite, however, that close approximation of Revenue and Expenditure, the Minister eased taxation in the following respects: —

(1) *Special Import Levy*. The list of articles was reviewed. Some 35 items were completely freed, the levy on others was reduced, and a protective duty was placed on others, so that the levy remained only on a short list of less essential goods from which the revenue was derived. This change reduced the anticipated revenue by £220,000.

(2) *Income Tax and Sur-Tax*. The standard rate of Income Tax was reduced from £7/6d. to 7/-, the 6/- rate to 5/6d. and the 3/- rate to 2/9d. The starting point for Sur-Tax was raised from £1,500 to £2,000 and the personal allowance for Income Tax was extended to Sur-Tax. These concessions reduced the expected revenue by £1.2m.

(3) *Entertainments Duty*. A reduced scale of duty was applied to Cinemas, Cine-Variety, Dances, Greyhound Racing and Rural Entertainments at a cost of £205,000.

Hence the effect of those three concessions meant that the anticipated revenue was reduced by £1,625,000. On the other hand, the Minister budgeted for increased expenditure on the Supply Services in the following items:

(4) *Social Assistance*. The rates for Old Age, Blind, Widows and Orphans (Non-Contributory) Pensions, and Unemployment Assistance were increased by 2/6d. a week, the cost being £883,000.

(5) *Pensions* in respect of Public Service and Military Service were increased at a cost of £81,000.*

155. The effect, therefore, of these increases was to add to the cost of the Supply Services £964,000, so that taking together this increase and the decrease in revenue and allowing for the original surplus of £89,000, the Minister had to find £2.5m. In the Budget for the previous year he had allowed £1.5m. for errors in estimation, and events showed that he was justified, because lower short-term interest rates had led to a saving on Central Fund Services, and

---

* The Budget for 1960 reduced again the number of articles subject to the Levy at a cost of £555,000, and reduced the Entertainments Duty on Cinemas and Dances by £350,000. It increased Social Insurance by £135,000, Social Assistance by £450,000, and Pensions and Allowances by £150,000.

revenue estimated at £124,783,000 had actually reached £126,410,000. The Minister, therefore, concluded that there would not be any undue risk in allowing at least a similar amount for overestimation in the current year, and in the confidence that the reduction in direct taxation would stimulate national output, and strengthen the revenue base, he took the calculated risk of increasing the allowance for estimation to £2.5m.

156. As regards Capital Account the Government's Programme for Economic Expansion for 1959/60 envisaged expenditure of £41.69m. and the White Paper in April, as we have seen, gave an estimate of £31m. for non-voted and voted capital services, but the Book of Estimates warned that we should await any items included in the Budget Statement. The Budget actually increased the capital account to £45.6m. — that is an increase of £3.9m. on the Programme, and about £14.6m. on the White Paper figures.[1]

To provide this capital of £45m., the Exchequer was to give £33m. (including fresh borrowings of £30), seven of the State-sponsored Bodies and Local Authorities were between them to raise £7m., and they were expected to provide £5m. from their internal resources.

FINANCIAL RESOLUTIONS

157. After the Budget Statement and a brief discussion by the Opposition, the Minister introduces what are called " The Financial Resolutions," one of which is of a general and the others of a specific nature. The latter are dealt with at once, and cover any new taxes, any variation in a temporary tax, or any removal of a temporary tax. The Provisional Collection of Taxes Act, 1927, authorises under certain conditions the immediate collection of the taxes imposed or varied pending the enactment of the necessary Finance Bill. In 1959, for instance, there were eight specific resolutions dealing with different aspects of the Budget and four of them ended with the Clause " It is hereby declared that it is expedient in the public interest that this Resolution shall have statutory effect under the provisions of the Provisional Collection of Taxes Act, 1927 (No. 7 of 1927)."

158. The General Resolution, the last to be moved, is drafted in the widest possible terms — e.g., " That it is expedient to amend the Law relating to customs and inland revenue (including excise) and to make further provision in connection with finance " — so as to give ample scope for discussion ranging over the whole field

---

1. See Appendix, para. 358.

covered by the Minister. The Debate continues over many sittings, but, when it is ended, the specific resolutions — each resolution was put and agreed to when submitted — are embodied in the annual Finance Bill.

FINANCE ACT

159. The Finance Bill may be said to deal with two subjects— (1) The Financial Resolutions passed in Committee of Finance, and (2) a number of minor subjects which may have been mentioned by the Minister, but which do not upset the Budget balance. Of the 82 sections in the Bill of 1959, about 45 relate to Specific Resolutions. The Bill goes through the legislative stages already described.

THE APPROPRIATION ACT

160. Meanwhile, the Dáil has been considering the departmental estimates of expenditure. Indeed, it may have begun to do so at the end of March or early in April but usually they are not completed until the following July or August. The procedure followed has already been described, and from it emerges the annual Appropriation Bill.

Here it is necessary to emphasise that the Appropriation Act does not deal merely with the supply resolutions taken on the estimates but also with the Supplementary Estimates and the Vote on Account. The Central Fund Act simply legalises the issue of money and borrowings in respect of the Supplementaries and the Vote on Account, but it does not state the services to which the moneys are to be appropriated. It does not legalise the appropriations-in-aid, because they are not mentioned, and because the supply granted is based on the net amount of the estimates. The Central Fund Act, in fact, leaves everything except the issue of money very much in the air. It is a temporary measure designed to enable the Government to meet its immediate needs and merely authorises the Minister to draw from the Central Fund in anticipation of the Appropriation Act.

161. The Appropriation Act, 1959, will illustrate what has been said. It is a short Act of four sections (including the Short Title) with a long Abstract containing two Schedules in which the supply voted in the Supplementaries, the Vote on Account and the Resolutions of Supply are definitely appropriated. Its Long Title sets out its purpose — " to apply a certain sum out of the Central Fund to the service of the year ending on 31st March, 1960, to appropriate to the proper supply services and purposes the sums

granted by the Central Fund Act, 1959, and this Act, and to make provision in relation to borrowing."

The Sections of the Act are as follows:—

1. The Minister for Finance may issue out of the Central Fund and apply towards making good the supply granted for the service of the year ending on 31st March, 1960, the sum of £77,619,270.

2. (1) This has the same wording as Section 3 (1) of the Central Fund Act except, of course, that the amount which may be borrowed is £77,619,270.

(2) As in Section 3 (2) of the Central Fund Act (Cf. para. 123).
() As in Section 3 (3) of the Central Fund Act (Cf. para. 123).

3. (1) "All sums granted by this Act and the other Act mentioned in Schedule A annexed to this Act out of the Central Fund towards making good the supply granted amounting as appears by the said Schedule in the aggregate to the sum of £119,308,252 are appropriated and shall be deemed to have been appropriated as from the date of the passing of the Acts mentioned in the said Schedule A for the services and purposes expressed in Schedule B annexed thereto. The abstract of schedules and the schedules annexed thereto with the note (if any) to such schedules shall be deemed to be part of this Act in the same manner as if they had been contained in the body thereof."

3. (2) "In addition to the grants out of the Central Fund referred to in the foregoing subsection of this Section, there may be applied out of any money directed under Section 2 of the Public Accounts and Charges Act, 1891, to be applied as appropriations-in-aid of the grants for the services and purposes specified in Schedule B annexed hereto, the sums respectively set forth in the last column of the said Schedule amounting as appears thereby in the aggregate to the sum of £7,698,476.

162. As regards Section 1, it will be noticed that the supply granted (£77,619,270) together with the Vote on Account (£38,000,000) exceeds by £72,200 the figure of £115,547,000 given in the Book of Estimates for Public Services. The explanation is that the Book gives 66 Votes, but the Appropriation Act shows that there were 67, the additional vote, an echo of the Budget Statement, being for £72,200 for payment of increases in certain pensions, etc., in respect of public service. That increased the cost of the supply services to £115,619,270. Of that total £38,000,000 was granted in the Vote on Account and the balance, £77,619,270, is granted by the Appropriation Act. The supply voted in both Acts is not the gross but the net.

163. In the Abstract of Schedules mentioned in Section 3 (1) the work of appropriation is done. The Schedules A and B are repeated twice, first to record the grants and to allocate them to the years for which they were voted, and, secondly, to repeat the grants and to appropriate them to the services for which they were voted. In the second instance Schedule B is divided into two parts, one (Part I) dealing with the allocation of the Supplementaries to the services, and the second (Part II) appropriating the whole current year's supply (Central Fund and Appropriation Acts) to their services. Thus, for 1959/60 the Schedules are:—

Schedule A — Grants

Grants out of the Central Fund £119,308,252

Schedule B — Appropriation of Grants

Year	Sums not exceeding	
	Supply Grants £	Appropriations-in-Aid £
1958-59 (Supplementary)	3,688,982	30,180
1959-60	115,619,270	7,688,296
Total	119,308,252	7,698,476

Schedule A — Grants out of Central Fund

	£
For the Service of the year ended 31st March, 1959, under Act No. 6 of 1959	3,688,982
For the Service of the year ending 31st March, 1960, under Act No. 6 of 1959	38,000,000
under this Act	77,619,270
Total	£119,308,252

164. Schedule B — Appropriations of Grants, Part I (Examples)

Schedule of Supplementary sums granted, and of sums which may be applied as Appropriations-in-Aid in addition thereto, to defray the charges for the several Public Services therein particularly mentioned for the year ended on 31st March, 1959.

Vote No.	Title	Sums not exceeding	
		Supply Grants	Appropria-tions-in-Aid.
(1)	(2)	(3) £	(4) £
26	For the Salaries and Expenses of the of the Minister for Agriculture including certain services adminis-tered by that Office and for pay-ment of certain Subsidies and sundry Grants-in-Aid	2,220,000	48,000*
67	For the payment of Remuneration	987,000	—
	13 other Votes	481,982	78,180
	Total 15 Votes	3,688,982	30,180

* Deficit.

Schedule B — Part II

165. Here it is to be noted that although only the difference between the Vote on Account and the total of the Supply Services was voted in Section 1, the net total of all the Services is appropriated in Part II of the Schedule which runs : " Schedule of sums granted and of sums which may be applied as Appropriations in addition thereto, to defray the charges for the several Public Services herein particularly mentioned which will come in course of payment during the year ending 31st March, 1960." Here are given a few examples :

Vote No.	Title	Sums not exceeding	
		Supply Grants	Appropria-tions-in-Aid
(1)	(2)	(3) £	(4) £
2	For the Salaries and Expenses of the Houses of the Oireachtas including certain Grants-in-Aid ...	241,100	—
4	For the Salaries and Expenses of the Central Statistics Office ...	129,040	600
10	For Employment and Emergency Schemes (including Relief of Distress)	821,530	35,000

11 For Remuneration for the Management of Government Stocks ...	66,300	—
12 For the Salaries and Expenses of the State Laboratory	27,600	1,160
Total of 62 Other Votes	114,333,700	7,631,536
Total 67 Votes	115,619,270	7,668,296
Total of Schedule B	119,308,252	£7,698,476

166. The Central Fund Act, as we have seen, simply empowers the Minister for Finance to issue in respect of the Supplementary Estimates and the Vote on Account the sums set out in the Act, but the Votes for the Public Services are not legalised until the Appropriation Act is passed. Hence, if a Supplementary Estimate or a Vote on Account be granted, but the Dáil dissolves before the Appropriation Act is passed, the Estimate must be reintroduced when the new Dáil assembles. Thus in December, 1932, a Supplementary for £25,000 was granted in respect of Army Pensions, and expenditure was incurred under its authority, but the Dáil dissolved in January, 1933, and the Estimate had to be re-introduced when the new Dáil assembled. The expenditure was not irregular or illegal, because Section 14 of the Exchequer and Audit Departments Act, 1866, prescribes that " When any sum or sums of money shall have been granted to Her Majesty by a resolution of the House of Commons, or by an Act of Parliament to defray expenses for any specified Public Service, it shall be lawful for Her Majesty from time to time by Her Royal Order countersigned by the Treasury to authorise and require the Treasury to issue, out of the credits to be granted to them on the Exchequer Acounts, the sums which may be required to defray such expenses, not exceeding the amount of the sums so voted or granted." Hence, once supply has been granted for a service, Finance has authority to issue the money required.

117

CHAPTER **X**

The Expenditure of the Supply Grants

167. With the passing of the Annual Appropriation Act, the financial work of the Oireachtas is completed, and now we have to turn attention to the manner in which departments expend the grants on the services, and for the purposes prescribed by the Act. We have, therefore, to see first how expenditure is incurred, and then how it is liquidated.

AUTHORISATION OF EXPENDITURE

168. In the first place, it is to be noted that the passing or voting of an estimate does not authorise a department to employ the credits voted, but that the authorisation of Finance is necessary to do so. In the case of a service already established, the required financial authority will already exist, but if it does not the sanction of Finance must be obtained for the expenditure (See para. 84 above.)

Expenditure entered into by different departments will vary according to their particular functions, but, speaking generally, all such commitments may be reduced to three main headings, according as they fall: (a) Under Acts, Regulations, Orders, Rules, Circulars or Warrants made under statute; or (b) Under Contract; or (c) Under General or Specific authorisations of the Department of Finance.

169. The Pay and Allowances of personnel are covered by Regulations, Warrants, Orders or Rules, which are issued either by the Minister for Finance, or by the Minister of a Department with the concurrence and counter-signature of the Minister for Finance. Such Regulations are, of course, subject to amendment from time to time, but otherwise they are permanent rules which continue in force until rescinded. In some departments the bulk of expenditure is made under such Rules or Regulations.

170. Commitments under Contract may be either Simple Contracts or Contracts under Seal according to the nature of the matter under consideration, or the requirements of either party to the contract. In placing contracts, departments are not allowed to follow their own devices. In 1923 the Government decided that the system of placing Government Contracts should be unified, and for this purpose set up a Government Contracts Committee to direct and control the placing of contracts by the various departments of the State.

The Committee consists of the Parliamentary Secretary, a representative of Finance, a representative of each of the three Central Purchasing Departments—the Office of Public Works, the Stationery Office, and the Post Office—and three from other departments. Departments must send annually an estimate of their requirements to the Purchasing Departments, and these are supplied either from stock or by a special purchase if the order be of some magnitude or has a special specification. The Purchasing Departments must each submit monthly to the Committee a list of purchases made or of contracts placed exceeding £300, and other departments if they exceed £100. Contracts exceeding £3,000 may not be placed without the prior consent of the Committee or, in a case of urgency, without its subsequent approval. Competitive tenders must be invited, and contracts must be placed with firms of financial standing and capable of performing the contract. Special tender and contract forms must be used, and preference given to Irish firms. The Committee's prior authority must be obtained for the acceptance of an excess amounting to more than £10 on a contract up to £200 in value, or more than 5 per cent. on a contract over £200.

171. The third heading under which expenditure may be incurred is under the General or Specific Sanction of Finance. The first is a sanction for a particular purpose but not restricted to a particular occasion. The stores supplied or the services rendered may be of a recurring nature, and the sanction allows the department to deal with them without having recourse to Finance on every occasion. They cover, in fact, all matters of a recurring nature which are not the proper subject of an order or regulation. A specific sanction, on the other hand, is for a particular purpose and is restricted to a particular occasion. If, for instance, officials are going abroad on a particular mission, the sanction of Finance is needed, and is restricted to the particular occasion.

DISCHARGE OF EXPENDITURE

172. Usually a Contracts Branch when ordering goods sends with its order three other forms to the Contractor and a copy of the order itself to the Claims Branch of the department. Having completed the forms, the contractor, when despatching the goods, sends the forms completed to the stores officer who is to receive the goods. The latter, after checking the goods, signs and certifies the forms, retaining one as a stores voucher and sending the others, one to the contractor and the third to the departmental Claims Branch.

When, therefore, the claim for payment reaches that Branch,

it has already before it, the order placed by Contracts, and the certified form of receipt from the Stores Officer for the accuracy of which he is personally responsible. After checking the account, the Claims Officer allocates the expenditure to the vote subhead under which provision was made in the estimate, and gives the voucher a serial number for subsequent identification. The claim is then sent to the Cashiers Branch for payment. The account (or memorandum) books kept by the Claims Branch will naturally vary with the nature and volume of the claims, but the more care taken before passing the account, the less trouble is likely to arise later.

173. It is in the Cashiers Branch that all payable orders are issued, and all disbursements in cash are made. When the orders are made out, they are signed by a responsible officer. In signing he has beside him the vouchers containing the contractor's claim, the contract's order, the stores officer's receipt, and the signature of the claims officer, so that the danger of collusion or fraud between the parties to the transaction is remote. While the payable orders are being completed, a schedule of all the payments to be made is also prepared. The orders are signed by a responsible officer, and the schedule by two other officers. The latter must be authorised by Finance and the Paymaster General may not accept less than the signatures of two officers so authorised. Before the orders are despatched, the vouchers are stamped, and the order numbers inserted.

As regards payments to a department's own personnel, if they be in cash, two records are necessary, one, a pay list certified either by the actual signatures of the payees, or by the signature of independent witnesses of the payments, and the other, a permanent ledger record of the transactions. The first is needed to vouch the payments, and the second to keep easily accessible records of all payments made to any one person. If payment be made by payable order, the ledger record will suffice, because the receipted drafts will vouch the payments.

174. When the Payable Orders and Schedules have been despatched, the vouchers with a copy of the Schedules are sent to the Accounts Branch for booking purposes. Here again the books kept and the method of registration will vary with departments, but at least two records would seem to be essential — (1) a Self-balancing Payable Order Register to record the date and number of the Order, the Payee, the amount paid, and the Subhead, together with a personal column for such payments as Imprests which are not final and cannot, therefore, be booked until they are cleared. (If as often happens in large departments a record by auxiliary

subheads be required, a self-balancing analysis book, containing the date, number, and amount of the orders and the auxiliary subheads should be kept. This book may prove useful for the purpose of statistics, costing, and for answering questions raised in the Dáil.) (2) A Ledger Record by Subheads to which postings are made direct from the Payable Order Register—payments which are not final being recorded separately.

175. From this ledger is compiled the Annual Appropriations Account. In addition to the postings mentioned, it should also record the grants made by the Dail, the Exchequer Issues to the Paymaster General on behalf of the department, the amount of payable orders issued, and the orders cleared by the Paymaster General. Postings to the relevant books should be continuous, and at the end of the year they will permit the Appropriation Account to be accurately compiled. The following example may illustrate what has been said: (1) A department was granted a net sum of £1,440,000 of which £520,000 was given in the Vote on Account, and the remainder, £920,000, in the Appropriation Act, together with appropriations-in-aid of £30,000. At the end of the year the Exchequer Issues to the Paymaster General for the department were £1,330,000, but £95,000 had to be written off the current grant in respect of the previous year's surrender. That surrender had been £180,000 to meet which only £85,000 had remained unissued from the Exchequer in respect of that previous year. The Exchequer Grant Account will, therefore, be:

	£		£
To General Account of Vote:		By Paymaster General	1,330,000
„ Vote on Account	520,000	„ Surrender (prior year)	95,000
„ Vote to complete	920,000	„ Balance (unissued)	15,000
	£1,440,000		£1,440,000

(2) The expenditure for the year over the various subheads totalled £1,200,000 and the appropriations-in-aid (£30,000) were realised. The General Account of Vote will be:

	£		£
To Subheads	1,200,000	By Exchequer Grants	1,440,000
„ Surplus (for surrender)	270,000	„ Appropriations-in-Aid	30,000
	£1,470,000		£1,470,000

This account is in effect a summary of the Appropriation Account for the year.

(3) The department's account with its banker, the Paymaster General, must also be taken into consideration. At the end of the

previous year he had on his books £160,000 in Exchequer Grants issued in favour of, but not used by the department, and during the year he had received, as we saw, grants totalling £1,330,000 together with the £30,000 lodged with him as appropriations-in-aid. On the other side, he had cleared departmental payable orders to the value of £1,190,000. The Paymaster General's record will be:

	£		£
To Balance — Exchequer Grants (prior year)	160,000	By Payable Orders (cleared)	1,190,000
„ Exchequer Grants during year	1,330,000	„ Balance	330,000
„ Appropriations-in-Aid	30,000		
	£1,520,000		£1,520,000

(4) The position regarding outstanding Payable Orders must be clarified, because there will be a number of them outstanding both on the previous and on the current year. At the end of the previous year they totalled £87,000 and during the current year the department issued payable orders to the value of £1,250,000. The Payable Orders Account will be:

	£		£
To Paymaster General (orders cleared)	1,190,000	By Orders (o/s prior year)	87,000
„ balance o/s current year	147,000	„ Orders issued	1,250,000
	£1,337,000		£1,337,000

The orders outstanding at the end of the previous year should be encashed during the current year in time to have them included in the Appropriation Account for that year — otherwise they will be cancelled. Similarly those outstanding at the end of the current year should be cleared in time to have them included in the account for that year. That the department issued orders to the value of £1,250,000 but that only £1,200,000 has been charged in the Appropriation Account is explained by the fact that some of the orders issued during the year represent imprests, or advances to contractors, agents and sub-accountants and will not be a proper charge to the Vote until a subsequent year. The balances of such orders will be carried to a suspense account until the full amount issued is vouched and thus cleared. They will be shown in the Balance Sheet of the department, attached to the Appropriation Account.

(5) Finally the Appropriation-in-Aid Account will be:

	£		£
To General Vote of Account	£30,000	By Paymaster General	£30,000

CHARGING OF EXPENDITURE

176. We have now seen how expenditure is authorised, how it is defrayed, and how it is accounted for. But every payment made during the year is not necessarily correct or proper, and it is now, therefore, necessary to see what conditions must be verified to render a charge in an account regular and proper.

First, it should be noted that no additional period is allowed during which payments in respect of the financial year may be made. In some continental countries such periods, varying from one to twelve months, are allowed, but in Ireland, Great Britain and the Commonwealth generally no extra period is permitted.

The conditions for a payment to be regular derive in the first instance from the wording of the Appropriation Act where in Schedule B, Part (II) it speaks of " sums granted . . . to defray the charges for the several Public Services which will come in course of payment during the year." That phrasing comes in turn from Section 24 of the Exchequer and Audit Departments Act, 1866, which runs : " An appropriation account of supply Grants shall exhibit on the charge side thereof the sum or sums appropriated by Parliament for the service of the financial year to which the account relates, and on the discharge side thereof the sums which may have actually come in course of payment within the same period : and no imprest or advance, of the application of which an account may not have been rendered to and allowed by the accounting department shall be included on the discharge side thereof." This has always been interpreted as meaning : (a) that the payment must have been made before the end of the financial year either by cheque, or by cash or by sending to the Paymaster General a schedule authorising him to pay the payable orders listed theron ; (b) that the payment must be in respect of a fully matured liability, and (c) that the payment should be final.

177. The first condition flows not only from the wording of the statutes quoted but also from the fact that the Appropriation Account takes the form of a Receipts and Payments Account which deals only with that part of the expenditure which is actually paid during the period. Hence arises the dictum that " the date of payment governs the date of charge." The period in respect of which the payment is made does not affect the date of charge, and the only determining factor is the date on which the payee received the cash or on which the draft was sent to him provided always that the payment was due. In connection with this condition the following points should be noted : —

(a)   The cretiting of a payee's Banking Account as confirmed by the Banker's receipt is regarded as an actual payment.

(b)   Payments made by Sub-Accountants or Imprest Holders must be included in the account of the period for which the payments were made.

(c)   Cash Payments are charged according to the date on which the payee acknowledge their receipt, or in cases where individual receipts are not forthcoming according to the date of the certificate of payment.

(d)   Payments by Cheque, Draft or Payable Order are charged according to their date of issue, so that delay in cashing on the part of the Payee does not affect the date of charge, provided that the Draft is presented within the prescribed period—that is, within three months of the end of the financial year in the case of a Draft drawn at the end of March.   In point of fact all Drafts not cashed within that period are automatically cancelled.

(e)   Cancellation of drafts is always absolute.   The items to which such drafts refer must be removed from the account, and re-charged to the year in which the new draft is issued.

(f)   The extending of a draft does not affect the year of charge.

(g)   If a department owes money to another but has a counter-claim against it, the amount of the counter-claim may be charged to the Vote as a payment though no cash payment be made.

(h)   Where short issues are made owing to deductions in respect of fines, forfeitures or defalcations, the short issue only is charged in the account, but in the case of Income Tax deductions, the gross amount is charged to the Vote, because that amount has been earned and is due, because section 10 of the Exchequer and Audit Act requires the payment into the Exchequer of " gross revenues," and because a receipt is given by the payee for the gross amount.

178.   The second condition requires that the payment must be in respect of a fully matured liability.   This condition implies conversely that when a liability has so matured, its payment should not be postponed, even though it should cause an excess on the Vote, or even though it is not provided for in the current, but in the following year's Estimate.   In the latter case, an irregularity occurred in entering into the commitment without having provided for it, but it would be still more irregular to defer its payment once liability for it has matured.   If, however, in entering into the commitment, the department, with the approval of Finance, agreed with a contractor to pay for work in instalments some of which would fall in one financial year and some in another, then the liability in regard to the latter would be deferred to the financial year in which it was

agreed it would be discharged. In this case, the liability is simply outstanding and is not postponed in the proper sense of the word. In connection with this condition generally, the following points may be noted: —

(a) Liability in respect of Stores, etc., does not fully mature until all the usual steps—inspection, examination, etc.—have been taken regarding them.

(b) It is not legitimate to ante-date or post-date a draft, so as to bring the charge within a particular year's account.

(c) It is not legitimate to draw a draft before it is due, and to retain it until it becomes due at some date after the close of the financial year.

(d) It is not legitimate to issue a draft, say, in March, to an agent for transfer to a payee, so that it may reach the latter on the maturity of his claim during the succeeding financial year.

179. The third condition demands that the payment must be a final discharge of a commitment which is legally due to a public creditor. This condition removes from the ambit of the account: —

(1) All Imprests, that is, advances made to carry on some public service. This, however, does not apply to grants-in-aid which are exempted from the condition that the money so granted must be expended within the financial year.

(2) All over-payments even where it is clear that a subsequent refund will be made.

(3) Advances which it is known will be repaid—unless special provision be made in the estimate to charge the expenditure, and to credit the repayment as an appropriation-in-aid.

(4) Advances made to contractors which do not represent stores delivered within the year of the requisite quality. These should be posted in the first instance to a personal account, and only that amount should be charged to the Vote which represents stores delivered and accepted within the year. In all such cases, however, due regard must be had to the conditions of the contract, which may, for instance, require payment within the year under a guarantee from the contractor that repayment will be made for stores which fail to pass the necessary inspection tests. Similarly, sums lodged in Court pending litigation, or deposited in a Bank pending negotiations for the purchase of property cannot be regarded as final payments and are not, therefore, legitimately chargeable to the Vote.

180. Loans made to contractors in order to enable them to undertake a contract are not in the same category as the advances which we have discussed, and against which there is no repayment,

but a delivery of stores. In the case of advances by way of loans, it is intended that they be repaid in full and provision should be made for the payment in the Estimate and for repayment under Appropriations-in-Aid. If such has not been foreseen, a special Subhead should be opened under the authority of Finance, and a note should be appended indicating that it will be repaid. Loans of any magnitude should be dealt with in this way and under no circumstances should they be simply carried to a Suspense Account —a Suspense Account with a Debtor Balance should be avoided wherever possible. If the loan has been provided for in the Estimate, then it may be finally charged out in the Account, preferably under a special Subhead, and if a special Subhead be not opened, then a special note should be appended to the Account.

181. A fourth condition to make a payment regular is that the claim must have been examined and passed. This does not arise from any statute but is a matter of sound practice and common sense. Moreover, it is inherent in the quality of a proper voucher, and it means that even if a department is aware of a certain debt it should not discharge it in the absence of a claim from its creditor. A complete voucher should contain the receipt of the payee, specify the service performed and show that the service was authorised and satisfactorily performed. To include a payment in an Account it is necessary that it should be fully vouched, and the most exact knowledge of expenditure does not justify payment for it in the absence of proper vouching. If a voucher be lost, the amount represented by it cannot be include in the Account without the specific authority of Finance. If, however, a Department considers that a certain item of expenditure fell properly for payment in the course of the year, although at the time it is not in a position to substantiate it, it may include it in the Account, but then it becomes itself open to the criticism of the Auditor General who may consider the evidence insufficient to justify its inclusion.

CLASSIFICATION OF EXPENDITURE

182. The rules for classifying expenditure according to the proper Subheads are briefly these:

1. Classification should always follow provision, that is, expenditure should be charged to the Subhead in which provision was made for it.

2. If no provision was made for it in the Estimate, it should be charged to the Subhead under which provision would have been made.

3.   If expenditure is fully covered by a vote, but a doubt arises as to the Subhead to which it should be charged, it may be charged either according to its technical description or according to the service for which the expenditure was incurred.   The latter method is preferable because the total cost of the service is then more easily ascertainable.

4.   Even if a service be not explicitly provided for in the Estimate, it may yet be authorised, provided that it be within the ambit of the Vote.

As regards Overcharges to Subheads and to Overpayments, the adjustment may be carried out in the following ways.

1.   If an error in classification it may be corrected at once by relieving one Subhead and debiting the other.

2.   If an actual over-payment has taken place, the debit subhead should be relieved, and the amount involved carried to a Suspense Account until recovery has been effected.

3.   If the Subhead had not been relieved prior to the recovery and the Account is still open, the credit should be posted at once to the Subhead; but if the Account be closed, it should be treated as an Appropriation-in-Aid if the vote has a Credit Subhead, or as an Extra Exchequer Receipt if it has no Credit Subhead.

Once an item has been included in an Appropriation Account on which the Auditor General has reported, the recorded expenditure is indelible, and the transaction is final as far as charge and classification are concerned, but the indelibility does not, of course, bar a claim to a refund if an over-payment has taken place.

CHAPTER XI

The Appropriation Account

183. The Exchequer and Audit Department's Act prescribes, as we saw, that the Department of Finance should decide what departments are to render Appropriation Accounts and that the Account itself should show on the charge side, the sum appropriated by Parliament for the particular service, and on the discharge side, the sums which came in course of payment during the year (Section 24). But Section 23 prescribes that: " A plan of account books and of accounts adapted to the requirements of each service shall be designed under the supervision of the Treasury and it may prescribe the manner in which each department of the public service shall keep its accounts." In accordance with those Sections, Finance has prescribed the subheads of each Vote under which the estimated expenditure is to be shown, and consequently it has also prescribed the manner in which the Appropriation Account is to be rendered. The purpose of these prescriptions is to show Parliament in the Estimates what specifically it is voting, and in the Accounts how its intentions have been carried out.

184. An Appropriation Account, therefore, may be described as an annual account of each of the Supply Services rendered to the Auditor General on behalf of Parliament showing by subheads the actual direct expenditure of a department as compared with the estimated expenditure approved by Parliament when voting supply. The direct expenditure only is shown, and the account does not show the cost of any services rendered by other—such as the Common Service—Departments as appears on the Total Cost Statement appended to Part II of the Estimate. By way of illustration we give the Account for the office of the Minister for Finance (Vote 6) for the years 1956-57. It is as follows:—

185. OFFICE OF THE MINISTER FOR FINANCE

Account of the sum expended in the year ended 31st March, 1957, compared with the sum granted for the Salaries and Expenses of the office of the Minister for Finance, including the Paymaster General's Office.

Service	Grant	Expenditure	Expenditure compared with Grant	
			Less than granted	More than granted
Office of the Minister	£	£	£	£
A. Salaries, Wages and Allowances	151,720	138,685	13,035	—
A1. Chief Medical Officer for the Civil Service	1,870	2,005	—	135
B. Travelling Expenses	300	655	—	355
C. Incidental Expenses	450	549	—	99
D. Telegrams and Telephones	1,600	1,654	—	54
Paymaster-General's Office				
E. Salaries, Wages and Allowances	19,620	18,984	636	—
F. Travelling and Incidental Expenses	180	168	12	—
Gross Total £	175,740	162,700	13,683	643

Surplus of Gross
Estimate over Expenditure
£13,040

	Estimated	Realised	Deficiency of Appropriations-in-Aid realised
Deduct —			
G. Appropriations-in-Aid	1,260	1,253	£7
Net Total	£174,480	161,447	

Net surplus to be
surrendered
£13,033

	Estimated	Realised
Extra Receipts payable to Exchequer Compensation for loss of an officer injured in accident	£	£
	—	29

Explanation of the Causes of Variation between Expenditure and Grant:

A. Saving due mainly to vacancies and to staff changes involving new appointments at lower points on the salary scale.

A1. No provision was made for the increase in remuneration granted as from 1st November, 1955.

B. Expenses which could not have been foreseen were incurred in connection with a journey abroad.

C. Unanticipated advertising of a temporary post on the staff of the Department caused this excess.

APPROPRIATIONS-IN-AID

		Estimated £	Realised £
1.	Expenses of management of Local Loans Fund	1,250	1,250
2.	Commission charged to sundry departmental funds on purchases of securities by Government Stockbroker	5	—
3.	Miscellaneous	5	3
		£1,260	£1,253

Extra Remuneration (exceeding £50).

An Assistant Secretary received £350 as Chairman of Irish Steel Holdings Ltd. and £500 as director of The Irish Assurance Co. Ltd. Another Assistant Secretary received £250 as director of Cemici Teoranta.

A Staff Officer, Grade III, received gratuities totalling £110 for the performance of extra duties and a Clerical Officer received £80 for overtime.

Notes

The Account includes expenditure of £1,112 approximately in respect of remuneration of staff lent, without repayment to other Departments and Offices. The Accounts of other Votes include expenditure of £695 approximately in respect of remuneration of staff lent without repayment to this Department.

Department of Finance,
14th August, 1957.

Accounting Officer.

I have examined the above Account in accordance with the provisions of the Exchequer and Audit Department's Act, 1921. I have obtained all the information and explanations that I have required, and I certify, as the result of my Audit, that in my opinion the above Account is correct.

Comptroller and Auditor General.

186. The Account itself does not call for any explanation but a few notes on the accompanying statements may not be out of place.

(1) *Extra Exchequer Receipts* are unexpected receipts not earned in the ordinary course of a department's business, and are therefore lodged direct to the Exchequer, and not to the Paymaster General's Supply Account. Since 1959/60 small receipts of this nature would be treated as Appropriations-in-Aid.

(2) *Causes of Variation.* The explanation of the causes should be simple and direct stating concisely the factors causing the excess or saving on each subhead.

(3) *Appropriations-in-Aid.* These are detailed to show that no receipts other than those estimated for have been appropriated in aid of the Vote, or, if they have, that Finance has exercised its power under the Public Account and Charges Act, 1891, and allowed the department to do so.

(4) *Extra Remuneration.* In accordance with the " Standing Instructions " any extra remuneration over £50 received by an officer from public funds must be shown in the Account, if it is not already set out in the Estimate. Officials must report annually to their Accounting Officers the receipt of any such remuneration however casual or variable. Remuneration includes pensions or compensation allowances, but not disability pensions or similar payments.

(5) *Surrender.* The surplus to be surrendered is the difference between the parliamentary grant and the department's actual audited expenditure. The Auditor General is responsible for seeing that this is effected, but the method is determined by Finance about 12 months after the close of the financial year. The surrender is made from the unissued portion of the exchequer grant, and any issued portion in the hands of the Paymaster General is ignored. If the balance in the Exchequer be sufficient to meet the surrender, the only year affected will be that to which the account refers, but if it is not sufficient, the surrender may have to be spread over succeeding years. It is to be noted that a surplus on the Appropriation Account is distinct from a department's exchequer surplus. The latter is the difference between the Grant and that portion of it not issued to the Paymaster General, whereas the former is the difference between the Grant and the department's actual expenditure which may be less than the exchequer issues made to the Paymaster General for the department.

(6) *Notes.* These cover a host of different items, their object being to bring to notice anything of a pecuniary nature which has come to light during the year concerning the present or past

accounts. Thus, they deal with expenditure in respect of Staff lent or borrowed without repayment between departments; Services rendered or stores transferred without repayment between department; Fees (stamps) received; Gifts; Compensation for damage or injury to persons or property where there is no subhead for such; Losses by Fire, etc.

187. *Losses of Cash or Stores.* The practice in dealing with such losses is not uniform. In the Account for 1956, for instance, two Votes — the Post Office and Revenue — have a regular Loss Subhead against which are charged any losses of cash or stores occurring during the year; three others—Lands, Defence and Social Assistance—opened subheads in their Accounts to record their losses; Justice has a separate " Statement of Losses ". Losses on any other Votes are recorded by means of notes. The Subheads, opened or provided, deal only with the losses which affect the year's account and all others are recorded by means of the Notes. All items, including those of the previous paragraph, are subject to the approval of Finance and its authority for write-off is quoted in each case.

Four classes of Losses are usually distinguished according as they are actual, virtual, technical or constructive. The first covers thefts, embezzlements, misappropriations, overpayments, overissues, bad debts, and deterioration of stores. The second includes nugatory payments for services or stores, forfeited contracts, ex-gratia payments where there was no legal obligation to pay, extra contractual payments, compromises and waivers of claims. Technical losses refer to the inadequate vouching of payments, and constructive include wasteful expenditure of any kind arising from any cause, even a change in policy, whereby the stores supplied or the services rendered are not of the specified standard or quality. Actual and virtual losses, whether accidental or not, must be recorded, but in the case of technical and constructive Losses, the recording is a question for the decision of Finance without prejudice, of course, to any action by the Auditor General.

If public money be lost the gross sum must be shown, but if there be statutory or other power to withhold payments against the loss, only the net amount will be recorded, the payment withheld being charged in the ordinary way against its proper subhead. Similarly where stores are lost, only the net loss is noted. It would be wrong to charge a loss in an account in order to increase the appropriations-in-aid or extra exchequer receipts by the credit of a recovery.

188. *Use of Funds other than Supply Funds.* If, in addition

to the Supply voted, a department uses other funds—whether public or funds held in trust—in carrying out its services, an account of their receipt and expenditure is added to the Notes. Thus in 1956 advances from the National Development Fund for various development schemes were received by five departments or offices which submitted, in the Receipts and Payments Form, an account of their expenditure, and the accounts were certified by the Auditor General.

Again, the Department of Education holds certain Trust Funds and Stocks for the development of Education throughout the State in Primary and Secondary Schools, and it furnishes an account of the transactions on each Fund.

Finally, the Department of Posts and Telegraphs supplies an " Abstract of Engineering Expenditure ", the Department of Justice, a Prison's Manufacturing Account, and an account of the Gárda Síochána Reward Fund; and the Department of Agriculture, accounts relating to the General Cattle Diseases Fund and the Dairy Produce (Price Stabilisation) Fund.

VIREMENT

189. The word " Virement " is not found in any standard English dictionary. It is indeed originally a French nautical term coming from the verb " virer " meaning to tack, veer, change course or transfer. It is used as a French financial term meaning " clearance " and has thence passed into other State accounting systems. It is employed to denote the process by which excesses are offset by veering or transferring savings, either between votes, or between subheads of the same vote, or are used to meet expenditure on a new subhead opened in a Vote.

The use of Virement varies from state to state. In some it is employed between different votes; in others only between subheads of the same vote, while in others it is entirely forbidden. In Great Britain it is not allowed between the various civil votes, but it is permitted between the defence votes subject to the restrictions (a) that it must be authorised by the Appropriation Act of the year in which the Estimates are passed; (b) that it must not be taken for granted, but must have the explicit approval of the Treasury; (c) that the Treasury itself must place a statement before the Commons showing where it has permitted virement, and (d) that legal effect must be given to its exercise by the Appropriation Act for the year following that in which it was employed.

In Ireland it is allowed only between the subheads of each Vote. For a period of six years from 1923 onwards, the Irish Committee of Public Accounts sought to restrict the power of Finance in exercising virement and various suggestions were put forward for that purpose. One was that it should be limited to 50 per cent. of the sum provided for the subhead, and another that it should not exceed a maximum of £5,000 in any one case. Both suggestions were shown to be impracticable, and in the end all attempts at restriction were abandoned, subject to the proviso that " If a service is of a novel character, or even remote from anything shown in the original estimate, or if a considerable sum is involved, a Supplementary Estimate must be introduced."

Departments may not exercise virement without the express sanction of Finance. The opening of new subheads by Finance, inherent in its power of virement, has no effect on appropriation, and the service provided for must not cause an excess in the Vote and must be within its ambit. Such subheads should be limited to non-recurring items, and if the service is likely to recur, provision for it should be made in the estimate .

DATE FOR RENDERING APPROPRIATION ACCOUNTS

190. A Schedule to the Exchequer and Audit Department's Act prescribes that Appropriation Accounts are to be submitted each year to the Comptroller and Auditor General by November 30th by Departments; by January 15th to the Treasury by the Comptroller and Auditor General; and by January 31st to the House of Commons by the Treasury, if the House is then sitting, and if not sitting then within a week after Parliament next assembles. The object of this was to give departments time to compile their accounts and to effect adjustments on any inter-departmental transactions relating to the year of the account. It also meant in theory, though not, of course, in practice, that the books of account could be kept open until November 30th. These dates also applied to Ireland.

But in his report on the Accounts for 1956/57 the Comptroller and Auditor General says: " With a view to the earlier presentation of the annual accounts of the Public Services, arrangements were made with Accounting Officers to close the books of account for the year on June 30th, 1957, and immediately after March 31st in future years. All the appropriation accounts for 1956-57 were received by October 3rd, 1957, approximately two months in advance of the statutory date."

From this it is clear that all accounts will now be closed on March 31st and that consequently inter-departmental transactions must be adjusted during the financial year. In Great Britain, the accounts are now closed on July 31st each year and reach the Comptroller and Auditor General by September 30th.

CHAPTER XII

Supplementary Estimates: Excess Votes: The Contingency Fund: Grants-in-Aid.

SUPPLEMENTARY ESTIMATES

191. A Supplementary Estimate is an estimate added to an annual estimate and presented to Parliament during the currency of a financial year in order to regularise expenditure. Such estimates are an evil, but unfortunately a necessary evil which cannot always be avoided. They are evil because they tend to, or actually sometimes do, upset the balance of the Budget which is based to a very large extent on the annual estimates, and they should, therefore, be restricted to the utmost limits consistent with efficient administration. They are, however, necessary at times, because the ordinary estimates being framed in the autumn preceding the financial year, accounting officers, not being clairvoyant, cannot possibly foresee everything that may happen during the following fifteen or sixteen months. Moreover, the pruning of the estimates by Finance will have left very little space for manoeuvre. A rise in prices or remuneration may easily throw out the original calculations, a new service may have to be introduced or an old service extended making it necessary to seek more money.

192. Hence supplementaries are necessary:—

(1) If any excess is foreseen within the financial year on the annual estimate.

(2) If a considerable excess is involved on a subhead.

(3) If a new service be created by statute or by administrative action, especially if the latter be of a novel character or remote from anything contained in the original estimate.

(4) In emergencies such as those arising from war or civil commotion.

(5) If Parliament, while approving of the annual estimate generally, desires to discuss some particular aspect of it. This is not a usual procedure but it was used in Ireland during the emergency *. Only a token sum is taken.

In framing supplementaries, the sum required is apportioned over all the subheads affected, but if the amount of the original

---

* The procedure was also employed in March, 1960, to debate the proposal to remove University College, Dublin, to a new site at Belfield.

subheads is sufficient, only a token sum as added. Savings on all subheads are bulked. If there be savings and surpluses, only the net sum required is shown.

All savings used in supplementaries are shown in the following year's estimate when comparing the subheads with those of the year in which the supplementary was taken. If, for instance, a saving of £10,000 was applied in a supplementary, the original, say £50,000, will be reduced to £40,000.

In the Appropriation Account the subheads on which savings were effected are shown at their original figures, but the revised figures are given for those on which increased expenditure was voted, even though only a token sum was taken.

The form of all estimates is a matter for Finance, subject to the approval of the Committee of Public Accounts. In the case of supplementaries Finance will ordinarily lean towards appropriating savings and surpluses, but if the service be completely new they will most probably be ignored, and the Dáil asked to vote the total sum required.

If it be necessary to take a supplementary and the appropriations-in-aid have not been realised, the grant is increased by the amount of the shortage which is shown in the Appropriation Act as a " Deficit." Thus in Schedule B, Part I of the 1959 Act, there is recorded a deficit of £48,000 on Vote 26, and £3,820 on Vote 31. In Vote 52, on the other hand, there is a token grant of £10, and appropriations-in-aid of £82,000. At the end of the Schedule the total given is £30,180 because the grants on the other two Votes have been increased by £51,820. The power of Vote 52 to use £80,000 is not affected.

EXCESS VOTES

193. If a Supplementary Estimate be an unavoidable evil, an Excess Vote is a capital crime, because it is not only irregular but illegal, and for that very reason departments are inclined to over-estimate rather than to under-estimate their requirements. An Excess Vote may be defined as a vote taken to cover expenditure already incurred in excess of that authorised by Parliament, and, therefore, taken in the year subsequent to the year in which the original expenditure was authorised. One never speaks of an Excess Estimate but always of an Excess Vote, because the excess to be voted is not probable but definitely ascertained.

Such votes are extremely rare, and it may be said that they are never incurred deliberately, not only because they are illegal but also because they involve for the department concerned a good deal of trouble with Finance, with Parliament and with the Committee of Public Accounts.

They do, however, sometimes occur, and then they may be attributed either to faulty accounting methods or to pure mischance. If in a large department accounts are not properly compiled, or if they are not kept up-to-date, the responsible official may easily make a mistake and over-estimate the money available to defray expenditure, and thus unwittingly fall into an excess.

An excess is always reported by the Comptroller and Auditor General to the Committee of Public Accounts, which deals with it before any other business, and which usually issues an Interim Report on the subject stating that the covering authority of the Oireachtas will be required. If the Committee is satisfied with the explanations offered, it reports to the Dáil that there is no objection to an Excess Vote. This is taken at the earliest opportunity, and certainly within the year of the Auditor General's report.

The Excess Vote follows the same procedure as a Supplementary Estimate. If there are surplus appropriations-in-aid, they will be used as an offset to the excess. Thus, in one case there was an excess of £1,608 over the whole vote, but there were surplus receipts of £9,618 of which £1,598 were used as an offset, so that the net amount voted was the token sum of £10. In this case the surplus receipts probably deceived the Accounting Officer and led him into the excess. If there be no offset, the total excess is voted; and if receipts are less than the excess, the net sum is voted. In all cases, however, the gross excess must be shown.

THE CONTINGENCY FUND

194. The Contingency Fund is a Fund of £20,000, formed by a Grant-in-Aid, voted by the Dáil to the Government for the purpose of defraying urgent or unforeseen expenditure (a) which is not covered by the ordinary votes, (b) which cannot immediately but will subsequently be brought to the notice of the Dáil, (c) which the Dáil may reasonably be expected to approve, and (d) which is subject to the audit of the Auditor General.

The Estimate for the Fund was first taken in 1923/24 and the definition given above is taken from a note to the Estimate at the time. It was later decided that the annual account of the Fund should be annexed each year to the Appropriation Account of the Vote for " Repayment of Advances on the Contingency Fund."

From 1927 to 1933 Finance and the Committee of Public Accounts were at variance as to the admissibility of certain charges in the account, but finally the matter ended on Finance promising to give due weight to the criticisms of the Committee.

Advances from the Fund are repaid either by a new and additional vote, if the advance be for a completely new service, or by a supplementary estimate, if the service is related to an existing vote, or by the Vote for Repayments itself for the odds and ends for which the Fund may be used.

The account of the Fund has accordingly two main headings according as the advances are made either (1) in anticipation of votes of Parliament and for services charged on the Central Fund; or (2) are repayable from the Vote itself. Examples of the first are advances for the alleviation of distress and for O.E.E.C. and of the second, bounties for centenarians and on the birth of triplets, and expenditure on Votes which have ceased.

GRANTS-IN-AID

195. A Grant is a sum of money voted by the Dáil for a service, and the various grants so voted fall into three types:

(1) *Statutory Grants.*—These are grants for a service or services which fall within the limits of the statute or statutes covered by the Vote, such as, for instance, the ordinary supply grants.

(2) *Extra Statutory Grants.*—These are grants for a service which is not quite within the ambit of the statute or statutes covering the Vote, but which are in some way appropriate to the Vote. Thus, in the Vote for Superannuation and Retired Allowances a token sum of £5 is taken in the Estimate for " Grants not covered by statute made in cases of distress or other exceptional circumstances "; and in the Appropriation Account, 1956/57, for Social Assistance a subhead was opened for the payment of £971 for " grants made on grounds of equity in cases where, owing to causes beyond the pensioner's control, payment of pension was impracticable within the prescribed period." Such grants require the sanction of Finance, and if specific provision has not been made in the Estimate, they should form the subject of a Subhead or Note to the Appropriation Account.

(3) *Grants-in-Aid.*—These are grants which are exempted from the condition that any money issued from the Exchequer must be expended within the financial year. On the other hand, any balances unissued from the Exchequer must be surrendered, unless with the approval of Finance they are issued and placed to the credit of a special deposit account.

If a Vote carries a grant-in-aid, the fact should be indicated in Part I of the Estimate, in the Resolutions of Supply, and in the

Appropriation Act. The audit of these grants is not a statutory function of the Auditor General, so that if it be intended that the grant should be so audited, the fact should be noted in Part I or Part II of the Estimate. Accounts so audited are usually appended to the relevant Appropriation Account.

A grant-in-aid may not be increased without the approval of Parliament and savings on other subheads may not be applied by Finance to increase it, but savings on a grant-in-aid may be applied by Finance to meet excesses on other subheads.

CHAPTER XIII

The Comptroller and Auditor General:
The Committee of Public Accounts.

196. The word "Audit" means an official examination of an account with verification by means of vouchers. Three forms are usually distinguished, according as the audit is antecedent, concomitant or subsequent. Antecedent audit means audit conducted before payment is made. In this sense, there is no audit by the Auditor General, because the voucher is not complete until payment is made and the receipt of the payee obtained. But there are antecedent or preliminary checks, first by the Comptroller General in seeing that the amount requisitioned by the Minister for Finance does not exceed that authorised by statute for particular services; secondly, by the Minister for Finance (a) in requesting the Bank to transfer a stated sum to the Paymaster General, and (b) by requiring his specific sanction for all items of expenditure.

197. Audit is concomitant or preventive when it is exercised during the process of making payment. Here again there is no such audit in the Irish system, but there are vital checks (a) by the Claims Branch in assembling the voucher, (b) by the Cash Branch in making out the payable order by reference to the voucher, and (c) by the Schedule Officers in examining the voucher and draft before requesting the Paymaster General to pay the drafts listed on the schedule.

198. It is with subsequent or final audit that the Auditor General is concerned, that is, with the examination of accounts, and with verification by means of complete vouchers. He is, of course, concerned with seeing that the departmental system of vouchering and paying is sound and can be relied on, but, once satisfied on that point, he relies on the final audit made by his officials.

199. As a constitutional organ of State, the Comptroller and Auditor General is appointed by the President on the nomination of Dáil Éireann, and holds office until the retiring age prescribed by Law. He may not be a member of the Oireachtas, and may not hold any other office or position of emolument, and he cannot be removed from office except for stated misbehaviour or incapacity, and then only by resolutions passed by both Houses of the Oireachtas. His position, therefore, is not only similar to, but almost identical with

that of the Judges of the Supreme and High Courts, so that, like them, he is independent in the exercise of his functions as an officer of State. In securing that position we are following the practice of most modern democratic countries. In Great Britain, for instance, the Comptroller and Auditor General is appointed by Royal Letters Patent, and holds office during good behaviour subject to removal by the Crown on an address from both Houses of Parliament. A similar position obtains in Australia, New Zealand and South Africa. In the United State of America the Comptroller General is appointed for fifteen years by the President with the consent of the Senate, and during that time he may not be dismissed except by a joint resolution of Congress.

200. Article 33.6 of the Constitution states that, " the terms and conditions of the office of the Comptroller and Auditor General shall be determined by law." The law on the subject is the Comptroller and Auditor General Act of 1923 (No. 1). Sections 1 and 2 of that Act deal with his appointment, salary and pension, and Section 3 with the age (70) of retirement. Under Section 4 the Minister for Finance is to provide the necessary staff and to regulate their numbers, salaries, conditions of employment and grades. Section 5 is " Anything which is by the law for the time being in force directed to be done by the Comptroller and Auditor General, other than the certifying and reporting on accounts for Dáil Éireann, may be done by a principal officer of the Department authorised for that purpose by the Comptroller and Auditor General."

Section 6 is: " The Comptroller and Auditor General shall have full power to make from time to time orders and rules for the conduct of the internal business of his Department, and to promote, suspend or remove any of the officers, clerks, and other persons employed therein, and also, subject to the approval of the Minister for Finance, to make regulations and prescribe forms for the guidance of departments and persons in making up and rendering their accounts to him for examination."

Section 7 is: (1) " It shall be the duty of the Comptroller and Auditor General to control all disbursements and to audit all accounts of moneys administered by or under the authority of the Oireachtas at such times and in such manner as shall from time to time be prescribed by law " (cf Art 33.1 of Constitution).

(2) " It shall also be (his) duty to report to Dáil Éireann on such matters and at such periods and times as shall from time to time be prescribed by law or required by resolution of Dáil Éireann " (cf Art. 33.4).

(3) " Unless and until it shall be otherwise provided by the

Oireachtas, he shall have and exercise all such powers and perform all such duties as are prescribed by this Act, or are conferred or imposed on him by any Act of the Parliament of the late United Kingdom having the force of law in (Éire) and adapted to the circumstances of (Éire) by or under the Adaptation of Enactments Act, 1922 (No. 2), and particularly by the Exchequer and Audit Departments Acts, 1866 and 1921."

201. The relevant sections of the last-mentioned Acts may be summarised thus:

(1) Finance must render annually to the Auditor General an account of all transactions on the Central Fund for the year (Sec. 21); (2) Departments must render him their annual Appropriation Accounts, and when certified and reported on, they must be laid before the Dáil (Sec. 22); (3) In examining the Appropriation Accounts he must satisfy himself that the money has been expended in accordance with the intentions of Parliament and with the authorisations of Finance (Sec. 26); (4) If he is satisfied with the departmental system of accounting, and if the department certifies the vouchers to be correct, he may in his discretion admit the sums so certified without further evidence of payment (Sec. 26); (5) He shall have free access at all convenient times to the books of account and to other documents relating to the accounts (Sec. 28).

From these sections it follows that he has to examine the Appropriation Accounts from three different angles. First, there is an Accountancy Audit in order to test the accuracy of selected vouchers; secondly, there is an Appropriation Audit to ensure that expenditure accords with the intentions of the Dáil; and thirdly, an Administrative Audit to ensure that the expenditure has been authorised by Finance.

202. The object of the Accountancy Audit is the same as that of a commercial audit, that is, to detect fraud, overpayments and technical errors. The Auditor General is entitled to see every voucher, but he is not obliged to test the accuracy of all of them. After satisfying himself of the soundness of the department's accounting method, he is entitled under the Acts to rely on a test audit, that is, a detailed audit of a percentage of the transactions.

203. The Appropriation Audit is the primary function of the Auditor General. It differs from a commercial audit, for, whereas the object of the latter is to see whether the assets and liabilities of the balance sheet are properly calculated, that of the former is to ensure that the parliamentary grants have not been exceeded, and that they have been expended for the purposes for which the grants were voted. The basis of this audit is the Estimate in so far as it

acts as a guide to the Dáil's intentions, and the Auditor General is, therefore, concerned as much with Part II as with Part I of the Estimate.

204. The Administrative Audit, being dependent on the directions of Finance, is not a statutory but rather a quasi-statutory obligation. In practice, however, the request of Finance always operates, and the audit consists in seeing that, irrespective of the terms of any subhead, the general or specific sanction of Finance has been given for all expenditure thereunder.

205. In addition to certifying the accounts as the result of the audit, the Auditor General has the duty of " Reporting " and the subjects of that report are best summed up in the words of the British Comptroller and Auditor General in his Report on the Civil Appropriation Accounts for 1947/48. " It should be borne in mind," he says, " that mention of a subject in my Report does not necessarily imply criticism. Some paragraphs are included in order to comply with statutory regulations; others in accordance with suggestions made by previous Committees of Public Accounts, or to provide information necessary to the correct interpretation of the accounts.

Large-scale fraud or financial irregularity affecting the public accounts is uncommon, and in the main my Reports deal with the following types of case where they appear likely to be of interest or concern to Parliament:

(i) Apparently wasteful or uneconomical expenditure.

(ii) Apparent lack of control over expenditure or failure to collect all due receipts.

(iii) New developments or extension of existing activities which involve considerable additional expenditure but have not been debated at length in Parliament.

(iv) Serious discrepancies between expenditure and estimate.

(v) Lack of statutory power, other than that of the Appropiration Acts, for continuing services.

(vi) Information about subsidies or other objects of expenditure in amplification of that given in the estimates or accounts.

(vii) Any other developments in the field of public expenditure likely to be of interest to Parliament."

206. As regards the Auditor General's right to see documents other than those relating directly to the accounts, it should be accepted as a principle that a department should not refuse him any papers, unless it is prepared to justify its refusal before the Committee of Public Accounts on the grounds of public policy or secrecy. A case in point occurred in connection with pensions granted under the Military Service Pensions Act, 1924. On the Appropriation Accounts,

1924/25, he reported that the audit of the pensions was confined to the amount of the pensions awarded by the Board of Assessors, but that the data on which the reports were based were not made available. The refusal was made on grounds of public policy, and the Attorney General advised that the Minister for Defence had no legal power to compel the Board to produce the documents. The Committee of Public Accounts held that the refusal was justified. In 1925/26 the Auditor General again referred to the subject, and the Committee on reconsideration held that his statutory powers were being limited, and asked that immediate steps be taken to remove the anomaly. This was done by the Military Service Act, 1930, which declared that " the findings of the Board of Assessors as set out in their report shall be . . . and be deemed always to have been final and conclusive and binding on all persons and tribunals whatsoever."

207. The Auditor General has no power to disallow an item in an Appropriation Account. He simply reports the facts as he finds them, and leaves the Committee of Public Accounts to reach their own decision. Even if the Committee recommends a disallowance, it does not become effective until the recommendation has been endorsed by the Dáil. Pending that endorsement the amount involved is not removed from the Account, because the expenditure therein is indelible. If the Dáil agrees to the disallowance, the amount is carried to a suspense account, and is removed from the statement of audited expenditure appended to the Committee's Report. The disallowance may be either personal if an individual be at fault, or technical if the expenditure was not proper to the vote and has, therefore, to be revoted. A personal refund automatically clears the suspense, and the receipt is surrendered to the Exchequer. But if there be no refund, or if the disallowance be technical, or if Finance with the Committee's approval waives recovery, the amount is withheld from a current grant until Finance decides either to take a supplementary estimate, or to open by means of savings a subhead in the current Appropriation Account, or to make special provision for it in a subsequent estimate.

THE COMMITTEE OF PUBLIC ACCOUNTS

208. The Auditor General does not report direct to the Dail, but to a Select Committee, " The Committee of Public Accounts," appointed to examine and report to the Dáil upon the accounts and to suggest alterations and improvements in the form of the Estimates. The Committee is appointed at the beginning of each financial year and consists of twelve Deputies, none of whom may be a Minister

or a Parliamentary Secretary, and four of whom constitute a quorum. As a Select Committee it has almost unlimited powers of investigation and may send for persons, papers and records. Witnesses may, if necessary, be examined on oath. It is not a judicial tribunal, because it does not decide questions but reports its findings, and its procedure, being informal, is that of a fact finding committee. Its investigation is not deflected by party bias, and it acts as the guardian of the financial rights of the Dáil.

When all the accounts have been examined, and the minutes of the proceedings completed, the Committee issues its Report which is signed by the Chairman. This will not deal with all the points raised by the Auditor General, but only with those which it considers should be rectified, and on which it desires action to be taken. The Committee has no executive power, and, therefore, its findings must be implemented by the Minister for Finance on behalf of the Government. Hence its influence on departments is indirect and consists mainly in the publicity of its reports. The Minister must reply to all observations of the Committee, not orally but by means of official minutes. If he agrees with the observations he issues instructions to the department concerned, and, if he disagrees, the subject is pursued at the next session of the Committee.

The Committee may not concern itself with policy and may not, therefore, question the amounts of the estimates. It may, however, consider the merits of expenditure and may not accept a plea of policy if it appears unwise, unnecessary or extravagant. Neither may it concern itself with matters of administration unless they are shown to be negligent, extravagant or ineffective. It may inquire whether the actions of Finance comply with the law, and its recommendations on financial order and principle are invariably accepted.

CHAPTER XIV

International Relations

209. Ireland's relations with other sovereign states are set out in Article 29 of the Constitution. After declaring Ireland's "devotion to the ideal of peace and friendly co-operation amongst nations founded on international justice and morality"; "its adherence to the pacific settlement of international disputes by international arbitration or judicial determination" and "its acceptance of the generally recognised principles of international law as its rule of conduct in its relations with other States", the Article goes on: "the executive power of the State in or in connection with its external relations shall . . . be exercised by or on the authority of the Government . . . and for that purpose it may to such extent and subject to such conditions, if any, as may be determined by law, avail of or adopt any organ, instrument, or method of procedure used or adopted for the like purpose by the members of any group or league of nations with which the State is or becomes associated for the purpose of international co-operation in matters of common concern ".

210. Sub-Article 5 deals with the position of the Oireachtas in relation to international agreements: "Every international agreement to which the State becomes a party shall be laid before Dáil Éireann ". "The State shall not be bound by any international agreement involving a charge upon public funds unless the terms of the agreement shall have been approved by Dáil Éireann". "This section shall not apply to agreements or conventions of a technical and administrative character ". "No international agreement shall be part of the domestic law of the State save as may be determined by the Oireachtas ". From this it would appear that the Government may enter into any international agreement provided that it is laid before the Dáil, that the latter's approval is necessary only when the agreement involves a charge on Public Funds, and that the Senate need not be consulted unless the agreement is to form part of the domestic law of the State.

211. When the Constitution was enacted, Ireland was associated at least externally with the Commonwealth Group of Nations, and it was a member of the League of Nations. The association with the Group formally ended with the passing of the Republic of Ireland Act, 1948, and during the Second World War the League was shattered not because its Covenant was not adequate

to prevent war, but rather because the Covenant was not implemented. Since then Ireland has become a member of a number of international organisations and the purpose of the present chapter is to outline their objects and structure.

THE UNITED NATIONS (U.N.)

212. The United Nations is a global organisation embracing some eighty sovereign nations of the world. Its objects, as set out in the Preamble and Chapter I of its Charter, are all embracing, but reduced to the simplest terms they may be described as the preservation of peace and the material welfare of nations. In 1945, some fifty-one nations assembled in San Francisco as the United Nations Conference on International Organisation, drafted the Charter consisting of 19 Chapters and 111 Articles, and it became operative on 24th October, 1945, when China, France, the Soviet Union, Great Britain, the United States of America, and a majority of the other signatory states deposited the ratified Charter in the archives of the United States Government.

The first meeting of the General Assembly was held in London on 10th January, 1946, but the permanent seat of the Organisation is in New York. It requires a majority of two-thirds of the General Assembly to amend the Charter.

213. The United Nations Organisation works through a Secretariat and five main Councils:

1. *Secretariat.* The Secretary is its chief administrative officer and is appointed by the General Assembly on the recommendation of the Security Council. His staff is appointed by him according to regulations made by the Assembly, and they have the status of international officials, being responsible to the Organisation alone. The Secretary reports annually to the Assembly but he may at any time bring to the notice of the Security Council any situation which he may consider a threat to international peace.

2. *The General Assembly.* This consists of all States that are members of the Organisation. Each State has one vote but may have five delegates. Its main functions, briefly, are to foster international co-operation in all fields of human activity, to promote the realisation of human rights everywhere, and to elect the non-permanent members of the Security Council. It meets in the ordinary way annually, but special sessions may be called to discuss any subject within the scope of the Charter, unless the Security Council is dealing with the subject. If the latter is not dealing with it, the Assembly may make recommendations either to its members, or to the Security Council or to both, if there be a threat to inter-

national peace. If action be necessary, the question is referred to the Security Council in the first instance, and the latter is required to report back to the Assembly stating what action (if any) it is to take. If it fails to act, the Assembly may itself make recommendations to its fellow members for collective measures, including the use of force, to maintain or to restore international peace. For decisions on major questions a majority of two-thirds is necessary, but in minor matters a simple majority suffices.

3. *The Security Council.* This organ consists of five permanent —Nationalist China, France, Soviet Russia, Great Britain and the United States—and six non-permanent members elected by the General Assembly, three each year, for a two-years term. The Council functions continuously, each member State having a permanent representative. Decisions require seven affirmative votes, but the concurrence of the five permanent members—hence the veto—is required, unless the question be one of procedure, or it is one in which a settlement of a dispute is involved—one of the permanent members being a party to the dispute. The main function of the Council is to maintain international peace and security and, when pacific measures fail, to use armed force if necessary, assisted by all members of the Organisation, who are required to hold available national air forces for combined operations. The Council has three committees: (1) The Military Staff Committe consisting of the Chiefs-of-Staff or their representatives of the permanent members and dealing with military requirements, the employment and command of the forces placed at their disposal, and the regulation of armaments including disarmament; (2) The Atomic Energy Committee consisting of one representative from each of the eleven member states of the Council and Canada; and (3) The Commission for Conventional Armaments composed also of representatives of the eleven members to make proposals for the regulation and reduction of forces and armaments.

4. *The Economic and Social Council.* This is made up of eighteen members of the Organisation elected by the General Assembly with six members elected each year for a three-years term. Each member has one vote and one representative, and decisions are by a majority of those present and voting. The Council meets twice a year, but special sessions may be held. Its functions are to work, on an international basis, for improving the standards of living, for the solution of economic and social problems, for co-operation in education and culture and for the observance of human rights. For those purposes it is directed to establish commissions of inquiry and to bring into relation with the United Nations any specialised agencies

dealing with the subjects. The following have now been so brought into the relationship: The International Labour Organisation; The Food and Agriculture Organisation of the United Nations; U.N. Educational, Scientific and Cultural Organisation; The International Civil Aviation Organisation; The International Bank for Reconstruction and Development; The International Monetary Fund; The International Telecommunication Union; The Universal Postal Union; The World Health Organisation; The International Refugee Organisation; and The World Meteorological Organisation.

5. *The Trusteeship Council.* This consists of the five permanent members of the Security Council, and of all States administering trusteeship territories, together with as many members of the Assembly as there are trustee members. It acts under the authority of the Assembly. It deals through the administering authority with territories formely held under mandate by various members of the Organisation. The Administering Authority may be the nation which formerly held the territory under mandate. The Council considers reports submitted by the Administering Authorities which have to answer annually a questionnaire on the political economic, social, and educational development of their peoples. Inspections are carried out periodically and petitions from the territories are considered. Each member of the Council has one vote and decisions are by a majority of those present and voting. The Council meets twice a year, but special sessions may be held.

6. *The International Court of Justice.* This Court—the judicial instrument of the Organisation—has its seat at the Hague and consists of fifteen judges elected by the Assembly and Security Council for a term of nine years. It is governed by a Statute based on that of the Permanent Court of International Justice to which only states may have recourse and it is an integral part of the Charter. Each member State of the United Nations is a party to the Statute, and, if a party to a dispute, undertakes to abide by the judgment of the Court. If it fails to do so, the other party may appeal to the Security Council, which may decide the appropriate measures to be taken. Non-member states may by arrangement subscribe to the Statute and take part in the election of judges.

Ireland's permanent representation at the United Nations is estimated for the year 1960/61 to cost £39,682. Its assessed share of the Organisation's administrative expenses is £30,400 and of its Emergency Force £9,000. Contributions to the Children Fund is put at £1,000, and a sum of £5,000 for technical assistance for undeveloped areas. Travelling and other expense take £11,650.

Ireland is also a member of the specialised agencies except

U.N.E.S.C.O. Its assessed share of the cost of I.L.O. is £9,050 with £2,000 for travelling and other expenses. The Food and Agricultural Organisation costs £7,420, the Telecommunication Union £7,500, the Universal Postal Union £2,500, the World Health Organisation £8,800, and the World Meteorological Organisation £1,150.

THE COUNCIL OF EUROPE (C.O.E.)

214. The idea of a Council of Europe, or of a United States of Europe, or of a Western European Union is not a modern conception. In the old League of Nations a French Minister pleaded for it, and produced a plan to support his plea, but though widely discussed and warmly approved at the time it came to nothing. Both before and after the last War there were several organisation working for the ideal of European co-operation and integration but they all finally merged into "The European Movement", which met at The Hague in May, 1948, and resolved to work for a European Parliament.

215. By a "European Parliament" was meant a parliament with supra-national powers composed of states, which would surrender as much of their sovereignty and independence as was necessary for the common good, and which would bring about not only a customs but even an economic union. A customs union, it was argued, would progressively produce a common market by the gradual abolition of tariffs and quotas, while an economic union, by co-ordinating financial and social measures, would lead to a political integration.

216. A number of important events in Europe helped towards the formation of the Council of Europe. As far back as 1922 Belgium had formed a customs union with Luxembourg, and in 1948 the Netherlands had joined to form "Benelux". In March of the same year, the Brussels Pact was signed by Britain, France, and the Benelux countries, and although that was primarily a military treaty for the defence of Europe—it was called the Western Union Defence Organisation (W.U.D.O.)—it, nevertheless, contained provisions for consultation between the signatory states regarding economic and social problems. In May, 1948, the European Movement called for a European Parliament, and in August called a meeting of the Brussels Pact States to consider the matter. Early in 1949, five other countries—Denmark, Sweden, Norway, Italy and Ireland— were called into conference, and from that meeting emerged in May, 1949, the Statute of the Council of Europe (C.O.E.). Greece, Turkey, Austria, Federal Germany and Iceland subsequently joined the Council.

217. The object of the Council was, in brief, to promote greater unity among its members, so as to foster the ideals of their common heritage, but all questions of defence were specifically excluded. It has its permanent headquarters at Strasburg and meets twice yearly each session occupying about 15 days. Its organs are:—

1. *The Council of Ministers.* This comprises the foreign ministers of member states. Each state has one representative and one vote and deliberations are held in secret. For important questions an unanimous vote is necessary, for others a two-thirds majority, and in minor matters a simple majority suffices. To make, for instance, a binding recommendation to a member state, unanimity is necessary; to admit new members two-thirds must agree, but on financial or administrative subjects a simple majority is sufficient.

2. *The Consultative Assembly* meets in public and is composed of delegations from the Parliaments of member states. The strength of each delegation varies considerably. Great Britain, for instance, has eighteen, and Ireland four representatives. In the Assembly each member of a delegation sits, speaks and votes as an individual, and not as a representative of his Government or Parliament, so that on any particular question members of the same delegations may express entirely opposite views. The functions of the Assembly are purely deliberative, and any conclusions reached therein are put to the Council of Ministers in the form of recommendations.

3. *The Joint Committee* co-ordinates the work of the Ministerial Council and the Assembly.

4. *The Secretariat* is administered by a Secretary-General and a Deputy appointed by the Assembly on the recommendation of the Council of Ministers. The staff is appointed by the Secretary-General in accordance with regulations made by the Council as a whole.

The Council of Europe has not any supra-national powers, nor indeed any powers in the customs, the economic, the social or the financial spheres, its sole usefulness consisting in the publicising, from time to time, of important issues.

In the financial year 1960/61 Ireland is to contribute £11,150 towards the expenses of the Council while Travelling and Incidental Expenses are estimated at £5,800.

218. The Council of Europe is distinct from the Western European Union. In 1950, the Western Union Defence Organisation of the Brussels Treaty Powers merged with the North Atlantic Treaty Command, and in 1954 Germany and Italy also joined the Pact. In that way the Brussels Treaty Organisation of five was

expanded into seven members, and in May, 1955, was re-named the Western Union. Its Council consists of the Foreign Ministers of the seven member states, and the Union, in addition to an organ for the control of armaments, has also various social and cultural organisations. Not only the Union but also the North Atlantic Treaty Organisation may be said to be an extension of the Brussels Treaty Organisation. N.A.T.O. now consists of fourteen states—the seven Brussels Treaty Powers, Canada, the U.S.A., Denmark, Iceland, Norway, Greece and Turkey.

EUROPEAN RECOVERY PROGRAMME (E.R.P.)

219. Towards the end of the last war and for some years after it, Europe, in common with the rest of the world, was in a serious economic plight, and measures were required to relieve its immediate needs, and to re-construct its economy. For that purpose the United Nations, with funds contributed internationally, set up the organisation known as the United Nations Relief and Rehabilitation Agency (U.N.R.R.A.) and the U.S.A. and Canada came to the help of Great Britain by means of loans on most generous terms.

220. U.N.R.R.A. was a world-wide organisation, and the United Nations, desiring to pay special attention to Europe, set up in 1946 a permanent " Economic Commission for Europe " (E.C.E.) to study and report on the situation. E.C.E. was not only a permanent commission, but it also embraced all the countries of Europe including Russia and the Iron Curtain states. The Commission still continues, and meets once yearly, and, though now completely overshadowed by other organisations, it still issues reports on the economic conditions of the different European nations.

221. The economic situation in Europe deteriorated in 1947. U.N.R.R.A. was being wound up, E.C.E. was only beginning its work, and the loans to Great Britain had been drawn on to a much greater extent than had been expected.

222. It was in such circustances that the United States decided to intervene to save Europe, and the pioneer of the intervention was its Secretary of State, Mr. George Marshall. In a speech delivered at Harvard on 5th June, 1947, he promised American financial help to relieve and rehabilitate Europe, provided that Europe itself would co-operate in framing a joint programme, and looking beyond the present, would plan future permanent economic co-operation, so as to make itself independent of American or any other help. That offer was made to all Europe including Soviet Russia.

223. In response France and Great Britain invited all nations desiring to avail themselves of the offer to meet in Paris, and fourteen

other nations replied—Austria, Belgium, Denmark, Greece, Iceland, Ireland, Italy, Luxembourg, Norway, Portugal, Sweden, Switzerland, Turkey and The Netherlands. (Federal Germany joined in 1949.) These sixteen states formed themselves into a Committee of European Economic Co-operation and issued a Report on 22nd September, 1947, and in the following year, on 16th April, 1948, signed a Convention setting up a "Continuing Organisation for European Economic Co-operation" O.E.E.C.), each country submitting estimates of their requirements for the following four years.

224. In 1948 the European Recovery Programme (E.R.P.) was formerly inaugurated, when the United States passed the European Economic Act. That provided grants and loans for the signatory nations of the Convention to be administered by the Economic Co-operation Administration (E.C.A.). The aid to Europe thus provided is better known as Marshall Aid. E.C.A., having completed the E.R. Programme, officially ceased in December, 1951, because in September of that year the Mutual Security Act established one organisation to administer all American aid projects. O.E.E.C. did not however cease, although its original purpose was simply to deal with the allocation of Marshall Aid Funds. It was a "continuing organisation" and it was to embrace all forms of European co-operation.

225. At the end of war, Ireland, though neutral during it, found its financial, especially its dollar, resources depleted, and its agricultural and industrial economy weakened and retarded. Marshall Aid came to its assistance with a grant of £6m. and a loan of £40m. In an Agreement between the two countries ratified on 2nd June, 1948, Ireland in return for the promised assistance agreed "to exert sustained efforts in common with other participating countries speedily to achieve through a joint recovery programme economic conditions in Europe essential to lasting peace and prosperity and to enable the participating countries .. to become independent of extraordinary outside economic assistance within the period of the agreement." In the ordinary way the agreement was to cease on 30th June, 1953.

226. On 28th October, 1948, there followed the Loan Agreement, under which the Export-Import Bank (called Eximbank) of Washington, as Agent for the American Government, agreed to "a line of credit in favour of Ireland to the extent of £20m. at the rate of 2½ per cent. on the unpaid principal balance repayable in semi-annual instalments beginning on 30th June, 1956, and ending on 31st December, 1983." On 23rd February, 1949, a second agreement increased the line of credit to nearly £30m. but a third

agreement of 22nd December, 1949, reduced it to about £29m. Finally, a fourth agreement of 30th June, 1950, set the sum at about £43m.

227. As regards the Grant as distinct from the Loan, an agreement ratified on 17th February, 1955, provided that the Grant should be used for (1) scholarship exchange between the United States and Ireland; (2) other programmes and projects (including the establishment of an Agricultural Institute) to improve and develop the agricultural production and marketing potential of Ireland, and to increase the production and efficiency of Irish industry; (3) development programmes and projects in aid of the foregoing objectives. It also provided that the two Governments should enter into sub-agreements setting out the projects on which the Grant was to be expended, that any money expended on the projects before the signing of the sub-agreements should not be met out of the Grant, and that a Reserve Fund not exceeding 6 per cent. of the total Grant should be set aside to meet contingencies or other projects in the categories set out above.

228. The first Irish statutory reference to the Loan is contained in Sec. 2 (4) of the Appropriation Act of 1948 which prescribed that the proceeds of any money borrowed from the Government of the U.S.A. or any agency thereof should be placed to the credit of an Account of the Minister for Finance with the Central Bank. This was followed by Sec. 4 of the Central Fund Act, 1949, prescribing that the Minister should establish a Fund to be known as the American Loan Counterpart Fund to be kept in the Central Bank, that he should pay into it from time to time money to the credit of the Account established by the Act of 1948, that any money paid out of the Central Fund for principal and interest on the Loan should be repaid out of the Fund to the Central Fund, and that the Minister might invest any money in the Fund in the same manner as he was authorised to invest moneys of the Post Office Savings Bank.

229. The advances in respect of the Loan were first lodged by the American Government to the credit of the account of the Minister for Finance in Eximbank, and were transferred thence to another account of the Minister in the National City Bank of New York. Those lodgments were then sold to the Bank of England and credited to the Counterpart Account at the Central Bank. The total amount borrowed at the rates of exchange then prevailing was equivalent to £40,701,046 and at the end of March, 1959, £40,007,873 had been invested in Ways and Means Advances. Since 1956/57 a sum of £710,234 had been repaid so that at the end of March, 1959, there was outstanding £39,990,803. In terms of dollars the amount

outstanding is $126,214,366 which at the rate of $2.80 to the £ would be equivalent to £45,076,560.

230. Section 4 of the Central Fund Act, 1950, dealt with the Grant as distinct from the Loan, and established the American Grant Counterpart Special Account to be kept at the Central Bank. It was to carry the equivalent in Irish currency of any grants made by the American Government, and out of it was to be paid any money required by the Agreement of June, 1948, to be paid to that Government, and the money required to meet expenditure on the projects agreed by both Governments. These included Ground Limestone Delivery, Bovine T.B. Eradication, Pasteurisation of Separated Milk, Grants to Rural Organisations, Technical (Agriculture) Assistance, Agricultural Institute, Technical Assistance (Industry and Commerce), Equipment for Industrial Research Laboratory.

ORGANISATION FOR EUROPEAN ECONOMIC CO-OPERATION (O.E.E.C.)

231. The Economic Co-operation Administration, as we have seen, officially ceased on 31st December, 1951. O.E.E.C., however, being a "continuing organisation," continued to work for the economic rehabilitation of Europe through the following organs of administration:—

1. *Council of Ministers,* consisting of one or more ministers of the member states with representatives of the two Associated States, Canada and the United States, meeting at ministerial level. For decisions to be binding the Council must be unanimous.

2. *Executive Committe,* comprising the Heads of Delegations elected annually from seven member states. It carries out a preliminary study of questions to be submitted to the Council.

3. *Ministerial Committee for Agriculture and Food.* In January, 1955, the Council decided to take over the work of the former European Conference on the Organisation of Agricultural Markets ("The Green Pool"), and to replace it by this Committee composed of representatives from the member states and Spain. Special meetings of Ministers of Agriculture are called to decide important questions binding the governments of member states.

4. *Committees.* Working to the Executive and the Council are several committees dealing with such problems as Payments, Energy, Manpower and Agriculture. In addition, there are other committees composed not of state representatives but of technical experts chosen for their specialist knowledge. Some of the latter are described as "vertical", because they deal with specialised

problems, and others as "horizontal", because they are concerned with more general questions such as Trade and Economics.

5. *Secretariat*. This is staffed by independent international civil servants under a Secretary General, and has six directorates or branches dealing with various aspects of the Organisation's work. They do the necessary preliminary work for the Committees.

232. Among the many contributions made to the economic recovery of Europe by the Organisation, two may be regarded as outstanding, viz., the liberalisation of trade, and the convertibility of currencies. In 1940, it began the process of liberalising trade among its members, and in this it was materially aided by the work of the European Payments Union (E.P.U.) and by agreement on tariffs negotiated in 1947 by the General Agreement on Tariffs and Trade (G.A.T.T.), but while G.A.T.T. concentrated more on tariffs the Organisation stressed more the liberation from quotas. A Code of Liberalisation defined the rights and obligations of members, and drew up three categories of products to be progressively freed by them, thus differing in this respect from the product-by-product arrangements negotiated under G.A.T.T. The three categories were Food and Feeding Stuffs, Raw Materials, and Manufactured Products, and the trade to be liberated was private trade and not that operated by Governments. The process of liberalisation was done by means of percentages fixed for each year and based on the trade figures for 1948. The percentage was 50 per cent. for 1949, 60 per cent. in 1950, 75 per cent. in 1951, and finally in 1955 it was fixed at 90 per cent. overall with at least 75 per cent. in the three categories.

233. The second outstanding achievement of the Organisation was to help to bring about the convertibility of currencies. This was due to the European Payments Union (E.P.U.) which was established in September, 1950, with a contribution from the American Government of over £120m., and which replaced the bi-lateral agreements previously in force between member states under Intra European Payments Agreements. It set up a multilateral system of payments for off-setting the deficits or surpluses of each member with all other members, thus creating a single balance owing to the Union. In this way temporary fluctuations in the balance of payments were overcome by the automatic credit given by the Union, together with the payment of dollars or gold, which increased in proportion to the indebtedness of the member. The position of each country included that of its whole monetary area, e.g., the position of the whole sterling area in relation to that of the dollar. The Union was administered by a Board of seven financial experts working under the authority of the Council. Its

agent was the Bank for International Settlements at Basle. Each member's Central Bank sent the Bank a monthly statement of outstanding balances which were converted into units of account defined in terms of gold and equal to one United States dollar. The net balance of each member with its partner in the monetary area was thus calculated and the monthly surplus or deficit ascertained. Transferability between currencies was thus ensured by enabling each member to offset its deficit with some members against surpluses with others.

234. In view of the approaching convertibility of currencies a European Monetary Agreement was signed on 5th August, 1955, providing for (i) A European Fund of £200m. formed by the transfer of £90m. from the capital fund of the Union and by subscriptions from member states. (ii) A Multi-lateral System of Payments (a) requiring each member to fix the buying and selling rates of gold, the dollar and other currency units; (b) enabling each member to obtain short-term advances up to a maximum of 30 days; and (c) arranging for the periodical settlement of accounts. (iii) A Board of Management to supervise the working of the Agreement, and to deal with applications for short-term credits.

Ireland's financial contribution on an assessed basis towards the expenses of O.E.E.C. in 1960/61 is £14,000 with travelling and other expenses of £2,800.

EUROPEAN ECONOMIC COMMUNITY (E.E.C.)

235. Economic co-operation among the member states of O.E.E.C. seems now to be coming to an end, Europe appears to be breaking up into rival trade groups, and the future of the Organisation seems to be somewhat obscure. In order, therefore, to appreciate Ireland's present position it will not be out of place to outline the events which led up to it.

236. In 1952 France, Federal Germany and Italy joined the Benelux Countries to form the European Coal and Steel Community (E.C.S.C.), the object of which was to rationalise their production of coal, iron ore and steel by abolishing national frontiers therefor, and by reducing tariff barriers. Its chief administrative organs were: (1) A *High Authority* of nine members elected for six years to deal with questions on an economic rather than on a national basis. It could impose quotas, if production slackened, and priorities, if consumption demanded. It co-ordinated investment schemes, and could make loans or grants to stimulate production or marketing. The contracting parties thus formed a single economic unit as far as the commodities were concerned; (2) *A Common Assembly* of 78

members elected by their Parliaments; (3) *A Committee of Ministers* representing their Governments; and (4) *A Court of Justice* to settle disputes.*

237. The six countries later explored the possibility of a full customs union, and, after considering the report of a special committee, they signed a treaty in Rome on 25th March, 1957, establishing the European Economic Community (E.E.C.). Briefly the treaty provides for:—

(1) *A Common Market,* to be established progressively over a period of twelve years (and not more than fifteen) divided into four stages of three years each.

(2) *A Customs Union,* wherein custom duties will be gradually lowered at set intervals during the stages, so that they will be entirely abolished during the third stage. Export taxes on trade between the Six will be abolished by the end of the first stage. In 1959 the Six began to cut their duties by 10 per cent. Export subsidies are banned.

(3) *A Common External Tariff* against all other countries, roughly the average of the tariffs existing between the Six on 1st January, 1957. It may not exceed 3 per cent. on most raw materials, 10 per cent. on most semi-manufactured goods, and from 15 to 25 per cent. on certain chemicals. It will be introduced progressively at the end of the three stages and may not be altered without the unanimous decision of the Council.

(4) *Quotas* — All quantitative restrictions between the Six will be abolished by the end of the first stage.

(5) *Agriculture.* Tariffs on agricultural products will be abolished but there will be special marketing and price fixing arrangements.

(6) An *Investment Bank* formed by contributions from the Six to aid undeveloped areas, and a Special Fund to lessen the dislocation of trade caused by the removal of tariffs.

238. For the administration of the provisions of the Treaty the following Organs were established:—

(1) *Council of Ministers* consisting of the foreign ministers of the Six to oversee the implementation of the Treaty. For the first four years their decisions must be unanimous, but thereafter a qualified majority suffices. It must act on proposals made by the Commission; (2) *The European Commission,* a permanent organ

---

* At a meeting of the Western European Union early in June, 1960, the British representative stated that Britain was willing to consider joining E.C.S.C. and Euratom. The latter is an organisation of E.E.C. for developing the peaceful uses of atomic energy.

appointed by, but independent of, the Governments of the Six to administer the Treaty. It can regulate the Escape Clause — the clause which frees a country from its treaty obligations, if its balance of payments be unfavourable — but a qualified majority of the Council may reverse its decisions. It may require governments to remove any internal subsidy or taxation impeding the even flow of trade, but may not interfere with their social, fiscal or financial policies; (3) *An Economic and Social Consultative Committee* to assist the Council and the Commission; (4) *A Common Assembly* representing the Parliaments of the Six; (5) *A Court of Justice*.

239. Britain did not join the Common Market because by so doing it would have to set up a Common Tariff against outsiders, and that would not be compatible either with free imports from the Commonwealth, or with imperial preferences. On the other hand, it was now being confronted with a Common Tariff Wall which would mean less trade with the Six, and more competition in world trade. Hence, at a meeting of the Council of O.E.E.C. in July, 1956, it put forward a proposal for a Free Trade Area in Europe for industrial products only in which the Six, as an economic unit, could trade with the other members of the O.E.E.C. Agricultural products were to be excluded, so that Britain would be able to protect its own farmers and continue to import from the Commonwealth 50 per cent. of their agricultural exports.

240. The proposal was examined by a " Working Party " of O.E.E.C. which reported that it was " technically possible ", but pointed out its many difficulties especially as regards processed articles and differing tariffs. As regards countries, like Ireland, where the industrial potential was low, and where as a consequence native industries had to be protected, it was suggested that, instead of lowering their tariffs simultaneously with the industrially developed countries, they should be granted a longer period subject to inspection. Negotiations within the framework of O.E.E.C. took place over several months, but eventually proved abortive, the position of France being that even if two such institutions were technically possible, they were, nevertheless, incompatible.

EUROPEAN FREE TRADE ASSOCIATION (E.F.T.A.)

241. The Common Market began to operate on 1st January, 1959, and some six months later another trading group was formed. There was already in existence a Scandinavian Union consisting of Norway, Sweden, Denmark, Iceland and Finland which in 1954 had set up a Common Employment Market to aid the mobility of labour and had been studying the possibility of a Common Northern

Market for trade. In June, 1959, Britain joined with Norway, Sweden, Denmark, Austria, Portugal and Switzerland in planning a European Free Trade Association (E.F.T.A.) and a Convention was formally signed on November 20th, 1959, subject to the ratification of each Parliament concerned. Briefly, the convention is: (1) To reduce all industrial tariffs by 20 per cent on 1st July, 1960. This sets up a rigid time-table for each product, while the Six are allowed a certain discretion regarding individual products provided that the overall percentage is reached; (2) To have special agreements on agricultural products after bi-lateral negotiations between the interested parties; (3) To have a special agreement on fish and marine products. Frozen fish is included but Britain retains the right to review the position, if Norway exports to the United Kingdom more than 240,000 tons yearly or if the Norwegian fishery limits be extended; (4) A Steering Committee without, as in the case of the Six, a large Secretariat, and without any supra-national authority, as with E.C.S.C., to implement the convention; (5) to maintain close co-operation with O.E.E.C.

242. A second reduction of 15 per cent. in tariffs within the Common Market is due in July, 1960, and the Six have decided to extend it to all members of the General Agreement on Tariffs and Trade (G.A.T.T.). This body originated in 1946 in the Economic and Social Council of the United Nations which drew up a charter (The Havana Charter) for the liberalisation of international trade mainly by reducing tariffs on a product-by-product basis and by conceding the most favoured nation treatment. When, however, it was foreseen that the United States would not ratify the agreement, twenty-three of the signatories met at Geneva in 1947 and signed it. It is now a global organisation and embraces thirty-seven nations operating over 80 per cent. of world trade. Ireland is not a member of G.A.A.T.*

243. Spain became a member of O.E.E.C. in July, 1959, and was given a credit of £37.7m. from the funds of the European Monetary Agreement. Hence, of the 18 nations which are now members of the O.E.E.C. only five—Ireland, Iceland, Spain, Turkey and Greece—do not belong to either of the rival trade groups, and with both groups tending towards free trade in industrial products, it would seem that Ireland may have to reconsider its system of high tariffs and protection.

244. Following on the Western Summit Conference in Paris in December, 1959, a meeting was held there on 14th January, 1960,

---

* Ireland is, however, considering joining the Organisation.

between the eighteen members of the O.E.E.C. and its associate members, Canada and the U.S.A. It was decided that they should link up with the members of E.E.C. so as to form a committee, which would examine, in general, their several commercial problems, and, in particular, the possibility of reconciling the difference between E.E.C. and E.F.T.A., paying due attention to the interests of other countries, and to the principles and obligations of G.A.T.T. As a result of the January meeting a Committee was appointed to draw up a new Convention embracing the eighteen members of O.E.E.C. with Canada and the United States as full members. The Committee has recommended that O.E.E.C. should cease and should be replaced by an Organisation for Economic Co-operation and Development (O.E.C.D.), the objects of which should be to co-ordinate trade policies, to develop trade between the member States and to aid the undeveloped countries.

Meanwhile the Common Market is considering the " Hallstein Plan " by which quotas between the Six would be abolished by the end of 1961, tariffs would be cut by 20 per cent. instead of 10 per cent. by July 1960, and a common external tariff wall introduced in July instead of December, 1961, subsequently amended to 31st December, 1960. It is, however, likely that, before any attempt be made at implementing the plan, negotiations will take place between The Six and The Seven.

CHAPTER XV

State–Sponsored Bodies

245. In previous chapters we have been mainly concerned with the administration of the public services by the different departments, but in addition to these services, the modern state also engages in industrial enterprises. In some cases, as in Great Britain, this engagement has followed on a theory of political socialism, but in Ireland it has been caused by the fact that private enterprise either failed to fill important gaps in the national economy, or in doing so broke down financially. We have already in the course of this work mentioned generally some of these enterprises, but in the present chapter we shall deal with the more important, selecting those which have a special bearing on the Finance Accounts of the State.

246. By State-sponsored Bodies are here meant industrial or commercial enterprises which have either been created by the State, or in which the State has a direct financial interest. Before going into details, a few general observations may not be out of place. First, all such Bodies are not financed in the same manner. Some, like the Public Services, are financed out of moneys voted annually by the Oireachtas which generally include grants-in-aid either for their statutory or administrative functions or for both, e.g., the Institute for Industrial Research and Standards. Some receive their finances direct from the Central Fund as advances or loans repayable with interest, e.g., The Electricity Supply Board, and Bord na Móna. Some are aided partly by voted moneys generally for administrative expenses, and partly by repayable advances for capital purposes, e.g., Bord Fáilte and the Sea Fisheries Board. Finally the Bodies may be helped by the State subscribing to their share capital, e.g., Aer Rianta and the Irish Sugar Company. The Bodies may also be aided, if the governing statutes permit, by the Government guaranteeing their borrowings or overdrafts. At the end of March, 1959, the amount of guaranteed overdrafts, etc., of State-sponsored Bodies was £8.6m.

247. Secondly, all State-sponsored Bodies have not the same legal status, and here it is necessary to distinguish between statutory and quasi-statutory corporations. The former are incorporated under special statutes which specifically prescribe the Body to be a

corporation, thus giving it a distinct personality, perpetual succession, and a common seal. This status is usually given to Bodies operating essential monopolistic services throughout the entire State, e.g., the E.S.B., and Bord na Móna. The Agricultural Credit Corporation is not a body corporate in this sense. Quasi-statutory corporations, on the other hand, are incorporated under the ordinary Companies Acts, and their quasi-statutory status consists in their being recognised either before or after incorporation by some special statute usually for the purpose of the State participating financially in their activities.

248. Here it must be noted that a body corporate or statutory corporation may be created either by Royal Charter, or by the Government, or by Statute. The Royal Dublin Society and the National University, for instance, have been so created by Charter; the Government, as such, has not created any; but by Statute the Land Commission is a body corporate. Again, a statutory board, that is, a body established by statute for a specific—usually a non-trading—purpose is not necessarily a body corporate. The Land Commission is such, but the Army Pensions Board is not.

249. The third general observation relates to Parliamentary control. A State-sponsored Body may come under the notice of Parliament, if a question be asked in the Dáil about its policy but not about its administration, or during a debate on the Central Fund or Appropriation Bills if the Estimates contain provision for it, or during a discussion on the Budget when capital expenditure is being discussed, or, finally, if a Bill dealing with the Body is under consideration. But the control exercised on these occasions is entirely indirect and largely nugatory. In nearly all cases the accounts of the Bodies are presented to Parliament, but, unlike the Appropriation Accounts, there is no machinery to scrutinise them, so as to ensure that money is being expended for the purposes intended by Parliament and that the expenditure is neither wasteful nor extravagant. In other countries the necessity for such a scrutiny is recognised by setting up select committees or special commissions. The need for some such examination is also admitted in Ireland, for it was moved at one time that within twenty-one days of an account of a Body being tabled, the Minister responsible should move in the Dáil for a select committee to examine its account and report back to the Dáil. The motion was withdrawn on the Minister then responsible stating that the Government intended to introduce immediately proposals, whereby the Dáil might have a systematic consideration of the activities of the various Boards. That was in 1950 but the proposals have not yet materialised.

THE CENTRAL BANK

250. Following on the recommendations in 1938 of the " Commission of Inquiry into Banking, Currency and Credit," the Central Bank in 1942 succeeded the Currency Commission, which was neither a corporation, nor a company, but a simple commission, that is, a group of persons established by statute to carry out certain functions, until its objects were accomplished or the statute was repealed. The Commission functioned from 1927 until 1942, its chief purposes being to issue legal tender notes " against money in any form which is for the time being legal tender in Great Britain " and to hold monetary reserves of gold and foreign assets. Legal Tender Notes were protected to the extent of 100 per cent. by a reserve of gold, British legal tender, or sterling balances, or British Government securities maturing within twelve months.

251. The Central Bank Act of 1942 dissolved the Commission and set up the Central Bank, which took over the functions, property, assets, funds and liabilities of the Commission. It prescribed, as the general function of the Bank, the safeguarding of the integrity of Irish currency, and the controlling of credit in the interests of the welfare of the Irish people. In particular, it vested in the Bank the functions of the former Commission, and it extended its powers so that: (1) It could, if any bank needed accommodation, act as a lender in last resort by re-discounting bills of exchange, by making advances against bills or against Government securities, and by fixing the rates of interest for re-discounting bills and making advances; (2) It could on its own initiative engage in open market operations by buying and selling Government securities; and (3) It could receive non-interest bearing securities from commercial banks and settle clearance balances between them. In fine, the Act vested in the Bank all the powers and functions usually associated with Central Banks elsewhere.

252. The Central Bank is a statutory corporation composed of a Governor and not more than eight directors, two of whom may be Civil Servants. The Governor is appointed by the President on the advice of the Government for a period of seven years which may be extended. All the directors are appointed by the Minister for Finance, but three are selected from a panel submitted by the Banks, and all hold office for a period of five years. The capital of the Bank is £40,000 of which £24,000 was at once subscribed by the Minister for Finance, and with it the shareholding banks of the Commission were repaid.

253. The Act provided for the extinction over a period of twelve years of Consolidated Bank Notes—that is, notes issued by

the Commission to its eight shareholding banks—to be replaced by an equal amount of Legal Tender Notes, and it also empowered the banks to write off " Dead Notes," that is, notes issued before 6th May, 1929, when the consolidated issue first appeared. The write-off was subject to the consent of the Minister for Finance who might require the bank to pay the Exchequer or the Central Bank a proportion of the amount written off.

254. Every banker must be licensed annually by the Revenue Commissioners and has to deposit with the High Court a sum of £10,000 during 1943-45 and £20,000 thereafter.

255. To encourage investment within the State, and to prevent an undue expansion of credit, the Central Bank is empowered to require a banker to lodge an interest free deposit, whenever his assets fall below a certain level. The Bank is responsible for the issue of token coins, the profits of the issue going to its General Fund which also bears the cost of the issue and redemption.

256. Two Funds are prescribed by the Act, a Legal Tender Note Fund, and a General Fund. Whenever the assets of the former show an increase in value, the Bank may. at its discretion, transfer the surplus to a currency reserve within the latter.

257. Since 1st November, 1958, it has been arranged that the commercial banks would deposit with the Central Bank a substantial portion of their liquid sterling assets in the form of interest bearing balances repayable in Irish currency, so that the clearing of cheques between the banks can now be effected by drawing on the deposits.

258. In accordance with the Currency Act of 1927, as amended, the Bank has to furnish the Minister for Finance at stated intervals with a statement showing the position of the Legal Tender Note Fund, and this is published in Iris Oifigiúil. The Accounts are audited and signed by the Auditor General. The Notes issued are backed by Gold (about £2m.), by British Money which is legal tender for unlimited amounts (about £60m.), by Sterling Balances at the London Agency or Northern Ireland (about £5m.) by American Securities and Currency (about £11m.) and by Irish Government Securities (about £1m.). The latter is a new backing introduced in 1959 for the purpose of replacing the value of gold needed to pay the State's increased gold subscription to the International Monetary Fund, and it is a liability of the Government.

In 1958/59 the Bank had a surplus income of £1.7m. which it surrendered to the Exchequer.

THE ELECTRICITY SUPPLY BOARD

259. The Irish State's first venture into the field of trading took place in 1925, when it passed the Shannon Electricity Act.

Conceived by an Irishman, Dr. T. A. McLaughlin, planned by a German Company, examined by electricity experts from Norway, Sweden and Switzerland, the "Shannon Scheme", as it is called, was brought to fruition by Messrs. Siemens-Schuckert of Berlin. The Act of 1925 provided for the production by the State of electricity by means of hydraulic power derived from the Shannon, and for the distribution and supply by the State of the electricity so generated. At that time there were about 180 local undertakings supplying electricity to towns and villages mainly for lighting, and the Act did not prevent them from continuing their operations.

260. When the Scheme was nearing completion in 1927, another Act, the Electricity (Supply) Act, was passed, and created a monopoly for the production and distribution of electricity throughout the State. It provided for the "reorganisation and regulation of the generation, transmission, distribution and supply of electricity throughout the State" especially for that generated in the works constructed by the State under the Act of 1925, and "for that purpose it made provision for the management, administration and control of the said works with a view to the efficient and economic operation thereof." The Act thus set up the Electricity Supply Board, and, making it a statutory corporation, empowered it to acquire the private electrical undertakings, if and when it was economically feasible to supply the demand from the national grid. The development of the Scheme thus begun on the Shannon can be traced in many statutes passed between 1925 and 1958, and in the annual reports of the Board.

261. The Board now operates (1) Hydro-Electric Stations at Shannon, Erne, Liffey and Lee; (2) Peat-Fired Stations at Portarlington, Allenwood, Ferbane, Miltown-Malbay, Cahirciveen, Screeb and Gweedore; (3) Coal and Oil Fired Stations in Dublin (three) and Cork. Their total output in 1959/60 was 2,096 million units of which 37 per cent. came from the Hydro, 32.4 per cent. from the Peat, and 30.6 per cent. from the Coal-Oil Stations.

262. The Acts authorise the Board to incur capital expenditure of £100m. for its general purposes, and up to the end of March, 1959, it had expended £75m. The capital required is provided by means of advances from the Central Fund, repayable at rates of interest determined by the Minister for Finance, and since 1954 the Board may borrow with the consent of the Minister. At the end of March, 1959, the advances outstanding stood at £64m., and during the year the Board had paid interest of £2.6m. on the advances. The State had also guaranteed two issues of Stock of over £14m.

263. The Board is now engaged on rural electrification

estimated to cost £30m., of which the State will contribute 50 per cent. of the capital cost within a limit of £15m. Already about five-sixths of the scheme have been completed at a cost of £25m. The project will not ever be an economical proposition—hence the State subsidy—and when finished it is estimated that there will be an annual loss of over £1m. The Board consists of a Chairman and from two to six other persons appointed by the Government for five years. All may be re-appointed.

BORD NA MÓNA

264. It has been estimated that one-seventh of the area of Ireland consists of bogland, that is 93 per cent. water and 7 per cent. solid matter. From time immemorial the bogs were worked by country folk to win turf, a combustible fuel, for their own domestic use and for sale to the inhabitants of the adjoining towns. The implements used were of the simplest kind—the slean, the barrow and the fork—and the cutting was confined to the edges of the bogs.

265. In order to explore the potentiality of this native source of wealth, and to develop the industry by improved methods of cutting and selling turf and its by-products, a special branch was at first set up in the Department of Industry and Commerce, but in 1934 this was replaced by the Turf Development Board, which was incorporated as a private joint-stock company with a nominal capital of five £1 shares held by directors nominated by the Minister. The Government made grants-in-aid to the Company to meet its administrative expenses, and other grants, repayable with interest, for its development work. The Company engaged in the large-scale production of turf in a bog at Clonsast, and its work was highly successful especially during the years of war.

266. Following on this experiment, the Turf Development Act was passed in 1946, and Bord na Móna—the Peat Board—was by an Order of the Minister made under the Act established as a statutory corporation. All the operations of the Board in producing the turf are highly mechanised, and its present activities cover about 100,000 acres of bog land. Its aim is to produce annually $3\frac{1}{4}$ million tons of peat—2 million for electricity purposes and the remainder for industrial and other uses—but the target will obviously depend to a large extent on the requirements of the E.S.B. for peat-fired electricity stations. Seven of these are planned, three are in operation, and two others are under construction.

267. The peat is produced in three forms—as sod or machine peat, as milled peat, and as peat moss. The first is cut out of the

bog several inches below the surface, after the heathery substance on top has been removed. The target here is one million tons a year including 500,000 tons for electricity. In 1958/59, of the total production of this form of peat 223,807 tons went to the E.S.B. stations at Allenwood, Portarlington and Lanesboro'.

268. Milled Peat consists of turf scraped or cut from the surface of the bog to a depth of about a half-inch by special milling machines and then gathered together. The Board's target here is about $2\frac{1}{4}$ million tons annually of which the electricity authority is expected to take about 1.6 million tons. In 1958/59, of the total production the E.S.B. station at Ferbane absorbed 425,498 tons. Milled peat, not used for electricity purposes, is processed at the Bord na Móna factory at Lullymore and is turned out in the shape of briquettes for industrial, domestic and other uses. In 1958/59 the briquettes manufactured totalled 32,290 tons. Demand here is greater than supply, and two new briquette factories are contemplated. It is estimated that the annual output of the three factories would be about 250,000 tons of briquettes.

269. Peat Moss is obtained from the light mossy deposits of peat found in the upper layers of the bog. After being gathered and processed in the factory, it is compressed into bales of varying sizes. It is used as a soil conditioner, as an ingredient for potting and seed composts, as deep litter for poultry, and as bedding for animals. It forms a valuable export. In 1958/59 production amounted to 110,590 bales.

270. The Board has its own Experimental and Research Department to deal with the mechanisation of all operations connected with the development of bogs, the production of peat and its by-products. In co-operation with Messrs. A. Guinness, Son and Co. Ltd., it is founding a Chair of Industrial Microbiology at University College, Dublin, with special emphasis on the problems of peat. It has statutory power to erect houses for its permanent employees, and so far it has built 578 houses in eight village schemes.

271. The Board is financed by advances from the Central Fund the amount outstanding at 31st March, 1960, being £14m. It has also borrowed £.5m. from Messrs. A. Guinness, Son and Co. Ltd. to finance part of its requirements for 1957/58 and 1958/59, and this loan is secured by a charge on its floating assets and is guaranteed by the Minister for Finance. The original advances, £6.4m., to the Board were free of interest up to 1952, and a second series of £5m. up to 1955/56; but all advances made are now carrying interest. At the end of March, 1959, interest repaid amounted to £448,201.

272. The Board is constituted by a Chairman, a Managing

Director and five Directors appointed by the Government on terms similar to those already described for the Electricity Supply Board. The Managing Director alone acts in a full-time capacity. Its accounts are audited by the Auditor General.

273. The Turf Development Act, 1959, increased from £14m. to £19m. the money which the Board might borrow from the Central Fund and other sources, and it removed the limit of £2m. which it might take from other sources, provided that the total borrowings from all sources should not exceed the limit of £19m.

CÓRAS IOMPAIR ÉIREANN

274. In 1910 there were 29 Railway Companies operating in Ireland, 26 of which were situated in the area of what is now the Irish State. They had a mileage of 3,411 and 261 directors. They had all been built by private enterprise, and there had been no central planning or organisation. From 1916 to 1921 they had been taken over by the British Government, which, on restoring them to their owners, paid compensation of £3m. In 1922, when the Irish State was established, the railways reserves were completely depleted, wages had increased disproportionately to rates, and road competition was on the way.

275. In 1924 the Irish Government intervened to undertake the overdue task of reorganising the railways. Under the Railways Act of that year the number of companies was reduced to four, all of which were subsequently, about 1925, merged into the Great Southern Railways. The Act also set up a Railway Tribunal for the fixation of rates, etc.

276. The finacial position of the railways was steadily deteriorating, and in 1933 the Government, under a Railway Act of that year, attempted a financial reorganisation by the watering down of their capital. By the Act 90 per cent. of the Ordinary Stock, 65 per cent. of the Preference, 50 per cent. of the Guaranteed Preference and 15 per cent. of the Debenture Stocks were written off, so that the total stock was reduced from £25m. to £11½m. The Great Southern operated 2,000 miles of the 2,500 miles of railway track in the State. In 1942, under an Emergency Powers Order, the Government abolished the seven directors elected by the shareholders of the Great Southern Railways, and appointed a chairman and four directors in their place—the chairman alone constituting a quorum.

277. In 1954 came the first of the Transport as distinct from the Railways Acts. That of 1944 provided " for the incorporation of a Transport Company to be called Córas Iompair Éireann and for the transfer to that Company of the undertakings the Great

Southern Railway Company and the Dublin United Transport Company Ltd." The capital was again watered down.

278. The Transport Act of 1950 (1) established C.I.E. as a statutory corporation, the Board to consist of not less than three or more than seven members all appointed by the Government; (2) empowered it to take over all the undertakings of C.I.E. and the Grand Canal Company; (3) substituted Transport Stock for C.I.E. and Grand Canal Securities—all being merged into 3 per cent. Transport Stock 1955/60, 1975/85 and $2\frac{1}{2}$ per cent. 1965/75; (4) allowed the Board to borrow temporarily up to £.5m. or with the consent of the Minister up to £1m.; (5) permitted the Board to issue stock up to a limit of £7m. for capital development, for the redemption of Transport Stock and for the acquisition of transport undertakings. The Board used this power to issue for capital purposes 5 per cent. Transport Stock 1972/77 and $4\frac{1}{2}$ per cent. 1972/77. The Railway Tribunal continued to operate.

279. In 1955 another Transport Act increased the limit for temporary borrowing from £1m. to £$1\frac{1}{2}$m., and for the issue of stock for capital and other purposes from £7m. to £12m. At the same time it allowed the Board to treat as non-repayable a sum of nearly £$2\frac{1}{2}$m. which had been issued as advances for capital purposes repayable to the Exchequer.

280. All these attempts at re-organising C.I.E., both administratively and financially, ended in failure. From 1950 to 1957 it had lost £$10\frac{1}{2}$m. and the deficit in 1957/58 had increased to £2.7m. compared with £1.7m. for the previous year. Hence in 1958 another Transport Act made a further effort to rehabilitate the undertaking by increasing its already great powers and by reconstructing its capital. Briefly, the Act provided (1) that the Board as its general duty should provide reasonable, efficient and economical transport services with due regard to safety of operation, the encouragement of national economic development and the maintenance of reasonable conditions of employment for its employees; and that it should conduct its undertaking, as soon as may be and in any case not later than 31st March, 1964, so that its operating costs, including all charges properly chargeable to revenue, shall not be greater than the revenue of the Board; (2) that the Board may fix such charges and attach such conditions for any service as it may think fit, and that, despite any enactment to the contrary, it may refuse any traffic offered to it. The Railway Tribunal, therefore, ceased to operate; (3) that, subject to certain specified precautions, enactments dealing with level crossings do not apply to those under the Board's control; (4) that it may terminate

any uneconomical service of trains for passengers or goods, and that it need not provide alternative road transport leaving it to private persons or bodies to do so; (5) that it may close any canal, or part of a canal, which has not been in use for three years or more; (6) that it may sell by private treaty the land under or adjoining abandoned lines to a Local Authority or public utility undertaking.

281. The financial clauses of the Act provided: (1) that the Minister for Finance would grant to the Board in each financial year and for five years beginning on 1st April, 1959, a sum of £1m. (increased to £1,175,000 under the Great Northern Act, 1958) to defray the interest on Transport Stock, and for the purposes of the undertaking without prejudice to the borrowing powers of the Board under Government guarantee prescribed in the 1950 Act; (2) that the Minister would take over from the Board the 3 per cent. Transport Stock 1955/60 amounting to £9.9m. and would treat it, to the exclusion of the Board, as a Government Loan, and that after 1st April, 1959, the Minister would pay the amount of interest due thereon; (3) that the Board should not be liable for the repayment of £4.8m. in respect of interest on Transport Stock, and £803,000 in respect of temporary borrowing, being repayable advances from the Central Fund.

During 1958/59, the Board paid the Exchequer £185,291 interest on advances, and its working during that year involved a loss of £1.8m.

BORD FÁILTE ÉIREANN

282. In order to encourage Irish citizens to spend their holidays at home, and to attract tourists from abroad, a voluntary society, called the Irish Tourist Association, was formed in 1925 and its members were drawn from the hotel and restaurant trades, Local Authorities, and transport companies.

283. In 1931 the Tourist (Development) Act provided inter alia (1) that the Minister for Industry and Commerce could grant a certificate of approval to any registered company, whose aim was to develop tourism including the advertising of health and pleasure resorts; (2) that Local Authorities might aid the Association's funds by striking a rate up to one penny in the £ on the rateable valuation of the particular borough, urban district, or town. The funds of the Association, which is still in existence, are, therefore, formed by contributions from the rates and from the subscriptions of its members.

284. In 1939 under the Tourist Traffic Act of that year the Government established as a statutory corporation the Irish Tourist

Board with powers to extend and develop accommodation and other amenities for holiday-makers, either directly or indirectly, by granting financial assistance to others for the same purpose. It could acquire land compulsorily, including fishing and sporting rights, and it could register hotels, guest-houses, hostels and holiday camps. It allowed the Minister for Industry and Commerce to contribute as a grant-in-aid up to £45,000 a year towards the administrative and other expenses of the Board, and to make repayable interest-bearing advances from the Central Fund for works, investments or loans of a profit-earning character—the limit of such advances being fixed at first at £.6m. but subsequently (in 1946) being increased to £1.25m. In 1944 the Board began the registration, classification, and inspection of hotels, etc., and those so registered had to submit their maximum tariffs.

285. The Tourist Traffic Act of 1952 — (1) changed the title of the Board to Bord Fáilte Éireann; (2) increased the grant-in-aid for administrative expenses, etc., to £250,000; (3) increased the limit of loans by way of repayable advances from the Central Fund to an aggregate of £3m. not exceeding £75,000 in any one year; (4) provided grants to cover interest on the loans for a period of three years (Guaranteed Loans Scheme); (5) increased the number of directors from five to seven; (6) provided that the accounts should be submitted to the Auditor General.

286. The Tourist Traffic Act, 1955, increased the Board's grant-in-aid for administrative expenses to £500,000 and another Act in 1957 (1) continued the operation of the Guaranteed Loans Scheme for another five years, and (2) extended the Government's guarantee in respect of interest charges to private loans raised by hoteliers. Finally in 1959, another Tourist Act provided that for a period of ten years and in addition to the £500,000 of the 1955 Act, the Minister, out of moneys voted by the Oireachtas, might make non-repayable grants not exceeding in the aggregate £1m. for the development of major tourist resorts, and not exceeding £500,000 for the development of holiday accommodation.

287. During 1958/59 under the Private Loans Scheme, 38 applicants applied for the guarantee of loans totalling £240,000 and the Board agreed to pay interest grants of £41,000 over a period of five years. Grants were also made to meet a fifth of the cost of providing new bedrooms, and one-third of the cost of their central heating. From 1960/61, grants of 20 per cent. of the total cost will be made for such works as the installation of hot and cold water, and central heating, for the adaptation of bedrooms as bed-bath units, and for the provision of extra bathroom and toilet accommodation,

but the works must be carried out between January, 1960, and 31st March, 1963. If a loan is approved, the applicant borrows from a bank or other financial institution under the Minister's guarantee at varying rates of interest, and repayment of the loan is made by equal annual instalments over a period not exceeding 15 years. The loan is secured by a mortgage on the property, and the Board may make a grant towards the payment of the interest for a maximum period of 5 years.

288. The Board has offices in Dublin, London, Manchester, Chicago and New York, and the Irish Tourist Association, which receives a subsidy from the Board, operates in the 32 counties of Ireland. Loans under the Acts outstanding at the end of March, 1959, totalled £237,332, Repayable Advances then outstanding stood at £146,065 and the Board paid interest thereon of £117. The Income and Expenditure Account 1958/59 showed a deficit of £4,410.

THE SEA FISHERIES BOARD (BORD IASCAIGH MHARA)

289. The Irish Sea Fisheries Association Ltd. was registered in 1930 under the Industrial and Provident Societies Acts, 1893/1913, at the request of the Minister for Lands and Fisheries, who had no express legislative authority for doing so. Under the Fisheries Act of 1931, the Minister transferred to the Association fishing boats and other property vested in him, together with responsibility for loans made by him for the purchase of boats, and the securities for such loans. The Association was in effect a private body of some 2,500 members acting as a Co-operative Society for developing sea fishing by co-operating in the handling and marketing of fish and in providing fishing boats and gear. Its administrative and development expenses were met by voted grants-in-aid, and by repayable advances from the Exchequer for the purchase of boats and gear. It had the power to control fish imports, and to regulate the quantity and price of fish in the home market. Four of the directors (including the Chairman) were appointed by the Government and four others elected by the members of the Association.

290. Under the Fisheries Act of 1952, the Association was dissolved, and in its place was established the Sea Fisheries Board as a statutory corporation, its objects being to take over the assets and liabilities of the Association and to carry on its work. The Act also provided for a society—An Comhlachas Iascaigh Mhara—composed of person engaged in the sea-fishing industry such as fishermen and persons occupied in the retail, wholesale or distributive aspects of the industry. The Board is composed of six directors (including the Chairman) appointed by the Minister for

three years and not more than three may be civil servants. The administrative and development expenses are met by a yearly grant-in-aid (£180,000 in 1959/60) and by repayable advances from the Central Fund within a limit of £3m. for capital purposes. Repayable advances outstanding at the end of March, 1959, are shown at £849,959 and the interest repaid £35,217. The Board is allowed with the consent of the Minister to borrow temporarily.

291. The Board's activities are widespread, but on the basis of its Report for 1957/58 the following may be listed:—

1. *Boatyards.* Four are maintained—situated in Killybegs, Meevagh, Baltimore and Dingle—for the purpose of building fishing craft. Nine were built in 1957/58 at a cost of £94,466. Three others were built privately, and seventeen others were under construction at an estimated cost of £135,900. In addition the Board was providing five boats for the special Fíor Ghaeltach Scheme built in its own and in private yards. When completed this special scheme will cost about £80,000.

2. *Hire Purchase.* During the year the Board financed hire purchase transactions in ten new boats at £103,000 and in other boats and fishing gear valued at £185,875. At the end of the year motor fishing boats under hire purchase totalled 107 at a value of about £648,970. The Board is enabled to accept a proportion of the fishermen's earnings on foot of hire purchase or credit sales transactions. The Board reports a steadily deteriorating position in the accounts of certain hire purchasers.

3. *Auction Centres and Depots.* Centres for the auctioning of fish are maintained at Dublin, Cork and Killybegs and 32 depots are kept around the Irish coast.

4. *Ice Plants* are operated at Killybegs, Galway, Dingle, Muirisk and Cleeghan to provide supplies of ice for the preservation of the fish landed.

5. *Fish Meal Plant.* This is at Killybegs and is of an experimental nature. It is not sufficiently large to make it an economic unit. Frozen Fish, Smoked Fish, Fish Meal and Fish Oil (used in the manufacture of paints) are produced from herring catches.

6. *Processing Stations* at Dublin, Cork, Limerick, Galway, Killybegs and Cromane are engaged in smoking fish for the production of kippers.

7. *Landing Points* for fish catches are provided at 53 points around the coast.

8. *Marketing.* During the year the Board marketed 216,681 cwt. of fresh sea fish (valued at £565,683), 18,936 cwt. of Mussels treated on a fee basis for fishermen at Cromane, and other shell fish valued at £5,415.

9. *Offshore Fishing.* The Board operated three offshore vessels bought in 1952, but they are now sold. Capital outlay on them was £106,727, and they were sold for £33,950. The operational loss was £52,250.

There was a loss on Revenue Accounts of £287,043 in 1957/58.

AER RIANTA Tta.

292. The Air Navigation and Transport Acts empowered the Minister for Finance to promote the formation of Aer Rianta, to take up shares in it, and to pay it subsidies. Aer Rianta was incorporated in April, 1937, as a public limited liability company under the Companies Acts, its object being to promote aviation, manage airports, operate air services, both inside and outside the State—either directly or through companies in which it has controlling interest—and, as a holding company, to take shares in Aer Lingus and Aerlinte Éireann.

293. Under successive Air Navigation Acts, its capital was at first £500,000, then £1m. and now since 1959 £10m. In March, 1960, the Minister for Finance held 3,698,540 fully paid shares of £1 each, a few others being allotted to the directors and subscribers to the Memorandum and Articles of Association. It manages Dublin Airport, and is a holding and managing company of Aer Lingus and Aerlinte Éireann. It now holds 95 per cent. (£1.9m.) of the Aer Lingus issued share capital, and all the Aerlinte Share Capital of £1,425,005 apart from directors' qualifying shares.

294. The Chairman and four directors of the company are all part-time officials appointed by the Minister for Finance. They are concerned only with matters of policy. The Company submits its annual accounts to the Minister for Finance, and they are audited by the Auditor General.

295. At the end of March, 1959, there was a profit of £87,115 on the Airport Management Account, and a loss of £35,929 on the Administration Account. Its liabilities include £798,000, an advance from Aerlinte, and £655,000 due to B.E.A. for loan capital and for the purchase of shares in Aer Lingus.

296. The Air Navigation and Transport (No. 2) Act, 1959, raised the share capital of the Company from £2m. fixed in 1947 to £10m., divided into ten million shares of £1 each, and restricted its State guaranteed debentures to £5m. In this way additional share (£8m.) and loan capital (£1.5m.) was made available to the extent of £9.5m. to provide £5.9m. for the purchase of jet aircraft for Aerlinte, £655,000 due to B.E.A. under the agreement of 1956, £798,540 due to Aerlinte and £2.1m. for the requirements of Aer

Lingus. The Minister had already guaranteed debentures of £3½m. for the Company in respect of commercial loans.

AER LINGUS Tta.

297. Aer Lingus is a private limited liability company established in May, 1936, under the Companies Acts in accordance with the Air Navigation and Transport Act, 1936. It is a subsidiary of Aer Rianta although it was established before it. Pending the passing of the necessary legislation setting up the present company, Aer Lingus was financed by a private British Company (Olley Air Services Ltd.), both trading in partnership as Irish Sea Airways under a joint committee.

298. In 1946 the British and Irish Governments entered into an agreement by which their selected air companies were to operate into and out of their national territories. Following on this agreement, Aer Rianta and Aer Lingus on the one hand and British Overseas Airways and British Eureopean Airways on the other, entered in 1947 into an agreement whereby (a) the capital of Aer Lingus was increased to £5m., the Irish Company taking 60 per cent. and the British 40 per cent. of the new share capital; (b) the majority of the directors were Irish; (c) Aer Lingus was given the exclusive right of operating the services between Ireland and Great Britain; (d) profits and losses were divided equally between the shareholders, except in the case of continental services, when the profits were to be on a 60 and 40 per cent. basis and losses on a 50 per cent. basis.

299. In 1956 the agreement was revised and under the new arrangements: (a) Aer Rianta purchased threequarters of the B.E.A. shares—B.O.A.C. having sold their holding to B.E.A.; (b) Aer Rianta took over the liability to repay B.E.A. loan capital contributed over several years; (c) the British directors were reduced from two to one; (d) B.E.A. may compete with Aer Lingus on the routes between Dublin — Birmingham, Cardiff, Manchester, Liverpool and London; (e) Aer Lingus has the right to operate continental routes through Manchester.

300. Up to 1957 Aer Lingus relied on its shareholders for its capital, but in that year, in order to buy new aircraft (Fokker Friendship), it raised the necessary money, £2.8m., from private sources—The Ulster Bank Ltd. and the Irish Assurance Co. Ltd.—by means of State-guaranteed debentures. Aer Lingus has not, since 1950, received any subsidy from the State to recoup operating losses, any such being carried forward to be met by any subsequent profits.

301. The Chairman and six directors of the Company (including the Chairman and two directors of Aer Rianta) are part-time

officials, and the accounts are audited by the Auditor General. Of the total issued capital (£2,073,000) of the Company, Aer Rianta holds £1,977,800 and B.E.A. £95,200. For 1958/59 there was a surplus on the Operating Account of £204,434.

AERLINTE ÉIREANN Tta.

302. Aerlinte Éireann was formed in 1947 as a private limited liability company, in order to operate services between Ireland and the U.S.A. Its authorised capital was £5m. of which £1,425,000 was taken up by Aer Rianta. In 1948 the Government decided that the service should be abandoned, and its assets — five Constellation Aircraft — were sold realising £1,882,010. Of this sum there was on loan to the Minister for Finance, £1,083,470, and to Aer Rianta, £798,540.

303. In 1952 the question of re-opening the service by means of leased aircraft was considered, and in 1957 negotiations took place with an American Company (Seaboard and Western Airlines). In 1958 Aerlinte was restarted with three Irish directors, and the new service began in April, 1958, with leased aircraft under a revised agreement with Seaboard to end on 1st May, 1960. All flights operate to Shannon, but by arrangement with Aer Lingus aircraft is used between Shannon and Dublin. The annual accounts are dealt with in the same manner as those of the other air companies. On the Operation Account, 1958/59, there was a loss of £804,084. With the Government's approval the Company has entered into capital commitments of £6m.

INDUSTRIAL CREDIT COMPANY LTD.

304. In accordance with the Industrial Credit Act, 1933, this Company was established in 1933 as a public limited liability company under the Companies Acts, to fill a gap in the national economy, because up to that time the ordinary banks and finance companies did not usually underwrite Irish industrial flotations. Its object, therefore, was the acquisition, underwriting, holding, and selling of shares, etc., the carrying on in Ireland of any trade or industry, and the lending or advancing of money for the purpose of establishing, carrying on or advancing any trade or industry in Ireland. It did not at this time promote new enterprises, but investigated proposals and advised on those regarded as sound propositions.

305. An Act passed in 1958—The Industrial Credit (Amendment) Act—envisages a large expansion in the activities of the Company. It now empowers the Minister for Finance (a) to take

up by subscription shares in the Company, and to purchase any held by any other person; (b) to guarantee the repayment of the principal and interest within a limit of £5m. of moneys due by the Company, and the payment of dividends on any shares held otherwise than by him. In return, the Company must give such security as the Minister may require in respect of the guarantees, and any moneys paid by him from the Central Fund on foot of the guarantees must be repaid with interest within two years of the date of the advance, otherwise any outstanding amount must be revoted to the Central Fund out of moneys provided by the Oireachtas—the Company, however, being still liable for the amount revoted; (c) after the end of each financial year the Minister must lay before each House of the Oireachtas particulars of any guarantee outstanding showing the principal paid and any repayment made during the year.

306. The Programme for Economic Expansion stated that no sound industrial project would be allowed to fail or be prevented from starting through lack of capital, and to that end it also stated that it would finance the Industrial Credit Company as the chief State-sponsored agency for the provision of industrial capital, by direct advances from the Central Fund or by State guarantees to banks, etc., providing capital. To implement this policy another Act, The Industrial Credit (Amendment) Act, 1959, increased the Company's share capital from £5m. to £10m., and its borrowing powers from £5m. to £15m., and it empowered the Minister to make repayable advances. With these increased resources it is intended that the Company will underwrite public issues of share and loan capital, will subscribe for industrial shares, make long and medium term loans to industrialists, and provide hire purchase facilities for industrial plant and machinery.

307. The Company has five directors, and as a majority shareholder the Minister may appoint three. It has its own auditors. At the end of March, 1960, the Minister held £4,499,000 fully paid £1 shares in the Company, an increase of over £1.5m. since 1958/59, and in 1959 he received in dividends (net) £49,968. The Capital Budget provided £3½m. for the Company. For the trading year ended 31st October, 1959, the Company made a profit of £188,554 or of £63,618 after providing for taxation and bank interest. This added to the carry forward of £11,177 from the previous year amounted to £74,795 and the Company decided to put £70,000 to reserve and to carry forward £4,793.

THE AGRICULTURAL CREDIT CORPORATION

308. Following on a recommendation of the Banking Commission of 1926, the Agricultural Credit Corporation was established under the Agricultural Credit Act, 1927, and incorporated as a public limited liability company under the Companies Acts. Its object was to promote the co-operative movement, especially by providing re-discounting facilities for co-operative credit societies, to make loans direct to farmers, and to take over loans formerly administered by the Office of Public Works, such as long-term loans for hay-barns, cow-byres, and other buildings.

309. At this time the paid-up capital of the Corporation was £500,000, of which £292,118 was held by the Minister for Finance, who also guaranteed a dividend of 5 per cent. on the remainder of the capital, and a refund in full in case of liquidation. The Corporation was also empowered to issue Mortgage Bonds guaranteed by the State up to a limit of £500,000; to raise money by borrowing on the security of certificates of charge up to £1m. a year, the maximum outstanding at any one time not to exceed £7½m. and the Minister guaranteeing the principal and interest on the certificates; and to borrow on debentures to an extent not exceeding its paid-up capital.

310. In 1929 another Act increased the capital from £.5m. to £1m. subject to the condition that only one-half of the issued capital would be repayable in case of a winding-up, and it also allowed the the issue of certificates of charge beyond the limit of £7½m., if excess certificates were needed to repay those already issued. The issue of loans was also facilitated by the creation of floating charges on the Corporation's assets. The shares were divided into 525,060 A shares of £1 each (10/- paid up) of which the most were held by the Banks and which carried a guaranteed dividend of 5 per cent., the remainder being held by the Minister or the public, and 475,000 B shares (10/- paid up), all held by the Minister, and on which no dividend was paid.

311. The Agricultural Credit Act of 1947 re-constructed the Corporation, the Minister being the only shareholder, all others having been paid in full. The Corporation lends money to any farmer for agricultural purposes, or to any body engaged in activities of a similar character. The securities on which it relies may be divided into three classes: (a) Land Mortgages. This type constitutes the bulk of its business, but a loan thereby secured cannot exceed 50 per cent. of the value of the land, unless some collateral security be forthcoming. (2) Chattel Mortgages, specific when they relate to an identifiable object such as a tractor, and floating when they apply to all the stock and chattels of the farm. (3) Collateral such as life insurance policies, securities and guarantors.

312.   The chief borrower from the Corporation seems to be the small farmer. From April, 1928, to the end of April, 1958, the Corporation issued 49,606 loans totalling £7.9m., those secured by land mortgage amounting to £4m., those relating to chattels £12,100, those—mainly short-term—guaranteed by the Minister for Agriculture £2.3m., and other loans £1.4m. Of the total number of loans 46,911 were for under £500, 2,039 for between £500 and £1,000, and 656 for £1,000 and upwards. The half-yearly instalments include both interest and sinking fund and vary with the period of repayments. Loans are usually on a long-term basis — for machinery 5 years, livestock, 7, funding of debt, 20, buildings, 35, and loans, given on personal security, for not more than 5 years ordinarily. Banks, on the other hand, seem to depend usually on land mortgage for large farmers, and for small farmers they discount bills with a tenure of three months with one or two guarantors.

313.   The number of directors is now five—including the Managing Director—appointed by the Minister for Finance. The authorised and issued capital of the Company since its reconstruction is £300,000 consisting of 600,000 shares of 10/- each. The Minister holds all the shares and received in net dividends £8,438 during 1958/59. The Capital Budget for 1959/60 provides £1m. for the Corporation, and the State has already guaranteed £2.2m. Mortgage Stock issued for the Company's statutory purposes.

THE IRISH SUGAR COMPANY LTD.

314.   In 1926 a Belgian Company started in Carlow the manufacture of sugar from beet-root. It was given a monopoly of the manufacture, a subsidy of £160,000 a year, and a preferential duty on imported raw sugar. It produced about one-fifth of the requirements of the State.

315.   In 1933 the Government decided to extend the scope of the industry, so as to make the country as self-sufficient as possible in sugar production, and to encourage the cultivation of beet in arable crop rotation. Hence, under the Sugar Manufacture Act, 1933, a new company, The Irish Sugar Company (Comhlucht Siúicre Éireann Teo) was incorporated under the Companies Acts as a public limited liability company with the object of acquiring, erecting and operating sugar factories in Ireland. It took over the Carlow factory, and built three others at Mallow, Tuam and Thurles. Under the Sugar (Control of Imports) Act, 1936, the Company was given a monopoly in the importation of raw sugar.

316.   The consumption of refined sugar in the country is about 120,000 tons a year, and if the factories do not produce that amount,

the balance has to be imported in the form of raw sugar. In 1958 the area under beet crop was 83,593 acres which delivered to the factories 784,000 tons of beet valued at £5m. The crop yielded 102,467 tons of white sugar, but in 1959 it was expected that the sugar produced from native beet would meet home requirements. The Company also produces Golden Syrup, Icing Sugar, Cube Sugar, and Molasses for live-stock feeding.

317. Other activities of the Company include (1) Seed Breeding Research—it has its own laboratories—to provide growers with the best type of seed; (2) Fertilisers in the form of Ground Limestone and Factory Lime for which it has two plants, one at Buttevant, Co. Cork, and the other at Killough, Co. Tipperary. In 1958 these sold 101,851 tons of Ground Limestone, and 27,684 tons of Factory Lime, most of which was spread on the farmers' lands by the Company's specially designed lorries; (3) Designing, Producing and Hiring agricultural machinery for its own use and that of growers; (4) Gowla Farm in Co. Galway where about 2,000 acres of bog land is being reclaimed to produce ultimately beet for the Tuam factory; (5) Freeze Drying Plants at Carlow and Mallow for the processing of fruits and vegetables.

318. The Company has seven directors, four being nominated by the Minister for Finance and three elected by members of the Company. The Directors act in a part-time capacity. The Accounts are not audited by the Auditor General, but are furnished to the Minister for Finance and laid before both Houses of the Oireachtas. The authorised capital of the Company is £2m. of which £1,935,905 has been issued, and which consists of (1) 500,014 fully paid ordinary shares of £1 each—500,000 being held by the Minister for Finance; (2) 500,000 fully paid 6 per cent. Cumulative Preference Shares of £1 each, and (3) £935,891 4 per cent. Debenture Stock guaranteed by the State. The Finance Accounts for 1958/59 show £15,625 net dividends received from the Company. The profit for the year was £127,237.

IRISH SHIPPING LTD.

319. Before the last war, only about 5 per cent. of Irish sea-borne trade was carried in Irish-owned ships and they traded only in British and near continental ports, so that Ireland was practically totally dependent on foreign shipping for the carriage of her essential commodities. The Department of Industry and Commerce administered the British laws for the safety of ships, crews and cargoes, but it had no powers to control the movements or trading of ships.

320. In 1941 it was apparent that if essential supplies were to be maintained there was no alternative but to procure Irish ships. Private enterprise was unable to do so, because of the international difficulties in obtaining the necessary permits to buy, charter or run any ships. In the interest, therefore, of the national economy, the Irish Government had to intervene, and to that end it formed Irish Shipping Ltd. to acquire, charter and operate ocean-going ships. The Company was incorporated as a public limited liability company in March, 1941, with a capital of 200,000 of £1 shares all subscribed by the Minister for Finance, who by a subsequent Emergency Order (No. 157 of 1942) was empowered to guarantee any borrowing up to a limit of £2m. Previous to the Order the Company had to rely on a guaranteed overdraft, but by the end of 1942 the Company had paid off its overdraft and was able to operate on its own resources.

321. Between 1941 and 1943 the Company bought fifteen old vessels, mainly those of foreign nationality, which had taken refuge in Irish harbours, when their countries had become involved in hostilities, and the necessary ships warrants were obtained from the Allied Powers. The ships were in a poor condition and in order to render them sea-worthy, the Company re-opened a disused dockyard in Rushbrooke, Co. Cork, by forming the Cork Dockyard Ltd. to which it contributed a capital of £87,500. Emergency legislation also gave the Company power to place chartered vessels on the Irish Register.

322. In addition to the difficulties of acquiring ships and of procuring the necessary permits, licences and warrants, the Company was faced with the difficulty of insuring the vessels. Quotations in London were excessively high, so the Company decided to carry its own war risk insurance, at first on its ships, later on cargoes, and finally on marine insurance generally. This proved highly successful, because at the end of 1946 the Company had a surplus of £3m. It then transferred the marine insurance business to the Insurance Corporation of Ireland Ltd. in return for the issue of shares at par. In addition to the Corporation, there are now four other Irish-owned companies operating Marine Insurance, both at home and abroad.

323. By 1946, the old war-time vessels had been sold and seven new ships were ordered at a cost of £2$\frac{1}{4}$m., all to be delivered by 1950. In 1947, under the Irish Shipping Ltd. Act of the year, the Company's capital was increased to £5m. and the Minister for Finance was empowered to take up shares, to pay subsidies, and to guarantee borrowings up to £2m. In 1950 six more ships were ordered at a cost of about £2$\frac{1}{2}$m. In 1954 two of the smaller vessels

were sold and replaced by two others of a more suitable type. In May, 1957, there were fifteen ships in service, and during the following year four more (including one Tanker) were delivered, so that at the end of April, 1958, there were nineteen ships of 140,115 tons deadweight and a second Tanker was under order.

324. During 1958/59 the issued capital of the Company had reached the authorised figure of £5m., of which the Minister for Finance held 4,394,993 £1 fully paid shares. The cost of the ships was about £10m., half of which was found by the Company, the other half being contributed by the Exchequer, but the cost of the Tankers was financed by bank overdraft. The ships ply between the eastern ports of the United States and Canada and Ireland and also between Baltic and Irish ports. Most of its freight has come from tramping operations.

325. By their Memorandum and Articles of Association the Company is precluded from paying any dividends or bonus, so that profits are diverted to the building of new ships or accumulated as reserves for other purposes. In the event of a winding-up the Minister is entitled to all surplus assets. The profit for 1959/60 was £208,780 on Working Account.

326. The Irish Shipping Ltd. (Amendment) Act, 1959, increased the share capital from £5m. to £12m. and the Minister's power to guarantee borrowings from £2m. to £5m. The Minister's power to pay the company subsidies is repealed. Its fleet in 1960 consists of 17 vessels. At the end of March, 1959, the Minister held £5m. fully paid £1 shares, and the holding was later increased to £7m.

327. The Verolme United Shipyards of Holland have now purchased the interest of the Company in Cork Dockyard Ltd. and as Verolme Cork Dockyard Ltd. have signed an agreement with the Industrial Credit Company providing for a contractual commitment of £2.3m. and a further conditional commitment of another £2.3m. There are six directors appointed by the Minister for Finance and the Accounts are audited by the Auditor General.

THE IRISH ASSURANCE CO. LTD.

328. In 1936 an actuarial valuation revealed that certain Irish Insurance Companies were financially unsound, and in order to protect their policy holders, an Insurance Act was passed in that year providing that no firm could undertake the business of assurance unless (1) it obtained a licence to do so from the Minister for Industry and Commerce; (2) it deposited a sum of £20,000; (3) it was incorporated in Ireland, and (4) it satisfied certain conditions regarding capital, ownership and control.

329.   In 1938 it was found that four Irish Insurance Companies were on the verge of financial collapse, and, again in order to protect the policy holders, the Government intervened and passed the Insurance (Amendment) Act, 1938.   This Act amalgamated the four companies into one new temporary Company, the Industrial Life Assurance Amalgamation Company, which issued share as compensation to the shareholders of the dissolved companies and assumed their liabilities.   A considerable amount of public money, well over £1m., was paid to meet the deficiencies and to compensate the officials of the four companies.   By supplemental agreements made under the Act, the British Friendly Society transferred to the Amalgamated Company both its life and industrial business and four other British Companies, their assurance business. Shares were issued in consideration of the transfer.   All the directors and officials of the Amalgamated Company were appointed by the Government.

330.   The Company then set up a subsidiary, The Irish Assurance Co. Ltd., to operate the business transferred, and new life and industrial insurance business.   In 1947, when the objects of the Act had been achieved, the Minister for Finance purchased the shares of the British Companies, and the Amalgamated Company dissolved distributing its assets in the shape of Irish Assurance Company's shares to its shareholders in proportion to their holdings. At first the Minister for Industry and Commerce appointed for a period the directors of the new company, but now they are appointed in the ordinary way by the shareholders.

331.   The authorised capital of the Company is 100,000 shares of £5 each, and the issued is 100,000 shares of £5 each on which £1 a share is paid up.   The Minister for Finance holds 90,253 shares (£1 paid) and in 1958/59 received £8,461 in net dividends. He is not, therefore, the only shareholder, but he holds the majority of the shares, and has the right of a majority shareholder.   The Company has no monopoly, and competes with other Irish and foreign companies in both its industrial and life assurance business.

CEIMICÍ TEO.

332.   The Industrial Alcohol Act of 1934 provided that the Minister for Industry and Commerce might undertake the manufacture and sale of industrial alcohol, that the money required for doing so should be voted by the Oireachtas, and that the Minister could compel importers and producers of petrol to purchase the product in quantities and at prices fixed by him.

333.   In 1938, following the passing of the Industrial (Amendment) Act of that year, a Company, Monarchana Alcóil na hÉireann

Teo., was established and incorporated as a public limited liability company, its object being to erect and operate factories for the production from potatoes of industrial alcohol. Five factories were built for this purpose at a cost of about £438,593. They are situated, one at Riverstown, Cooley, Co. Louth, a second at Carrickmacross, Co. Monaghan, a third at Corroy, Ballina, Co. Mayo, a fourth at Carndonagh, Co. Donegal, and a fifth at Labbadish, Manorcunningham, Co. Donegal. The issued capital was originally £260,763 of £1 shares fully paid, with £25,000 debentures. Practically all the shares and all the debentures were held by the Minister for Finance who appointed all the directors.

334. In 1947 another amending Act changed the Company's title to Ceimicí Teo. and extended its objects so as to include the manufacture and sale of any chemical products. Originally the factories were intended to use surplus potato supplies, but they now use native and foreign molasses and maize starch. The alcohol is now manufactured at Cooley and Carndonagh, and starch at Labbadish and Corroy. The Monaghan factory is closed.

335. Since 1946 the Company has been exploring the possibility of producing from Irish raw materials a nitrogenous fertiliser at first as sulphate of ammonia, and later as ammonium nitrate which at present is entirely imported. In 1953 it reported that the nitrate compound could be produced from milled peat, or from anthracite duff in combination with limestone in a factory specially built for that purpose. The Government decided to reserve Blackwater Bog as a source of milled peat for the production of the nitrate, but though the factory is being planned, its construction has been deferred, because the price of imported nitrates has fallen considerably, so that at present prices the factory would not appear to be an economic proposition.

336. The authorised capital of the Company is now 500,000 shares of £1 each, of which 495,756 have been issued. All are held by the Minister and in 1958/59 he received net dividends of £15,492. There are five directors, three of whom are appointed by the Minister and all of whom are part-time officials except the Managing Director who is a technical expert. The accounts are audited by the Auditor General. The profit for the year ending 30th September, 1959, was £153,318.

THE DAIRY DISPOSAL COMPANY LTD.

337. In 1926 there were some 580 creameries and condensing plants operating in the Irish State Some, called proprietary, were carried on by limited liability companies, and others by

co-operative societies. There was uneconomic competition for the farmers' milk, not only between the two groups, but also between individual creameries operating in the same area. Of the 180 proprietary creameries operating in the State the most of them were owned by the Condensed Milk Company of Ireland (1924) Ltd. and by the Newmarket Dairy Company Ltd. In order to end the uneconomic trading, and to bring the industry under the control of the State, the then Minister for Agriculture, without any legislative sanction, agreed to buy for £365,000 the assets of the proprietary companies which consisted of 113 creameries, 10 condensing stations and a variety of other properties such as a toffee factory, houses, lands, shops, etc. About £210,000 represented the price for the creameries, and the remainder that for the condensing plants and other assets.

338. The Ministerial intention at the time was that any properties acquired which were not redundant should be sold or re-sold to existing or new co-operative creameries, and that those which were redundant should be closed down at the expense of the State and their assets sold to co-operative societies or other buyers. To implement this intention the Minister formed, in 1927, a private company, the Dairy Disposal Company Ltd., with a paid-up share capital of £7, all the shares being held by his nominees, three civil servants, who acted as whole-time directors of the Company. In effect it was, and still is, a holding Company having as subsidiaries the Condensed Milk Co. of Ireland (1928) Ltd., the Newmarket Dairy Co. (1932) Ltd., Cleeves Confectionery (Limerick) Ltd., and the Northern Irish Condensed Milk Distributors Ltd., the last being at present in the process of being wound up.

339. The Appropriation Act of 1927 provided £500,000 for the purchase of creameries, but, beyond authorising the payment of that sum, it did not give authority for any administrative action either on the part of the Minister or that of the Company. Subsequently, the Creamery Acts of 1928 and 1934 validated certain actions of the Company, and by vesting in the Minister an absolute discretion in the granting of licences to operate the creamery business, or any milk product, or by-product, it gave him complete control over the industry. The £500,000 was used mainly to purchase 183 creameries and to erect four new creameries. Eighty were closed as redundant, and 42 transferred to new societies—the redundant equipment being used to open up creameries in new areas. By 1944 only one proprietary creamery operated in the State.

340. From 1927/28 until 1944/45 the Company was financed by moneys voted by the Oireachtas—the highest amount provided

in the estimates being £90,000 in 1930/31 and the lowest £2,000 in 1943/44. Until 1931/32 the Subhead was simply " Purchase of Creameries," but in that year its purpose was set out more definitely thus: " To provide funds for the purchase of creameries and associated businesses; the extinction of redundant creameries; the re-organisation and sale of non-redundant undertakings to co-operative Creamery Societies; and the expenses and liquidation and carrying on business pending re-organisation and sale." In 1932/33 an additional subhead was opened entitled " Extension of the Creamery Industry " to provide funds for the erection of creameries and the carrying on of creamery business in Co. Clare; and in 1933/34 the title of both subheads was changed to " Improvement of the Creamery Industry " combining the ambit of the old subheads. From 1944/45 to date only a token provision of £5 is taken for the subhead, the expenditure being met out of the profits of the Company.

341. The original intention of closing redundant plants and of dispensing of others to co-operative societies, appears to have been abandoned, for the Disposal Company is still in existence and, as we have already seen, other private companies have been formed in association with it. Between them the companies now operate (a) a Condensed Milk Factory and two Sub-condensaries; (b) two Milk Powder Factories; (c) seventeen Creamery Groups and ancillary enterprises; (d) three Wholesale Butter businesses; (e) one Bacon Factory; (f) two Main Cattle Breeding Stations with satellite sub-stations.

342. In the evidence taken by the Committee of Public Accounts for 1956/57 the following observation by the Comptroller and Auditor General occurs: " The consolidated Balance Sheet as at 31st December, 1956, of the Dairy Disposal Company Ltd. and associated companies disclosed a liability of £584,603 in respect of issues from voted moneys for the purchase of creameries etc. This amount together with the balance of £648,290 to the credit of the Profit and Loss Account brings the total amount due to the Exchequer to £1,232,893 at that date. It was decided during the year to charge interest at the rate of 6 per cent. per annum from 1st April, 1956, on the outstanding balance of voted moneys, and £35,076 was received by the Department and brought to account as an Exchequer extra receipt." At the end of March, 1960, repayable advances stood at £1.3m. and the Exchequer in 1959 received interest of £35,076 in respect of capital liability.

343. The nominal capital of the Company is now 20,120 shares of £1 each, and the issued is 20,072. There are six directors—two

being seconded civil servants, one acting as Deputy Chairman and the other as Secretary. The Company does not publish any balance sheet of its own, but a consolidated balance sheet of itself and of its Associated Companies, which is published as an appendix to the Report of the Committee of Public Accounts. It has its own auditors.

IRISH STEEL HOLDINGS LTD.

344. The steel works at Haulbowline, Co. Cork, are the only works of their kind in the Irish State. They were originally owned by a private company, Irish Steel Ltd., but in 1947 a State-sponsored limited liability company took over the works as a going concern. The capital of the new company was 100 shares of £1 each of which only three have been issued, and they are held by the Minister for Finance. There are three directors, civil servants, appointed by the Minister for Industry and Commerce and they act in a part-time capacity.

345. The Capital requirements of the concern were first provided by a bank overdraft up to £300,000 guaranted by the Minister, and also by using any profits accruing from the under-taking. This arrangement has now been superseded by a long-term loan of £150,000 from an insurance company, the loan being guaranteed by the State and a guaranteed bank overdraft of £125,000 which has now been cleared.

346. The works produce steel moulds in open hearth furnaces from native scrap metal, and these in turn are converted into bars, and finished articles of a limited range. In addition imported steel is galvanised and corrugated. The annual profit in recent years has been between £55,000 and £70,000, and this has been helped by tariffs on imported steel, and by export restrictions on scrap metal. Plans costing about £3½m. have now been approved by the Government for developing and extending the factory, and legislation is to be introduced empowering the Minister for Finance to subscribe share capital to that amount. Meanwhile, by means of a supple-mentary estimate, the Company has been given £300,000 to meet its immediate commitments.

THE IRISH NATIONAL STUD
(Cólucht Groighe Náisiúnta na hÉireann Teoranta)

347. The National Stud Farm at Tully, Co. Kildare, comprises about 870 acres of which 674 acres were held on a yearly tenancy of £813 a year. The farm was originally owned by Lord Wavertree, who presented it together with about 30 brood mares to the British

National Stud, and it was worked by the latter from 1916 to 1943. It became vested in the Minister for Agriculture under Section 6 of the National Stud Act, 1945, and under Section 8 it was granted under annual licence to Cólucht Groighe Náisiúnta na hÉireann. Persuant to the Act the Company was incorporated under the Companies Acts in April, 1946, for the purpose of running the stud farm.

348. The maximum capital of the Company was at first £250,000 but it was later increased to £500,000. Shares are taken up from time to time by the Minister for Finance according to the Company's financial requirements, and at the end of March, 1960, he held 395,870 fully paid £1 shares. In 1957/58 the landlord's interest in the 674 acres was purchased for £17,000 provided by a supplementary estimate.

The five directors are all part-time officials, and are appointed by the Minister for Finance in consultation with the Minister for Agriculture. The Company made a profit of £3,393 during 1958.

ALGINATE INDUSTRIES (IRELAND) LTD AND ARRAMARA TEO.

349. The sea plants, or Algae, which are washed up by the sea on the western coast of Ireland, yield, when processed, Seaweed Meal, Carrigeen, and Sea Rod Meal. Seaweed Meal is manufactured by private firms, and Carrigeen with Sea Rod Meal was also originally produced by a private company, Alginate Industries (Ireland) Ltd., at its factory in Kiltiernan, Co. Galway. The sea rods are gathered and partly dried by the local inhabitants who sell them to the factory at Kiltiernan where, after further drying, they are made into sea rod meal. This meal is then sold to a British Company, Alginate Industries Ltd.—a large shareholder in the Irish Company— to be further processed in their factories in Scotland. The processing yields alginate which unites with certain metals to form a salt, which, inter alia, is used medicinally as a lubricant and emulgent.

350. Alginate Industries (Ireland) Ltd. was first registered as a private limited company in 1947, the majority of the shares being held by Irish citizens in accordance with the Control of Manufactures Acts. In 1949 the Alginate Industries (Ireland) Ltd. (Acquisition of Shares) Act authorised the Minister for Lands to acquire shares in the Company to the extent of £5,100. The money was used to buy out the Irish shareholders, and, with a further contribution from the British Company, to increase the capital. In 1954 a similar Act allowed the Minister to increase the value of his holding from £5,100 to £43,000 and a further increase in capital

took place, part being taken by the Minister and part by the British Company. In September, 1955, the name of the Irish Company was changed from Alginate Industries (Ireland) Ltd. to Arramara Teoranta, and the change was duly registered. The principal activities of the Company are the purchase of sea-rods and carrigeen and their preparation for marketing, but it is understood that another Irish private firm has recently undertaken the production of alginates.

351. The Minister holds 29,000 fully paid £1 shares in Alginate Industries (Ireland) Ltd. The Company has five directors and its accounts are not audited by the Auditor General. The Accounts and Report are submitted to both Houses of the Oireachtas. The present authorised capital of Arramara Teo. consists of 50,000 ordinary shares of £1 each of which 36,000 have been issued. The Minister holds 29,000 of the shares and the British Company the remainder.

INDEX

(The numbers refer to paragraphs)

A

Abbey Theatre, 88D.
Above the Line, 132.
Accountancy Audit, 201, 202.
Accounting Officers, 11-14.
Accounts, 127-130.
Accredited Herd Scheme, 92G.
Administrative Audit, 201-204.
Administrative and Executive Group, 22.
Administrative Law, 26.
Aer Lingus, 297-301.
Aerlinte Éireann, 302, 303.
Aer Rianta, 292-296, 301.
Agencies, United Nations, 213.
Agency Services, 118.
Agricultural Credit Corporation, 308-313.
Agricultural Grant, 62, 88.
Agricultural Institute, 92C, 227, 230.
Agricultural Production, 92A.
Agricultural Schools and Farms, 92.
Agriculture — Department, 6, 7, 86, 87, 92, 355, 356.
Airports, 87.
Alginate Industries (Ireland) Ltd., 349-351.
Allied Services, 117, 118.
Ambassadors, 106.
American Grant Counterpart Special Account, 92G, 92H, 230.
American Loan Counterpart Fund, 109, 228, 229, 359, 361.
Ancillary Group, 22.
Annuities, 95A, 109.
Appropriation Account, 183-190.
Appropriation Act, 160-165.
Appropriation Audit, 201-203.
Appropriations-in-Aid, 115, 144, 186.
Arramara Teo, 98, 349, 351.
Aras Mhic Diarmada, 93D.
Army, 105.
Army Pensions, 105.
Arterial Drainage, 88B.
Assets—External, 134.
Assets—Public, 138-140, 361.
Attorney General, 3, 8, 44.

Audit, 196-198.
Audit Office, 86, 200, 355.
Australia, 54, 199.
Austria, 54, 216, 223, 241.
Aural Services, 94E.
Aviation and Meteorological Services, 87, 99, 102.

B

Bank Advances, 135.
Banking Commission, 140.
Bank of Ireland, 61, 123, 142.
Belgium, 54, 214, 223.
Below the Line, 132.
Benelux, 216, 236.
Bills, 20, 41, 42, 44, 45, 46-50.
Blind Pensions, 93B.
Bord Fáilte Éireann, 103, 282-288.
Bord Ghaeltarra Éireann, 98.
Bord Gráin, 92K.
Bord Iascaigh Mhara — See under Sea Fisheries.
Bord na Móna, 99, 110, 264-273, 361.
Borrowing, 134, 135.
Bovine Tuberculosis Eradication, 89, 92G, 230.
Bretton Woods Agreement, 70, 75, 138, 37.
Broadcasting, 104E.
Broadcasting Authority, 362.
Brussels Pact, 216, 218.
Budget, 149-156.
Bureaucracy, 27.
Butter Marketing Committee, 92J.
Butter Subsidy, 92J.

C

Canada, 218, 214, 231, 244.
Capital Investment Advisory Committee, 62, 140.
Capital Services, 70, 87, 156, 354, 358.
Capitation Grants, 91B.
Causes of Variation, 186.
Ceann Comhairle, 50.
Ceimicí Teoranta, 332,336.
Census, 22.

191

BIBLIOGRAPHY

Administration, Vols. 1 to 7.

Annual Estimates, Appropriation Accounts and Reports of Committee of Public Accounts.

Annual Reports of Departments.

Annual Reports of State-sponsored Bodies.

The Civil Servant in the Law and the Constitution by C. S. Emden.

Delegated Legislation by C. T. Carr.

European Free Trade — Irish Management Institute.

Journal of Statistical and Social Inquiry Society of Ireland.

O.E.E.C. at Work — Official Publication.

Parliamentary Grants by A. J. V. Durell.

Public Administration in Ireland, Vols. 1 to 3, by F. C. King.

Report of Commission on Banking, Currency and Credit, 1938.

Report of Commission on Vocational Organisation, 1943.

Western European Union by R. G. Hawtrey.

APPENDIX

ADDENDA

i. NUMBER OF CIVIL SERVANTS

352. The number of civil servants for subsequent years is:—
      1st January 1957: 30,723 (12,401 unestablished).
      1st January, 1958: 30,285 (11,848 unestablished).
      1st January, 1959: 28,039 (9,417 unestablished).
      1st January, 1960: 28,107 (9,039 unestablished).

ii. REORGANISATION OF CIVIL SERVICE

353. In the Budget Statement 1960 the Minister for Finance announced that the civil service would be reorganised on the following lines: 1—Certain duties would be transferred from the clerical to lower grades, and the latter would be amalgamated into one new grade (Writer Clerk Grade); 2—Three of the Staff Officer Grades would be suppressed and their personnel absorbed in the Executive Grade; 3—The open competition examination for clerical officers would be suspended after 1960; 4—A number of the highest successful candidates at the next executive officer competition would be given, at the expense of the State, an opportunity of pursuing a nominated university course with a view to appointment to such grades as Statistician, Economist or Administrative Officer; 5—The minimum salary for Administrative Officers will be raised and more definite prospects of promotion will be offered. (Dáil Debates, Cols. 157, 159.)

iii. ESTIMATES OF EXPENDITURE, 1960/61—ALL SERVICES

354. The estimated State expenditure on all sources for 1960/61 is:

		£000	£000
1. Supply Services — Non Capital		105,883	
Capital		17,557	
			123,460
2. Central Fund Service (exc. Road Fund) ...			24,650
3. Capital and Other Services			23,480
4. Road Fund			6,000
		Total	£177,590

iv. ESTIMATES OF EXPENDITURE, 1960/61—SUPPLY SERVICES

355. By the amalgamation of certain estimates the number of votes has been reduced in 1960/61 from 66 to 59, and the expenditure on the Supply Services (including Voted Capital Services) is distributed as follows:

	£	Vote
Dept. of Taoiseach	31,180	3
„ „ Finance	16,610,330	1, 2, 4, 6-22
„ „ Justice	6,112,430	23-31
„ „ Local Government	5,131,890	32

		£	Vote
Dept. of Education		16,588,810	33-41
„ „	Lands and Fisheries	5,121,640	42-44
„ „	Gaeltacht	522,730	45
„ „	Agriculture	12,250,350	46
„ „	Industry & Commerce	2,471,000	47
„ „	Transport & Power	3,646,670	48
„ „	Posts & Telegraphs	10,259,500	49, 50
„ „	Defence	9,190,370	51, 52
„ „	External Affairs	554,600	53, 54
„ „	Social Welfare	26,112,600	55-57
„ „	Health	8,816,360	58, 59
„ „	Audit Office	39,600	5

Total: £123,460,060

v. VOTED CAPITAL SERVICES, 1960/61

356. These are for practically the same services as outlined in para. 87, and include Public Works and Buildings (£2.8m.), Local Government (£2.1m.), Forestry (£1.6m.), Agriculture (£8.1m.), Industry and Commerce (including Tourism) (£1.1m.), Transport and Power (£1.6m.), Universities (£15,000), Fisheries (£47,000), Gaeltacht (150,000). The services total £17,577,017)

vi. CENTRAL FUND SERVICES, 1960/61

357. These include: 1—Service of Public Debt, Interest and Sinking Funds (£23.3m.); 2—Local Taxation Grants (£1.1m.); 3—Judicial and Other Salaries, Pensions, Allowances and Expenses (£220,000).

vii. CAPITAL AND OTHER ISSUES, 1960/61

358. These embrace advances for all items listed in para. 70 except 12, 13 and 14. There are three new items: Broadcasting Authortiy Act, 1960 (£.5m.); Grass Meal Production Acts, 1953 and 1959 (£.09m.), and Irish Steel Holdings Ltd. (£1.7m.). The Grass Meal Project was first set up in 1953 but was subsequently abandoned. It is revived by the Act of 1959, the object of which is to authorise the Minister to promote a limited liability company with a capital of £200,000 for the acquisition, drainage and cultivation of bogland in the Bangor Erris area, for the processing of grass and other plants, and for the carrying on of kindred and incidental activities.

The total of the Capital and Other Issues as estimated in the April White Paper is £23,48m. to which must be added £17.58m. for Voted Capital Services, that is a total of £41.06m. which may be divided thus:

	White Paper £m.	Budget £m.
State-sponsored Bodies	16.26	25.74
Voted Capital Services	17.58	17.58
Telephone Capital	1.75	1.75
Other Issues	5.47	9.30
Total	£41.06	£54.37

The Programme of Capital Expenditure issued with the Budget Statement puts the total at £54.37m. as shown in the third column above. To meet its proposed expenditure of £54.37m., the Government is to find £41.78m., the State-sponsored Bodies £4.59m., and the balance £7.70m. is to be raised by the issue of stocks, or by borrowing from financial institutions.

viii. ESTIMATES OF RECEIPTS, 1960/61

	£000	£000
359. These are as follows:		
(i) Tax Revenue:		
Customs	38,675	
Special Import Levy	1,675	
Excise	31,400	
Estate, etc., Duties	2,800	
Stamp Duties	2,800	
Income Tax	24,700	
Sur-Tax and Super-Tax	1,600	
Corporation Profits Tax, etc.	3,300	
Motor Vehicle Duties	6,000	
		112,950
(ii) Non-Tax Revenue:		
Postal, Telegraph & Telephone Services	9,650	
Land Annuities, etc.	1,750	
Interest on Exchequer Advances, etc.	7,791	
Central Bank — Surplus Income	1,800	
Counterpart Fund	1,647	
Wireless Licence Fees	440	
Fee Stamps	430	
Miscellaneous	400	
		23,908
(iii) Other Receipts:		
Repayment of Capital and Other Issues	1,237	
Capital under Telephone Acts	1,750	
To be met by Borrowing or Otherwise	37,745	
		40,732
Total		£177,590

ix. THE PUBLIC DEBT

360. In para. 137 the gross indebtedness of the State at the end of March, 1959, was given as £428m., but this figure included a double reckoning of £42m. If this be deducted, the amount of the debt will be £386m. On the same basis the Public Debt at the end of March, 1960, was £424m. made up as follows:

	£m.
Ways and Means Advances	101
Exchequer Bills	16
Saving Certificates	24
Prize Bonds	14
Loans (13 issues)	189
Other Borrowings	50
Direct Liabilities	394
Indirect	71
Total	465
Less Double Reckoning	41
Outstanding Public Debt	£424

Hence, in the space of the year the Public Debt increased by £38m. Meanwhile the National Income rose from £480m. in 1958 to £503m. in 1959. The debt of Local Authorities rose to £145m.

x. THE PUBLIC ASSETS

361. At the end of March, 1960, the Assets of the State totalled £250m., and were made up of: (i) Repayable Advances, £176m.; (ii) Shares of Sundry Undertakings, £22m.; (iii) Balances on Sundry Funds and Accounts (including £41m. of Counterpart Fund), £52m. During the year, therefore, the Assets increased by £14m. The increase is mainly due (a) to advances of £4m. to the Local Loans Fund and of £1m. to Bord na Móna; (b) to an increase in the holding of Shares in the Industrial Credit Co. (£2m.), in Aer Rianta (£1.7m.), in Irish Shipping Ltd. (£2m.); and (c) to an increase of £1.6m. in payments under the Bretton Woods Agreements.

xi. THE BROADCASTING AUTHORITY

362. The Broadcasting Authority Act, 1960, established, as a body corporate, an Authority to be known as Radio Éireann consisting of not less than seven and not more than nine members to be appointed by the Government for a period not exceeding five years on terms to be fixed by the Government, which will appoint one member to act as Chairman. The Authority itself is to appoint a Director General as its chief executive officer and all its other officers and servants. The Authority must seek the Government's approval before appointing or removing the Director General, and its other officers must be appointed by public competitive examination unless they were already employed in the broadcasting service or they possess specialised qualifications, or the appointment is for a limited period up to two years. The Authority is to fix the terms and conditions of service of its officers and servants.

The Authority is to establish and maintain a national television and sound broadcasting service and has all such powers as are necessary for or incidental to that purpose. In performing its functions the Authority must bear constantly in mind the national aims of restoring the Irish language, and preserving and developing the national culture. It may broadcast advertisements and may fix the charges and conditions for such, and it may reduce the charge for Irish advertisers.

The Minister may appoint advisory committees, or advisers, to help the Authority in the discharge of its duties but neither the Authority nor the Director General is bound by the advice.

To finance the Authority, the Minister may for five consecutive years out of voted moneys pay the amount of the net wireless licence fees together with any further reasonable sums not exceeding in the total £500,000. For Capital purposes the Minister for Finance may make repayable advances within a limit of £2m. in the aggregate. It is, however, enacted that the Authority should at the earliest possible date secure that its revenue will be sufficient to meet sums chargeable to its current account and to make provision for capiatl expenditure. To meet current expenditure the Authority with the consent of the Minister may borrow temporarily from its bank and for capital purposes it may also borrow by means of the creation of stock or other forms of security.

The Minister may direct the Authority to refrain from broadcasting any particular matter, and to allocate time for Government announcements.

The Wireless Broadcasting Estimate for 1960/61 is for £145,000 against £436,500 for 1959/60, but the provision is for four months only, because it is expected that the Authority will function before the end of that period. A new Vote will then be necessary, and it is estimated that an extra sum of £350,000 will be needed.

xii. THE INDUSTRIAL GRANTS ACT, 1959

363. The Estimates 1960/61 provide for the Industrial Development Authority only administrative expenses (£43,000), but for An Fóras Tionscal provision is made for two grants-in-aid — one of £500,000 under section 12 of the Underdeveloped Areas Act, 1952 as amended by section 6 of the Industrial Grants Act, 1959, and the other, £475,000 under section 2 of that Act for industrial development outside the undeveloped areas. Hence the Authority is now confined to promotional activities, and An Foras deals with industrial grants both for the developed and undeveloped areas.